FROM CAERAU TO THE SOUTHERN CROSS

From Caerau to the Southern Cross

by

Rachael Ann Webb

Rachel Ann Webb

ALUN BOOKS
3 Crown Street, Port Talbot, West Glamorgan

ISBN 0 907117 46 5

Dedicated to the memory
of my
beloved son
Jack

Photoset, printed and bound in Great Britain by
WBC Bristol and Maesteg

ONE

My name today is Rachael Ann Webb, but I was born Rachael Ann Bowen, the third surviving child of John Bowen, of High Street, Ogmore Vale, and Rachael (née Davies) his wife; the date was April 16th, 1903.

My father was the son of Rees Bowen, a hotelier, of the Corner House Hotel in Swansea. My grandfather was six foot tall, but my grandmother, his wife, was only five foot one, a petite little lady who ruled her household with a rod of iron, as she did her son, my father. Father was a Baptist, a religious young man who felt a call to enter the ministry, but my grandmother insisted that a minister's living was not good enough, and he must become a barrister. Hers was the ruling voice, and so he entered the University College of Wales, Aberystwyth, going from there to Cambridge to study law.

My mother, Rachael Davies, was the daughter of a detective (referred to in those days as a plain-clothes policeman), living in Blackwood in Monmouthshire, and my parents were married in Pontllanfraith, though they spent the early part of their married life in London, near my father's work. They both loved children, and longed for a family of their own, but, very sadly, their six babies all died in infancy. Eventually their doctor told them that they would never rear a family because of incompatibilities in their blood; but then, to their great joy, a seventh child was born, a beautiful, healthy child whom the doctor assured them they would keep.

In later years I often heard my mother say that she could hardly believe that this child was hers; she would pick her up and squeeze her so tight, just to make sure that she was not dreaming, that sometimes the baby would cry out. She named the baby Emily Gwenllian, and as she grew older the child showed every promise of becoming as beautiful as her mother, with chestnut curls and eyes like deep, liquid pools, fringed with dark eye-lashes that caressed her cheeks. Then three years later

Benjamin David arrived, another fine healthy baby, exactly like his sister in colouring and features, whose arrival made his parents' joy complete.

When Emily was five and Benjamin was two, my mother discovered that she was going to have another child. She was quite annoyed by this, and told my father that she did not want another baby – she had already borne eight children, and she thought it would tax her strength to the limit. After her sixth child died, she had decided that she did not want to live in London any more because she felt that the smog and fumes of the city had been the cause of all those deaths, and so she and my father moved to Wales, to the clean, pure air of the mountains. They settled on the outskirts of Swansea, and there their two children were born. Now, however, she was upset at the prospect of another nine months of pregnancy. My father was always distressed by seeing her upset, and he said, "Never mind, Rachael, there's never one comes that the Lord won't provide for. You've got your boy and girl, I shan't have a look in with them, so the next one shall be mine".

My mother was nearing her time (though she still had several weeks to go before the birth was due) when she went on a visit to Ogmore Vale to see Mrs. Lewis, a friend of hers, who was also expecting a baby.

My mother had intended her visit to be only a short stay, but while there she was taken ill herself, and they had to send to London for my father. Three days later she was delivered of a baby girl, six weeks premature, and thus I made my entrance to the world at Ogmore Vale, not Swansea.

I was not a beauty as Emily and Ben were, and I did not resemble them *or* my mother. Instead I had my father's colouring, fair hair and blue eyes, and when my father saw me, he said I was lovely and exactly like his mother.

For many years my father had been very friendly with the Blandy Jenkinses. They lived in a mansion at Southerndown, and Lady Blandy Jenkins owned much of the land between Southerndown and Ogmore Vale as well as many properties in Ogmore itself. It was a country of rivers, with the Ogwr Fawr running down through Ogmore Vale and the Ogwr Fechan through the Garw Valley, to join at Blackmill and flow on to Tondu to yet another meeting of rivers. All these rivers were so pure that salmon swam up them through the valleys to spawn,

6

providing excellent salmon fishing, while the mountain streams were full of fresh water trout.

My father was a keen angler, and his main hobby was fishing, either with a rod or catching trout by hand; this particular year Lady Blandy Jenkins had asked him to be the judge in her annual salmon fishing contest – which was to be a competition to find the fisherman who was most skilful at catching trout by hand. (She always insisted on his being the judge if he was available). After the judging my father was to present the prize trout to Lady Blandy Jenkins in the Llanharan Arms in Ogmore Vale High Street, just opposite the house where I was born, and a photographer was in attendance to take pictures of her ladyship receiving this tray of prize-winning fish. In due course my father received one of the photographs; it was excellent, a 12″ x 14″ picture, but it was also very plain to see that my father, though a total abstainer, had not only celebrated the occasion, but had also wet the baby's head. His bowler hat, which he always wore sitting straight on his head in a dignified manner, was for once roguishly tilted backwards, proof that this time Lady Blandy Jenkins had succeeded (where on every other occasion she had failed) in getting him tipsy!

Two and a half years later, this time back home in Swansea, my mother gave birth to another baby boy. Since I was so young, I do not recollect his birth, and my memory starts some two years later, when I was four and a half years old. At that time I remember coming down a wide staircase, holding on to the bannister until I reached the newel post at the bottom, where my mother picked me up, and said to me, "Come, Ritty, Mammy's going to show you something". (Although I had been christened Rachael, because that was also my mother's name my father decided to call me 'Ritty' rather than 'Little Rachael').

My mother held me over a little white box, and said, "Can you see what's there, Ritty?" (They had already realised that I was only partially sighted.)

"Yes", I said to her, "it is a beautiful dolly. Is it for me, Mummy?"

"No", said Mother, "this is your sister, Sarah Margaretta, who came to stay with us for a little while, but now she is going back to Jesus".

I touched the baby's hand, and saw that she was holding a bunch of forget-me-nots. "Hasn't she got tiny hands, Mummy?"

I said, and in answer my mother read out the words on a card on the baby's chest: 'Safe in the arms of Jesus' I looked again, and noted that Sarah had a beautiful bonnet on her head – so beautiful that I asked my mother if I could have it; but she said, "No, Ritty, you can't have Sarah's bonnet, she's going to Heaven and she must take her bonnet with her". At that I got into quite a rage and shouted, "I want that bonnet, I want that bonnet!" I did not understand, of course, and thought it very unfair that Sarah should look so beautiful, with the forget-me-nots all around her, wearing that lovely bonnet. At last I screamed at my mother in rage, "Sarah can go to Jesus if she wants to, but she's not taking that bonnet". I was in disgrace after that, but I did not forgive my mother for a very long time for letting Sarah take that bonnet.

We did not see a great deal of my father at that time, but he came home at weekends whenever possible, and his return was a great occasion, when we went to the railway to meet him. There was always a present for me when he came, and the one I remember most of all was the one I liked best – a little wooden wash-tub and washing board, with a little wooden pail.

When my father came home on these weekends, he would take Emily, Ben and myself to Chapel on Sunday morning; we were well-dressed children, with first, second and third outfits, and Sunday mornings were the time for our second-best clothes. For Sunday School in the afternoon we also wore our second best, but after Sunday School we changed to our third-best clothes, which we were permitted to wear when we went for a walk. On one particular Sunday, a lovely day, Emily and Ben were allowed to take me with them on one of their favourite walks down by the riverside, but only after my mother had stressed that they must look after me and not let me soil my clothes. A neighbour's son who was about twelve years old at the time and was rather sweet on Emily who was about ten, often came with us on our walk, and joined us that day.

When we got down to the river, Emily and Ben and the boy wanted to cross to the other side, but I was afraid and hung back. At that the boy offered to carry me on his back, but I was afraid he would drop me in the water, and said, "No, I don't want to go across the river". However the boy insisted, and told me to get on his back and hold on tightly, and he would take me safely across. (Obviously he wanted to impress Emily with his

8

strength). So I got on his back, but halfway across the river he slipped on a stone and we both fell in and had a good drenching.

Emily and Ben expected to be severely punished for letting me get drenched, and we walked home very dejectedly, wondering what would happen to us when Mother saw us. Luckily, because it was Sunday when everyone was on their best behaviour, we got off lightly, with Mother just saying that it could have been worse, I might have drowned, and my clothes would soon wash clean. Meanwhile I was quickly washed myself and dressed in my first-best outfit ready to go to church with Mammy and Daddy. (Baby Garfield was left at home with Lizzie Dibble the nursemaid; babies were not taken to church in those days until they were able to sit quietly). It was a Sunday when Daddy was taking the service, and I loved listening to his sermons because he was always so gentle – the other preacher was a 'blood and thunder man' whom I did not like very much.

My father was not in the best of health just then, and the next time he came home for the weekend, he took us to stay at our grandmother's hotel in Swansea. We like staying with our grandparents because they had a big nursery with a large rocking horse, a great attraction to us little ones. While we were there, my mother took us for a walk to see the horse in a field behind the hotel; we didn't go into the field, but talked to the horse through the railings. After that, the first opportunity I had, I slipped quietly out of the hotel and went to look for this horse, climbing on to the railings to talk to it, and though the animal ignored me, I wasn't bothered, being too busy learning to spell its name. I kept calling out to the h o r s e, and then ran back to the hotel, dashing through the open door and shouting, "I can spell horse, I can spell horse!"

Suddenly I collided with a big man who was coming out of one of the rooms, and fell, striking my head on the marble floor of the hall. The doctor came and told my parents that I would never wake up. I would just die in my sleep. (Doctors were not very skilful in those days!) However, my mother's only sister, who was seventeen years older than my mother, was a lady doctor, and the first ever to practise in Blackwood, and Mother sent for her to come to Swansea immediately. She came as fast as she could, and once she had arrived and examined the unconscious child, she asked for a glass of port wine. Mother was surprised, because her sister did not drink, but she supposed

9

that perhaps after the journey she needed something, so a glass was quickly brought – but instead of drinking it, she forced the wine between the lips of the unconscious child. Naturally my parents were alarmed, and my father said, "You can't do that to her, Margaret, you'll choke the child". But my aunt said, "You go now, and don't worry. Leave this child to me, I know what I'm doing". Later she called them back into the room and told them to listen to my breathing, telling them, "Don't worry, this child is sleeping peacefully now. She wasn't sleeping before, you know, but she'll be as right as rain when she wakes up. She isn't going to die". And she showed them the empty glass.

Indeed, she was as good as her word, and when I woke from my long sleep I had no recollection of anything that had happened; as far as I know, I was none the worse for my ordeal.

My aunt Margaret was very much loved as a doctor, particularly in Bargoed and Blackwood. When her mother died, Aunt Margaret was twenty years old and had just married Charles Harris, the head gardener at the Crystal Palace in London; her first two children were like brother and sister to my mother, who was only three at the time.

About then an epidemic of diphtheria swept through Monmouthshire. People were dying like flies, and Aunt Margaret was called to Bargoed, to see a little girl of twelve years old, who was choking and near to death. The people in the house were frantic and, as my aunt told my mother, "I had to do something, Rachael, or they would have torn me to pieces". There were no isolation hospitals in those days, and no known cure, so, though doctors did what they could, it was usually futile.

Aunt Margaret looked around for inspiration, and since, like most people in Wales, she believed in the power of prayer, she silently prayed for God's help. Then her eyes alighted on the kitchen table, covered with the remains of the last meal, and with a sweep of her hand she cleared the table completely, except for a baby's feeding bottle. Then she said to the child's father, "Put the child on the table at once". In those days a baby's bottle was like a modern milk bottle, but with a big cork in the neck of the bottle, through which a rubber tube was pushed. This connected with a glass tube which ran down through the whole length of the inside of the bottle, and on the end of the rubber tube was a teat which went into the baby's mouth. Aunt Margaret cut a piece from the rubber tube and sterilized it, then she made an incision in the child's throat and inserted the tube into the neck, so that the child could get air into her lungs. The child recovered, and from that day on Aunt Margaret never lost a patient from diphtheria.

The little girl was a Jewess, and at that time there were a large number of Jews living in Bargoed; as a result of the child's cure they made Aunt Margaret an offer they felt sure she wouldn't be able to refuse – they would pay her any sum of money she cared to ask for if she would become doctor to the Jews alone. No price would be too high, they said, for her services. But she refused, saying, "I serve both Jew and Gentile alike, not one more than the other", and so she became very much loved by all the people of Bargoed.

There was another case in Bargoed when a young woman in her twenties was believed to be demented; many people said her illness was caused by evil spirits. Aunt Margaret went to see the girl at the request of her parents, and found her lying naked on the floor of her room, thrashing about like someone in an epileptic fit; her body was covered in what appeared to be blue bruises. My aunt said to the girl's mother, "This girl is not in a fit; I can cure her, but you must do what I tell you. Do you make your own bread?" "Yes, I do", said the woman. "Then I want you to make a large batch of dough, as much as you can get into the bread bin", Aunt Margaret told her. "And don't give your daughter anything to eat for twenty four hours. I am going to leave you now, and when I return I want to see a large batch of dough, as I've ordered. If you have carried out my orders, I can cure your daughter immediately".

Twenty four hours later Aunt Margaret went back to the girl's house, to find that her orders had been carried out to the letter, and the girl was in a sorrier plight than when she had seen her previously. She asked for a large white sheet which she laid out on the floor, and then she took the dough and spread it all over the sheet. Next she lay the naked girl on the sheet and wrapped it all around her, and waited for the results. When the girl became calmer, and her threshings ceased, they knew she had been cured, so they lifted her out of the dough. Her bruises had all gone, and the dough was covered in black beetles. Aunt Margaret told the story herself, and it seems that the cure was complete.

11

TWO

My brother Garfield Llewellyn was a very delicate child, and the doctors had given my mother strict instructions that she was never to feed him with solids, only with milky foods. Mother repeatedly implored the doctors to let her give Garfield solid foods, because he always seemed to be so hungry, but they always refused, and so at meal times Miss Dibble had to wrap him in a shawl and take him out while we ate our food. Miss Dibble was courting at the time, and often used these moments to meet her young man; one day while she was supposedly looking after Garfield, he disappeared. He was about two years old then, and very weak on his legs, so it was not thought that he could have got far, but Miss Dibble was crying, "I only put him down for a minute and he disappeared!"

They searched the grounds, and though Garfield was nowhere to be seen, the garden gate was open. Then my mother saw him coming towards her, with his face and hands covered in jam and a big grin on his little face. We were Welsh-speaking children, and little Garfield could only understand Welsh, so my mother ran to him, picked him up in her arms and said to him, "Pa le chi wedi bod, bach (Where have you been, my little boy?") He just grinned and said, "Bopa bara jam." (Auntie bread and jam.) Mother took him inside and washed and changed him. She could not tell where he had been, but at least he seemed to be more contented and satisfied. Exactly the same thing happened another day: again he was found covered in sticky jam, and once again he gave the same answer when he was questioned.

The third time Garfield disappeared, he was not to be found at all, though once again Lizzie (as we called Miss Dibble behind her back) swore she had only put him down to stretch his legs. At last my mother found him sitting on the doorstep of a little workmen's cottage, with what we called a 'culf' of bread (a whole round of a large loaf), covered in jam, in his hand, and

12

looking as happy as a sandboy. When she heard my mother's voice as she spoke to Garfield, a little old lady came to the door and said, "I'm sorry I've kept your little boy longer today but when he came banging on my door with his little fist as usual, and calling out 'Bopa, bopa, bara jam os gwelwch yn dda', I didn't have the heart to tell him I didn't have a bit of bread or jam in the house. I thought, if it takes the last penny I've got in the world, he shall have his bara jam – and it *was* all the money I had in the world, too." (All this she explained in Welsh, for she could not speak English.) "I sat him on the doorstep," she went on, "and said to him, 'Don't you move from there, Bopa is going to the shop to get you some bara jam.' And, bless his little heart, he sat there quietly and waited until I came back. I didn't know whose child he was, but I couldn't understand how a child so well dressed could be so hungry."

My mother explained what the doctors had said, that on no account was she to give Garfield solids to eat because he was suffering from drinking diabetes, and was only to be given liquids. The old lady flushed, and said, "I'm sorry, I didn't know. I'm so sorry if I've done wrong." But my mother said to her, "No, my dear, you've done no harm, instead you've taught me a lesson I'll never forget. This child will never have to ask for bread and jam again, and by your kindness you have probably saved his life." When my father came home, my mother told him about the old lady, and Father said, "For what she has done for us, that old lady will never want for anything while I am alive;" he kept his promise.

Meanwhile, when the doctor next called to see Garfield, he said to my mother, "You've been feeding this child." "Yes, I have," my mother replied, and at that he was very annoyed, and told her that she could be prosecuted for going against his instructions. "Go ahead and prosecute me then, if that's what you want, but this child will not need to knock at anyone's door again and ask for bread and jam," she told him. "So good day, doctor, your services are no longer required, and please don't call again to see my child," and she closed the door on him. With each new day Garfield grew stronger and more loveable, and he and I became so close that we could not bear to be apart from one another.

My father seemed to be at home more often now, coming back every weekend, whereas before he had only been able to come home when he was able to take time off from work. In fact, it appears that one day some time ago my father had gone out, taking Colonel, his retriever, with him; he had promised my mother that he would bring her back a hare, and he had carried his gun with him. Colonel returned home without my father, and a search party which set out to look for him found him lying on his stomach at the foot of a quarry where he had fallen. He was now in a private nursing home in Swansea, from which he could come home at weekends. We children had not been told of Father's accident, and when he came home at weekends we thought he was coming from London, because we still had our presents.

By now Garfield was coming up to his fourth birthday, and that was the date when my parents planned to have him breeched. In those days, when little boys were born, they were dressed in petticoats and dresses just like little girls, and their hair was left to grow long. Now, on his fourth birthday, that October, Garfield would become a little boy for the first time in his life, and once the date of the great day had been arranged, it was all a hustle and bustle of preparations. Emily and I had to go backwards and forwards to our dressmaker for fittings for our new outfits, which were to consist of lined dresses of fine red serge, with lace collars and cuffs, and red serge coats to match, with maroon velvet collars and cuffs. Meanwhile my father took Ben to his tailor to be fitted for a suit; Father was also having a new suit for himself, while Mother went to her own dressmaker for fittings for her own gown of plum velvet. Garfield's suit was to be of the same plum velvet.

All we could talk about was that our little brother was going to become a boy and be breeched on his fourth birthday, and there was great excitement. At last the big day arrived – a Sunday, because a breeching had to take place on a Sunday. (Our Sundays were very strictly observed, and we were never allowed to play or knit or carry out any of our weekly activities on Sunday, instead we had to curb our excitement and act soberly because it was a holy day.)

I was very sad because Garfield's beautiful golden curls had to be cut. Meanwhile Miss Dibble dressed us in our beautiful new dresses and coats, which had button-up boots and stockings to match. Emily and I were dressed exactly alike, and we wore white panama hats with white rosettes on a buckram frame at

14

the front. My mother was tall and stately, and her long velvet gown had a small waist, with a small bustle at the back (large bustles were out of fashion). It had a closely fitted bodice with a high neck edged with fine white lace, and leg-o'mutton sleeves. Her hat was of white velour, bowler style, with a large ostrich feather which went from the front of the hat over the crown and down the back. She looked very elegant.

When we were ready, Miss Dibble brought Garfield in, all dressed for us to see. He wore a plum velvet suit, with knickerbocker trousers that came down over the knees and fastened tightly just below them, and a velvet jacket which came down on to the hips and was fastened all the way up the back with a row of pearl buttons; the jacket had two rows of pin tucks on each side of a row of pearl buttons which came down the centre from the neck, and white lace round the neck and the bottom of the sleeves. He had a little boy's shoes, with a buckle on the front of each shoe, and a white panama tricolan hat (this was a three pointed hat, with the brim folded back, to form three points, one on each side of the hat, and one at the front; on each side of the front peak was a white rosette on a buckram base), and kid gloves. Ben also had a knickerbocker suit, of the same material as my father's suit, and we all wore kid gloves, like Garfield.

Now we were all ready, and with Garfield perched on Daddy's left shoulder, Emily and I on either side of him, and Ben escorting my mother, we proudly marched off to chapel. People came out on to their door steps to see the little Bowen boy going to chapel for the first time dressed as a boy. That was a very special day, and everything we did on it was special. Daddy took us to Sunday School, and in the evening we all went to Evensong, with Garfield perched on Daddy's shoulders as he had been in the morning.

We took our pew, with Daddy sitting on the end, Mammy next to him, with Garfield on her lap, then me, Emily and Ben. We children were not allowed to fidget or make a sound, but I did not like the preacher, who was the 'blood and thunder' man, and I was terribly bored. The pockets in our coats were meant for holding our handkerchiefs and our collection, not for putting our hands in, which would pull the pockets out of shape, but to prevent myself from fidgeting, I did put my hand in – and to my great surprise I found a new penny. The preacher was in the

15

middle of his sermon, but I forgot I was in chapel and shouted out, "I've got a penny, I've got a penny!" There was a terrible hush, and then everybody seemed to be hissing at me like a lot of snakes, telling me to 'ssshh'. The preacher stopped in mid-sermon to glare at me in anger, and I shrank down in my seat in horror.

I had committed an unpardonable offence, and I knew my punishment would come when the service was over, so I had to think of a way to get out of this predicament and get a word in first. When we came out, after the bowing and nodding and congratulations were over, we started our walk home, and I turned to my mother and said with great force and sincerity, "I'm not going to Heaven when I die." My mother looked at me severely, and asked, "Why, pray, are you not going to Heaven when you die?" "I don't like that God," I told her, "He points His finger at me in chapel and says, 'You are heading for damnation, you are going to be burnt in the fire of Hell.'" I stamped my foot, and said, "If that's your God, I don't want to go to His Heaven."

I thought I had floored my mother with this, and I would be safe from punishment. My father explained, "That's not God, Rachael, that man was only a preacher," but my mother said, "Now that's over, let's get down to the business of you shouting in chapel." "It's been a busy and exciting day for her today," said Father. "Don't you think we can forgive her this once?" But my mother always had to have the last word, and she replied, "John, I was never so humiliated in my life." At that I said I was sorry, and wouldn't do it again, but I had been so excited I had forgotten where I was.

THREE

At the time of Garfield's breeching, our baby sister was a year old, and my father had been in hospital for three years; gradually there were changes in our home. My father went back to the hospital on Sunday nights, and although I was too young to understand, I knew things were no longer the same for our family. Though we still had presents from Father as we had done when he was working in London, they were things that had been given to him after his sister's children had finished with them. Emily and Ben had been away in boarding school, but from whispered conversations I gathered that they would have to come home and they would not be going back to their schools after Christmas. These things did not worry me because I was so young, but I realised that my father and mother were worried, and I heard my father say, "It's no good, Rachael, you can't go on paying, I'll have to leave the hospital."

Mother said, "No, John, you mustn't leave, you need the treatment. We'll manage somehow."

I remember that Christmas so well – though neither my father or my mother knew then that that would be the last Christmas we would spend in our lovely home. My parents had always bought us expensive presents in the past, but this year we were limited to one toy each; my present was a wax doll. By now some of the rooms in our house were locked, because they were not being used and were kept closed to save fuel, while the room that had formerly been used only by my parents was now used by all of us. I remember asking my mother that day if I could bring my dolly in to warm herself by the fire because she was cold; of course we had a fire in our playroom, but it had a protective guard, and I could never get close enough to it, especially as there were now five of us sitting round it. I wanted to warm my dolly's little face, which felt very cold, and I wrapped her in a shawl and put her inside the fender to keep warm while I looked through my stocking. She was a beautifully dressed doll, but I was disappointed because I had wanted a pink doll and Father Christmas had brought me a blue one.

A little while later my mother came into the room and said to me, "What are you doing with your doll inside the fender?"

"I'm warming her," I said, "her face was cold."

My mother bent down and picked up the doll, saying, "Dolly's face is supposed to be cold, she is wax." But it was too late, the doll's face had melted. I was heartbroken, and had I but known it, that was the last expensive doll that I was to have. Mother looked sadly at me, because she already knew this, though I, of course, did not.

There had been no wages coming into the house for the past three years, and there were Father's fees to find, and his pocket money and money to travel back and forward to the hospital, so my mother decided to take in school teachers as lodgers to help her financially. However this was not a success, and one weekend, when he was home from hospital she discussed future plans with my father. They decided they would have to leave Swansea altogether and mother would go back to Blackwood. My father took a week off in the August of his fourth year in hospital to help get things settled. We had already said goodbye to Miss Dibble, because Mother could no longer afford her, and the other servant had left some time before. Much of our lovely furniture had also gone a long time ago, sold, I suspect, to keep our home going. Piece by piece it had disappeared in an effort to keep my father in hospital, but now the remainder of the furniture had to go. A sale was arranged, and soon all that was left to remind my mother of our lovely home was the fire-guard. The bedding and our clothes and the mattresses etc, were packed up and stored.

Then my father and mother and we five children set off to visit Aunt Margaret in Blackwood. When we arrived at her house, Aunt Margaret was waiting for us, and gave us a warm welcome. She told my mother she thought I was looking tired so I was taken off to the smallest room in the house to rest for a while; it held just a three-quarter bed behind the door and a small dressing table. However there was also a beautiful patchwork quilt on the bed. My favourite book had always been 'Little Red Riding Hood', and her grandmother had had a patchwork quilt on her bed just like this one, so when Aunt Margaret lifted me up on to the bed (because though I was seven, I was very small

18

for my age), and covered me over with the quilt, I was no longer Ritty Bowen, I was Little Red Riding Hood in her grandmother's bed.

Aunt Margaret had a grown-up family. Her eldest daughter, Margaret Ann, who was my mother's age, was married, with her own family of growing children; she had a beautiful soprano voice and in her younger days had been known as 'the darling of the music halls', especially by the people of Bargoed where she was always in great demand. (We had several records at home of her singing, and my one secret ambition had always been to sing 'The Children's Hour' and 'The Better Land' like Margaret Ann.) Aunt Margaret's second daughter, Maud, who was also married, was a trained harpist, and the youngest daughter, Emily Gwen, who was twenty years old, was organist at Llansantffraid Church, Blackwood.

Aunt Margaret's husband, Charles Harris, had been head gardener at the Crystal Palace, but then he came down to live in Pwllglas, near Blackwood, where he had bought several acres of land where he grew flowers for sale and prize blooms which he entered in all the flower shows for miles around, taking many first prizes with them. Later, with the help of his sons, he became the only florist and photographer in Blackwood, while Aunt Margaret's daughter, Margaret Ann, made all the wreaths and crosses for the funerals there. Every year, on Guy Fawkes Night, he would have a large bonfire built on a piece of his spare land; then he would get five poundsworth of fireworks, buy sacks of potatoes and chestnuts, and invite all the children in Pwllglas and Blackwood to come to his bonfire. Every child, irrespective of where he or she lived, was welcome to come and enjoy the bonfire and roast potatoes and chestnuts over the fire.

At Christmas he would put up a large Christmas tree in his garden, and the same children would be invited to come once again and enjoy themselves, tucking into the barrel of apples and cases of oranges that he provided for them. Each child from Pwllglas was given a present from the Christmas tree. Uncle Charlie was a much-loved man, as might be expected. He had family connections with St. Petersburg, and was uncle to Baden-Powell of the Boy Scout movement.

Next day we left baby Violet with Cousin Margaret Ann, and all the rest of us went to visit my late grandfather's home. We went down a winding lane, like a carriage drive, between rows of

19

fine trees whose leaves intertwined making a canopy over the road, to a place called 'The Waterloo' down the Rhiw. Then we came to a wicket gate on the side of the road, through which ran a stone path leading through a beautiful flower garden. On the right hand side we came to a large thatched cottage, while on the left hand side of the path was a long, flat-topped wall about four feet high, with two or three steps leading up to a kitchen garden, part of which was an orchard with gooseberry and red and black currant bushes heavy with fruit. In the centre of the cottage was a porch, with windows on both sides, but what attracted my attention most of all was an apple tree in the garden, leaning towards the cottage, which was laden with beautiful red apples.

The cottage door was opened by a trim little maid, who said, "Madam is expecting you," and then a little old lady, beautifully gowned and wearing a lace cap on her head, threw her arms round my mother, calling her 'Miss Rachael'. After that each of us was presented to the old lady in turn and told that this was Aunt Hannah. When it was my turn to be embraced by Aunt Hannah, she said to me, "So you are little Rachael the third;" I noticed she smelled of lavender perfume. Later we sat down to a meal of Aunt Hannah's home-made cakes and bread, and afterwards she told us that she was not really our aunt, but had been our grandfather's housekeeper; then she said, "If you children would like to go out into the garden while I talk business with your Mammy, Benny can give the apple tree a gentle shake – not too hard, mind – and the apples will fall down for you. Then you won't have to climb on the tree and spoil your good clothes!" It was a wonderful sight to see those beautiful apples falling down into our hands.

At the bottom of that large garden, which Daddy said was two acres in size, was a stout wire fence, dividing the garden from the railway line. We heard a train whistle blow, and all climbed on to the fence to wave to the train as it went past. I had travelled in a train, and I had seen one in the station, but now I was seeing one travelling on its tracks through the countryside, and it was very exciting indeed! Then we went home, and Mammy promised to bring us back the following day to spend a whole day with Aunt Hannah while Mammy and Daddy went off to do some business.

Next day at Aunt Hannah's, when we were tired of playing, we sat with her and she told us stories of how, when she was a girl of fourteen, she had gone into service, to a big house in Caerphilly. Her master was a wealthy landowner, who owned all the land that Cardiff was being built on. The Powell Dyffryn Collieries were sunk on his land, and he claimed royalties on every ton of stone, coal or muck that came up from those collieries, while he also owned the Taff Vale railway line – the line on which the train at which we had waved had been travelling. The Taff river passed through his land, as did part of the Cardiff canal.

"He had three children," said Aunt Hannah, "a daughter Ann who was twenty-one and had just left finishing school, a son Richard who, at eighteen, was away in school and had a fine baritone voice, and a younger daughter, whose servant I was, who was the same age as myself. When my mistress was sixteen, they gave a coming of age party for her elder sister on her twenty-first birthday.

"In those days," explained Aunt Hannah, "young ladies in society were not allowed to be friendly with men until they had had their coming of age party. As the time of the party drew near, all the wealthy young men and women were invited, and a detective was hired to protect the jewels that these guests would wear to the celebration. This was William Davies, who was thirty-six years old and unmarried; these days he would be known as a plain clothes policeman, but then he was called a detective. As the ball was going on, William Davies met a little sixteen-year-old servant walking in the grounds, and this was the start of many secret meetings, during which they fell in love. Later William asked her to be his bride, and she explained to him that she could not tell her mistress, because the master did not allow the maids to have 'callers', so they must continue their courtship in secret. William told her that he had bought a large plot of land, on which a cottage was being built for them; as soon as it was finished they would get married – though she said they would have to elope because she had no-one whom she could tell of her marriage. And in due course they did elope."

Ben interrupted the story here, and asked, "Was that you, Aunt Hannah."

"No, my dear," she said. "That was my mistress who had been passing as her own maid. She was wearing my cloak and bonnet on the night when she met William Davies, and she told me that she had been afraid to reveal her identity to him once she

21

realised she was in love with him, because she knew he would have discontinued the courtship. And she was in the grounds on the night of the ball, and disguised, in case her family saw her, because though she was still considered to be a child, being in the schoolroom, she wanted to see the guests arriving. A twenty-first coming out party, you see, was meant as a chance for the girl to meet all the eligible, wealthy young men, in the hope of finding her a suitable husband who would be approved by her father. – Ann, whose party it was, later met and married Colonel William Lewis, better known in the valleys as Colonel North.

"Eventually," Aunt Hannah went on, "Rachael and William Davies married quietly, with Dr. William Price of Llantrisant (who was William's first cousin) as one witness, and myself, her maid, as the other. (I had left my master's employment to go with my little mistress and her husband.) When they were signing the register after their marriage, she signed herself Rachael Thomas, and it was only then that William knew he had married the youngest daughter of the house and not her maid. She told William that she had left a note for her father, telling him that she had eloped, and hoping that he would forgive her – he was such a loving father that she was sure he would do so. But her father was so angry at what she had done that he forbade her ever to see her father or her mother again because she had dishonoured his household. Their family crest bore the words 'Gwell angau na chywilydd,' which translated means 'Better death than dishonour;' Mr. Thomas told Rachael that she had chosen dishonour, and therefore death, and henceforth she was dead to her family. She never saw her father or her mother, her sister or her brother again in this life, and died at the age of thirty-six, leaving your dear grandpa and three children – Margaret, David and your dear Mamma who was only three years old."

My mother had never told us anything about her early life, so we were very interested in what Aunt Hannah had to tell us – particularly Ben and Emily, because they were old enough to understand. Little Garfield looked at Ben, who was his hero, and asked, "Aunt Hannah, was the big apple tree here when grandpa came here to live?"

"No, Garfield," she said. "This land was just like a field covered in stones then, and your grandpa knew it would have to

22

be cleared before they could plant trees and bushes on it. He told his cousin, Dr. William Price, that it was going to be a back-breaking job, but they would have to start doing something about it, and Dr. Price told him, "Leave it to me, I'll think of some way to clear it without all that backache." The next time Uncle William Price arrived at the cottage, he was wearing a fur hat that he had made from the skin of a fox, with the nose of the fox over his forehead and the tail hanging down his back. William Davies roared with laughter when he saw him, and said, "What mad prank are you up to now?" "Firstly," said the doctor, "we have confused the people long enough. They're always asking me which I am, Dr. Price or William Davies, and as we are so alike, this will show the difference. Secondly, I have found a plan to get rid of the stones without hardship to either of us. I have distributed some posters in the village, to let all the boys know that there is to be a competition at the Waterloo to find the best stone thrower."

"Soon all the boys began to gather at your grandfather's gate. They had come for the contest. Uncle William Price told them that they were each to gather a large pile of stones and the boy who built the largest pile of stones would receive a prize. Next they were to throw the stones, over the fence onto waste land and the one who could throw the most was the winner. So in a very short time, at the cost of a few prizes, William Davies's two acres of land was cleared of stones. Uncle William Price was a great joker, and very witty, and next time you come to see me, I'll tell you some more of his pranks, but now your Mammy and Daddy have come to take you back to Aunt Margaret's. You *will* come and see me again, won't you, children?" We promised her that we would and then we went home.

When we got back to Aunt Margaret's that night, I told my mother that I would like to sleep in Cousin Margaret Ann's house. Emily and Ben had told me that they had had a lovely night there because they and Cousin Margaret Ann's children were allowed to sing in bed. So that night we slept like sardines; I slept in the same bed as my sister Emily and my cousin Mercy Flossy, while in another bed were my cousin Ethel, who was a year older than me, Maggie who was a year younger, and Emily Maud who was younger still. In the next room Ben and Garfield slept with my two cousins Richard and James. Cousin Margaret Ann's children had all inheritied her lovely voice, and after we

23

had been put to bed, with her permission to sing, Dick called out from his bedroom the name of the song we were to sing. We did not know the song he asked for that night, so he said, "Listen to me and I'll teach it to you." Then he sang and taught us 'If I should plant one tiny seed of love in the garden of your heart.' We sang it over and over until we each fell asleep.

We paid several visits to Aunt Hannah while Mother and Father went out looking for a house where we could set up home again, and we would ciammer for more stories. I asked Aunt Hannah, "If Grandpa Davies had children, why didn't Uncle William Price have any?"

"Uncle William once had a little son," explained Aunt Hannah. "He named him Iesu Grist (Jesus Christ), and he loved him very dearly. He was broken-hearted when the boy died, and said he couldn't bear to put the little body in the ground for slugs and worms to devour. So he built a large pyre on the mountain in Llantrisant, wrapped his little child's body in burial clothes, carried him to the pyre and cremated him. It caused an uproar amongst the inhabitants, and he was brought before the court, but he proved to them that it was the cleanest way to dispose of a body, and he won his case. The people termed him the 'Mad Doctor', though. Then he turned his affection to little mother-less Rachael and, with her father William Davies, brought her up with loving care. They made her all her clothes, which they would cut out on the kitchen table, then, taking the material, they would go up on to the mountain, where they would sit and sew by hand.

As there were no schools as we know them today, there was no compulsory education. Instead anyone, provided they knew their three Rs, could open a private school in their own parlour; they would charge a penny a week, though a better educated person could charge two pence a week. Rachael was taken to a twopenny school because the penny a week school was not considered good enough for her, and the two Williams would take it in turns to carry her there – there was no surface on the roads in those days, and there were large holes in the road which became very muddy on wet days." (Little Rachael wasn't allowed to wet her feet; in fact Aunt Hannah had once told us that Mammy wasn't allowed as much as to do up her own shoes until she was married.)

Aunt Hannah also told us of one occasion when Uncle

William was summoned by a farmer to attend court. Dr. Price called Rachael his lucky charm and she had to go with the two Williams everywhere they went, so she accompanied my grandfather and Uncle William to court that day. In court the farmer stated that he had the only bull in Llantrisant at his farm, and since Dr. Price's cow had had a calf and there had been no business transaction involved, he was suing Dr. Price for illegal servicing by the farmer's bull. Dr. Price's reply was, "I should be suing that farmer for illegal trespass by his bull on my land. He jumped over the fence into my paddock and assaulted my cow without as much as a 'by your leave!' This caused much laughter in the court and the case was dismissed. (Aunt Hannah told us many more tales, but for the moment I cannot recollect them, except one that she told us of Dr. Price giving my mother a Welsh spinning wheel on her fifteenth birthday.)

To Mother's extreme sorrow, Dr. Price died at the time of her sixteenth birthday. According to his last request, he was cremated on a large pyre on the mountain in Llantrisant, at the spot where his little son had been cremated before him.

FOUR

One day Mammy and Daddy told us that they had found a nice little house, with three rooms up and three rooms down, which Mammy could look after herself. It had a nice garden, and fields all around in which we could play. Now, then, there was the excitement of moving into our new house, which was in Edward Street, Pengam, between Blackwood and Bargoed. Our old furniture would not fit the new rooms, so we had to get furniture of a cheaper kind to fit into this small terraced house, and it was thoroughly exciting the day this new furniture arrived, because it all seemed so funny to us and had a strong smell of varnish and new wood.

The living room furniture consisted of a high backed wooden armchair (called by some 'the father's armchair'), a rocking armchair (sometimes called 'mother's chair'), a nursing chair, six wooden dining chairs and a white-topped table with red legs. I didn't like the smell of the new furniture, which made me feel sick. For the parlour we had a leather seven-piece suite, which was a couch and two fireside chairs and four leather padded chairs. At mealtimes my mother would warn us, "Don't put your feet on the rungs of the chairs or you'll scratch them, and don't kick the table legs until I've put their drawers on." I thought that was very funny, because little girls wore drawers! In the evening I saw my mother sewing, then, when she had finished she raised up the table and slipped something which resembled a sleever over each leg. They were made from cretonne and had a drawstring at the top and the bottom to keep them in position; they were used to protect the paint on the legs of the table. What I liked most of all was when, after the living room floor had been swept, my mother would throw fresh sand over the floor to keep it clean, and it looked so cosy.

Once we were settled into our new home, Daddy went back into the hospital. He told my mother that she would not have to pay his quarterly fees any more as it had been arranged that his aunt, Lady Mary, would pay his hospital fees as long as necessary, as well as the expenses of his weekend journeys home.

Our house was the last but one at the top of the street, and at the end of the last house was a grassy bank leading to a field of gorse and broom, which was in full bloom at that time. A little further on was a beautiful wood with very large strong oak trees, and some of the men had put up rope swings with wooden seats from the boughs of the trees; they were there for any child to use. Edward Street had a row of houses each side of the road, and on one side the houses were three-storeyed. The bottom house ended some yards lower down the street than ours, and so we had a clear view of all the surrounding countryside. There were no mountains, but we were on a high rise and from our house we could look down, over a grassy slope ablaze with gorse and broom, to the main road from Pengam to Fleur-de-Lys. Between the main road and our street was a lovely hay field called Bebb's Field, and in the part of the field near our home was a quarry, surrounded by trees and blackberry bushes, called Bebb's Quarry and Bebb's Wood, which was a short cut to Fleur-de-Lys.

At the back of our houses was a lane which was used by the coal carts when they delivered concessionary coal to the miners, and bordering the lane were some beautiful large hay fields. In the first field behind our house they were building the foundations for what was to be the largest council school in Monmouthshire, Fair View School. Among others it would accommodate the children of Edward Street who were then attending a small school at Pengam.

Soon after we moved into Edward Street an Irishwoman who lived further down the street came up to make herself known to my mother. She was bowing and scraping and kept calling my mother 'Ma'am' while she welcomed us to Edward Street; she said she had just come there to live from Ireland and had a number of children. "Oh, it's lovely having a real lady coming to live down here with us," she said. My mother was puzzled, for we were complete strangers and no-one knew us there, so she thought the woman was just flattering her. Despite this, she seemed a nice enough little woman – but later we found out that the flattery was just a means of using us, and there was scarcely a day passed without her sending up one of her children with a cup

27

in hand to borrow something or other. Her larder seemed to be permanently empty, and she told us that her husband was drinking heavily and spending all her money. My mother could ill afford to give so much to her, but she could never see anyone go without.

Lower down the street, in one of the cellar houses, lived a little girl of my own age with whom I became very friendly; her name was Dolly Parry. Next door to us, in the end house, lived a young couple with a three-year-old girl, who kept themselves to themselves, and would not mix with anyone, preferring to be left alone. They would not even come out and pass the time of day with their neighbours, so people ignored them, thinking that the young couple felt themselves a cut above their neighbours. Then one day we heard terrible screams coming from the house, and my mother, ignoring the fact that they might order her out, ran into their house and found the little girl on fire and the mother standing by, petrified and screaming, unable to do anything. My mother beat out the flames with her bare hands, but it was too late, the little girl was dead.

Straight away my mother ran into our house and unhooked the fireguard which she had brought with her from our old house, and ran back next door with it; then she telephoned for the police and the doctor. It was an offence by law to have an unguarded fire when there were children, but my mother said the young mother had suffered enough sorrow through losing her little girl not to have to be put through the ordeal of explaining to the police the reason for having no fireguard. The young husband was at work, but he had been sent for, so my mother stayed with the grieving woman until he got home.

It was then that the young mother explained why she did not bother with any of her neighbours in the street – she had a little boy upstairs whom she did not want anyone to see. My mother asked if she could see the boy, so the young woman took her upstairs and showed her a six year old boy who looked like a six year old baby except for his face, which was old for his years. He was suffering badly from St. Vitus Dance, and was in a very poor state; the child could not walk, and had never been able to do so. My mother stood silently looking at this little boy for a while. We were a family that believed strongly in the power of prayer, and I know my mother was praying for the child in that moment. Then she told the young woman, "You won't lose this little boy.

28

If you leave him to me I will get him to walk, and cure him of his disease in six months. Give me permission to give the child a medicine that I shall make for him and I guarantee that within the six months that the doctor has given him I will have him walking."

When my mother came back into our house, she told us about the little boy, and started to make the medicine for him at once because she wanted to start the treatment without delay. Each day she went in and attended to the child. She told his mother to discontinue the doctor's treatment; it had not done the boy any good, and it was no use mixing the two, Mother's and the doctor's. Every day after school I would go up to Charlie Harris's house, which was only two fields away; when I got there, Uncle Charlie would say, "What would my little apple-woman be wanting today?" and I would say, "Sweet peas, please," and he would take me into his flower garden and, with a special silver scissors, cut me a nice bunch of flowers. Then I would take the bunch down to our sick little friend's bedroom. My mother was as good as her word, and in six months the little boy was walking and completely cured of St. Vitus Dance.

Enough of the new Fair View School had now been built for it to be possible to hold a celebration of the coronation of King George and Queen Mary. One day my little friend Dolly Parry and I were coming home from school together when we passed a couple of little boys who were using swear words. Dolly and I were shocked, though they were not swearing a lot, they were just trying to impress us; we were shocked because we were unaccustomed to hearing such words, and we were sure these boys were headed for damnation because our preacher had always said so. If they were, then they would burn in hell fire, and we knew we must do something about it, and think up a way of saving them from damnation. It would take a lot of thinking, of course, as it was a very serious thing for two little girls to consider.

After some deliberation we decided that the deed would be done on Saturday morning early, after breakfast. We would go down to Bebb's Wood, where no-one could see or hear us, and we would throw back those naughty words into the face of the devil; then he would be defeated. When Saturday morning came, I had a self-imposed task to do for Daddy before he came home from the hospital – to get him a pint of milk, straight from

29

the cow and still warm, which he would drink as soon as he got in. Once that task was done, I waited for Dolly to call for me; then, clasping hands, and heads down, too ashamed to look at each other because of the terrible deed we were about to commit, we went down to Bebb's Wood and selected a secret little place among the blackberry bushes, there to defeat the devil.

I got into the bushes, then I helped Dolly in, and heads up, hands clasped, we shouted at the top of our voices the two naughtiest, wickedest, most terrible swear words ever uttered – 'bugger' and 'damn'. And so the devil was defeated. As for us, we hung our heads down, too ashamed to speak, as we walked to our separate homes. I felt very uncertain of myself as to whether I had done right or wrong, but I did not want to dicuss it with anyone, and for the rest of Saturday I had no inclination to play or go for walks with my brother and sister, because I was trying to come to terms with myself. I was not at all happy about what Dolly and I had done.

That night, after our usual supper of bread and butter and cocoa, I went to bed and, prayers said, I was soon fast asleep. Some time later in the night I awoke, to find an angel standing at the side of my bed, pointing a finger at me and uttering words which, coming from an angel, were very harsh indeed. "Little girl, you are going to die," the angel said, and repeated this over and over again until I could bear it no longer. I got out of the other side of the bed and ran out onto the landing, screaming, "Come quick, Mammy, Daddy, come quick, I'm going to die!"

My mother and father came out onto the landing, asking, "What's the matter, Ritty?" and I said, "Oh Mammy, Daddy, come quick. There's an angel standing by my bed, pointing a finger at me and saying I'm going to die. Please, Mammy and Daddy, can I come downstairs and tell you about it?"

"All right," they said, "You can come down for a while and tell us all about it if that will help."

Safe by the warm fire, with my parents to protect me, I told the whole story of the little boys and what Dolly and I had done to save them from hell fire; it must have been very sinful because now the angel had come to tell me I was going to die. They took me back to the foot of the stairs and said, "Now you go back upstairs, say your prayers, and tell God you are very sorry for what you have done and for the naughty words you've said, and then he won't let that angel come again to frighten you."

One cold, wet Saturday night in September my mother was giving us our supper before sending us to bed, when there was a knock on our front door, "Who can that be?" asked my father.

"Probably one of the Peters' children come to borrow something," said my mother. She went to the door, and there stood an Irishman in his thirties.

"Ma'am," he said, "I'm looking for lodgings."

"I'm very sorry, but we don't take in lodgers," said Mother.

"Oh Ma'am, I've been looking all day for lodgings, and can't get anyone to take me in. I'm a steeplejack," he explained.

"I'm very sorry for you being out on such a terrible night, but I have no room in my house for a lodger, and if I did, I wouldn't be able to look after you, I have an invalid husband and five children to look after," said my mother.

However the man was disinclined to go away, although my mother repeatedly told him she did not take in lodgers and she could not get him off the doorstep. She called my father and told him that he would have to deal with the man, so father told him that they could not take him in, and if he did not go soon, he would find himself on the road all night. The man took his foot from the door, and made to move away, calling out to someone as he did so, in a very sad, tired voice. "Come along," he said, and a little boy of about nine years old who had been sheltering in the doorway next door, joined him and they started walking down the street.

My mother called to the man, "Stop a minute, is this child with you?"

"Yes", he said.

"Do you mean to tell me," said mother, "that you are dragging this child all around the countryside with you in this weather?"

"Yes, ma'am," he replied. "He's all I've got."

"It's disgraceful," she told him, "This child should be in a nice warm bed, or at least by a warm fire, not trudging the roads, soaking wet as he is, with you. I can't see this child out all night, you'd better leave him with me until you can find somewhere to stay."

The man readily brought the child back, but he looked so wet and dejected himself that my mother said to him, "Oh, for goodness sake come in. But remember I can't give you lodgings;

31

you can sleep on the couch, but you must go in the morning."

My mother got the little boy out of his wet clothes, and put him in one of Ben's night shirts; it was too big for him, but as my mother said, it was better than being in wet clothes. She gave him some supper and asked the man how long it had been since the boy had eaten. His father said they had been on the road all day, and Mother saw that he would need more than the one slice of bread which was our usual supper, and told him to eat as much as he wanted. The man said that the boy's name was Donald Kelly (or Murphy – I can't quite recall).

Then we were all put to bed and Donald slept with Ben and Garfield. Next morning Donald's father set off to look for lodgings, leaving Donald with us, because my mother would not hear of him taking the boy with him. Instead she told him to go on his own, because that way he would have better luck, but to be sure to tell them he had a little boy, and to come back and fetch him when he had found somewhere. "Don't worry about your boy," Mother said, "he will be well looked after." And Donald himself was quite happy and contented to stay with us.

Donald's father went, and my mother could see that the little boy had a bad chest, because he was dribbling badly and his chest was soaking wet, so Mother set to work to find out what was causing the dribbling, and in the meantime she put layers of brown paper across his chest to prevent the water from getting on to it. It was the school holidays, and Mother sent us to pick blackberries (there was an abundance of blackberries down the woods and in Bebb's Wood). We set off, Emily carrying a large basket, and we children each carrying a container which we were to fill, then empty into Emily's basket. However Mother did not want Donald to put his blackberries in the basket because of his dribbling, so she gave him a large container and told him to save his berries in his own tin, then she would see what a good blackberry picker he was. "I will save your blackberries," she said, "and make a tart especially for your daddy when he comes to fetch you." She assumed that Donald's father would come that day to fetch him, but he did not, and after we were all put to bed except Emily, who was now in her teens, my mother flushed Donald's blackberries down the toilet – she didn't have the stomach to eat the fruit after he had dribbled over it.

Despite his dribbling, Donald was a lovely little boy, and we were all very fond of him. Days turned into weeks, and weeks into months, and still his father did not come. When Christmas arrived Donald was still with us, and by now we had accepted him as one of our own and begun to look on him as a brother; we could not think about the time when he would have to leave us. I heard my mother say to my father, "I wonder if he has abandoned this little child? If he has, I'm not turning the boy over to any authority, we'll keep him. We won't miss the little bit he eats."

Then one day his father turned up to fetch him. Donald was pleased to see the man, but he did not want to go with him. His father apologised for not coming to fetch him sooner, and said, "I could find plenty of lodging places, but when I told them I had a little boy travelling with me, they didn't want to know, so I took advantage of your kindness and left him where I knew he was happy. Several times I have come to satisfy myself he was happy, though he has not seen me; but the job has finished now and we are moving to another place, so if you'll just let me know how much I owe you, I'll settle up and take the boy with me."

"Never mind what you owe me," said my mother, "use it to get this little boy some good clothes, which he needs badly. I didn't keep him for money, I kept him because we love him, and we hate to part with him. He hasn't had the best of everything, but he has had the same as my own children, and that's a share of everything going; I'm sure you'll be pleased to see that Donald has changed considerably. He doesn't lisp now, he speaks properly, and he doesn't dribble."

Donald proudly showed his father his chest – "Nice dry chest now, Daddy," he said. He went with his father quite willingly, but tearfully, and we were all broken-hearted saying goodbye to our little 'brother'. He had been with us a long time, and we would miss him; we hoped we would see him again. My mother told his father, "Don't you let me find out that you have been dragging this little one around the country, he is not a gipsy and he needs a home."

Some weeks later my father was reading the newspaper when he called to my mother, "Come here, Rachael, listen to this. What was the name of the place that man was taking little Donald to?" My mother told him, and my father said, "You had better read this, then." Mother took the paper and read it. We knew something was wrong, for the blood had drained from her

33

face; she read that a steeplejack had fallen to his death, and he was survived by one child, a ten-year-old son. She turned to my father and said, "He's got no mother or father now, they'll put him in the workhouse, and then God help him. We can't let that happen."

"If you are willing to have the child, Rachael," said Father, "I'd like to see him coming back to us."

We children were so excited that we forgot the sorrow of the death of Donald's father in the joy of having our little brother back. Mother said, "We can't give him much, but we can give him a home and love, and he won't go hungry any more than the rest of us will. So get a letter off tonight, John."

My father sent a letter off with the next post, saying we would like to take the boy, and considered we had prior claim on him because he had lived with us for a twelve-month before his father came for him.

We did not have a reply for several weeks, and were anxiously wondering how the little boy was faring; when the letter did come, it was a great surprise to my parents, and a disappointment to us children, for we were not to have our little brother back. I recollect seeing this letter, though I can't quite remember the details; but I know the letter had a seal and crest on it, and I well recollect the wording on it, even though I was only Donald's age. It thanked my father and mother for their kind concern about Donald, but told us to have no anxiety about the young man, who was well cared for; he was his father's only son, and his father had been an eccentric millionaire. There was also a little message from Donald to us all, thanking us for all our care of him and the love and kindness we showed him when he lived with us in Edward Street, Pengam.

(If this book should ever reach Donald, and he remembers, I should like him to know that this is Ritty, and I'm sending my love.)

FIVE

Life in Edward Street was very happy although my parents often found it difficult to make ends meet; it was a paradise for children and a lovely place to grow up in. The new school behind our house was now complete, but at the time of which I am writing only the infants and small children were being educated there. We had celebrated the coronation with a party at the school's opening, when we were given a mug with a picture of King George and Queen Mary on it, and I had brought home a piece of cake for my mother's tea, wrapped in a nice clean handkerchief which Mother had given me especially for that purpose. Dolly, my friend, and I were now attending the school, and I had a new friend now, who lived a few doors down from me; her name was Violet Pretty. Her family had come to Edward Street from France, and in the mornings after a night of rain Violet would ask me to help her find slugs and snails for her father's breakfast. I thought at first that she was teasing me, but she told me her father loved them and all the French people ate them! When Violet was twelve and her brother Tommy was eleven, Mr. Pretty took Tommy to Cardiff for the day, leaving Mrs. Pretty and Violet at home. Tommy fell in the canal, Mr. Pretty dived in to save him, and they were both drowned.

My father's stay in hospital had now lasted a little over five years, and he carried his portfolio back and forward just as he had done as a barrister in London. He studied botany, and he was also very concerned about my very poor vision, as he had been told that any shock could make me lose my sight completely. Hence he was preparing me for blindness. Early every Saturday morning while the dew was on the ground, he would gather fresh herbs and put them in brown paper bags which were then hung from the back kitchen ceiling to dry. Doctors were not free; their services had to be paid for, and since many could not afford to pay, the doctors were often not called out when there was anyone ill in Edward Street. There was always someone knocking at our door, complaining about practically everything from boils to tummy bugs, and my father would treat them free with the medicines he made from the herbs.

Every day when he was home, he would take me for a walk through the fields and the wood; it was a game my daddy played only with me, teaching me the names of every herb and flower, by feel and touch and perfume. Thus at a very early stage of my life I could tell the age of every tree in the wood by the feel of the bark and the girth of the tree, and I became very popular with my teachers when we went on nature rambles. They would test my knowledge and ask me the age of trees, and they were amazed at the accuracy of my answers.

He played another game with my little sister Violet; he would take us for a stroll and we would walk until Daddy felt it was time to go home. He would walk on for another few yards and drop a penny behind his back, then he would turn to us and say, "Come on, let's go home, there are no pennies here today." We would turn around and go back the way we had come, then Violet would find her penny, and we would go home. That was Violet's game.

One day, while I was learning to tell a flower by its smell, there was a large bumble bee on the bloom. I leant down to smell the flower and saw the bumble bee, and I thought how beautiful it looked at close quarters, so I said to it, "Kiss me, little bee." Afterwards I told my daddy, "I only wanted him to kiss me, and he bit me on my lip, so I don't like him!"

One Sunday we five children went to our new chapel, Fair View Chapel, Pengam, with Daddy and Mammy. During the service the minister asked if Rachael Bowen would come up to the pulpit and give them a recitation, and Violet Adelaine Bowen come up and sing a little song. Violet's song was 'Into a tent where a gypsy lay, Dying alone at the close of the day,' which she knew right through to the end and sang very well. She was only three and a half years old, a chubby little thing, in no way bashful or shy, and after I had said my piece, she stood up proudly in the pulpit, and viewed the whole congregation with a cheeky look on her face as if to say 'Silence, the singer is on her feet.' Everyone started to laugh at the expression on her face, and she put her hands on her hips, stared everyone in the face, and shouted, "I won't sing now, you buggers," and got down

36

from the pulpit. I expect my father must have scolded her for using a swear word, because when we got home Violet took the fireside shovel, and stormed out of the house in a rage. My mother told fifteen-year-old Emily to go out and see what Violet was up to. She was furiously digging up the soil at the side of the end house, and when Emily asked her what she was doing, Violet told her she was digging a hole to put Daddy in. When Emily told my mother, she said she didn't like that, it sounded like a bad omen.

In his briefcase my father carried documents relating to the inheritance of my grandmother, Rachael Davies (nee Thomas), which we assumed had died with her. Father told Mother, "Another few months and I will have got it all settled," and Mother said, "I wouldn't worry for myself, John, if I never had it, but I would like it for our children." "Well," said Father, "it will be more than you will want, Rachael, or the children, or the children's children."

Father had found full proof, that in my great-grandfather's will he had left everything to his second wife, my step-great-grandmother, but that after her death it was to be shared equally between his three children, Ann, Richard and Rachael Thomas. However after her death it had been learned that my step-great-grandmother had forged my great-grandfather's signature to a will leaving everything to her three sons by a former marriage, and they had been living in luxury on the wealth which should have gone to her late husband's own three children. My father had discovered this, and the estate had been taken away and put in Chancery; there were only a few months left now before Ann, Richard and Rachael could claim their inheritance. All this was the result of my father's hard work when he was in the hospital.

Now my father had decided not to go back to the hospital, because he felt well enough to stay at home and save the expense. My paternal grandfather had died some time before, leaving his estate entirely to his wife during her lifetime, after which it was to be divided equally amongst his surviving children; now she had also died. My father and mother went to the funeral in Swansea and to the reading of the will, and on their return Daddy told us that he had something important to tell us. We all gathered round him; I sat on one of his knees and Garfield sat on the other, and he said, "Now, children, I am going to tell you something, but it has to be a secret, just between us here. Firstly, we are going to leave Edward Street. Daddy and Mammy are going to buy a nice big house for us."

At that I said, "Oh Daddy, I don't want to leave Edward Street, because I love Dolly Parry." Daddy said, "Oh, there'll be plenty of other Dolly Parrys," but I insisted "but I only want this Dolly Parry."

"You'll have a nice big room to play in," suggested Father. "No more playing on the streets."

"But I like playing on the streets," I chipped in again.

"That wasn't the secret," Father went on. "But what I am going to tell you now must be a secret for a while. Daddy has had a word in his ear (that's what makes it a secret) that I am going to be the headmaster of the new Fair View School. So now, with the money that we are going to have from Grandfather's estate, we are going to buy that nice big house, suitable for a headmaster, and Benny can go back to school, and there will be no more poverty for us, thank God. And some day, Benny my son, you will be a good barrister, I hope."

At that Benny began to act a little boastful, and my father said to him, "Now Benny, don't get a swollen head, I'm not a headmaster yet."

Ben replied, "Daddy, if you do become headmaster, will we be allowed to speak Welsh in the playground? The way it is now, if we are caught speaking Welsh to anyone, we are sent to the headmaster for punishment, because Welsh is not allowed to be spoken in Monmouthshire."

Father said, "Yes, Benny, I'll see that it is allowed. This is Wales, and I shall endeavour to introduce Welsh into the school. But, Benny, I want you all to understand that if and when I am headmaster, at home I may still be 'Daddy' to you, but at school you will address me as 'Sir'. You will be no different to me than any other boy at the school."

At about this time there was a faint rumour going around of war, but it meant nothing to us, for as children we knew nothing of war, and it was not spoken of at home. In our school we had a teacher who, though only a young man, had seen active service in the Boer War and was very embittered. (I believe that they took very young boys for the Boer War, because Aunt Margaret's son, Jim Harris, went as a drummer boy at the age of fourteen.) For some reason or other our teacher taught us to sing the Marseillaise, the National Anthem of France, which he translated into English. He also taught us a song he had composed himself, the words of which are as follows:

Mad dogs of war are on the track,
Barking at the Union Jack.
Oh, what a surprise, ah!
We will give the Kaiser,
Those mad dogs will soon be wiser.
When they hear the sound of
Rule Britannia and God Save the King,
Then they'll know that we fear no foe,
When they hear our voices ring.
We are all under the same old flag,
Brothers in arms are we,
One King and one Empire,
One flag and one desire.
England, Ireland, Scotland, Wales and
Comrades on the sea, unite to fight
For a cause that is right,
To conquer Germany!

That song was the first indication I had, as a child, that there was unrest in the world. The teacher talked a lot about fighting war, and he said that German Zeppelins would soon be over Blackwood. But Zeppelins was a word I knew nothing about, I had never heard of it before, and I didn't know what he meant.

The children of Edward Street were very friendly; it was a long street, and many children played there together, but there were no fights or squabbles amongst them. We could play in safety in the street, because we lived away from the shopping centre and the only traffic we were ever likely to see was the delivery cart, and the coal cart on a Friday evening, and about once a week the chip cart, which would come round in the evening. The chip cart was a new invention, and a tremendous thrill it gave us, to hear the horse trotting up the street and see the cart with the chimney on top, and the smoke billowing through it from the pans inside the cart. We would all gather around the cart and watch the man making chips, which fascinated us as we had never seen chips being made before. If we were lucky and had a halfpenny to spend, we would have a nice bag of chips, and we could put our own salt and vinegar on them.

But the most exciting thing that ever happened to me was to watch out every night before it got dark, and sometimes even after dark, for the magic man with his pole. He would walk up our street, stopping at every lamp post, and when he came to our post, I would always say to him, "Hello, Mr. Magic Man." Then he would prise up the catch and open the door of the lamp on top of the lamp standard. With one little wave of his magic stick inside the lamp, it would burst into light, and I would say, "Thank you, Mr. Magic Man, you must be very clever." Then off he would go, on his way. I would gaze up at that light and imagine I was a little fairy living inside the lamp, warm and safe, locked up inside that little lamp for always.

I never joined in the children's play although I would be out in the street watching them; instead I would jump up onto the shop window, which would be brilliantly lit, and I would no longer be little Ritty Bowen; I was transported into fairyland myself.

It was now the beginning of October, 1913, just after we had had the news of good things to come, when one night there was a strange light in the sky. All the children stopped playing, and looked at the sky, shouting, "There's a tremendous big sausage in the sky!" Parents came out to see what was happening, and quickly hurried the children indoors, because it was a German Zeppelin, one of many that flew over Pengam. Mothers would use it as a threat to get their children in at night, and the saying was no longer 'the bogey will get you', but 'If you don't come in, the Zeppelin will get you and carry you off to Germany.' We didn't know what Germany was, but we were sure it was something terrible. Now we played a new game, in which we were soldiers, and all the children, myself included, would march up and down the street, singing at the tops of our voices 'The mad dogs of war' and the Marseillaise. We usually ended up with 'John Brown's Body Lies a Mouldering in the Grave.'

There was a family in our street, the Robertsons, who had eight children, but their mother was very ill and my mother had been going back and forward, making food for the children. Mother did not expect Mrs. Robertson to live, but when she died, my Mother was very upset, and wanted to go to the funeral. Yet when I heard Father say, "Are you going to the funeral, Rachael?" Mother replied, "No, John, I'll do what I can for Mr. Robertson and the children, but I won't go to the funeral." "You go, Rachael," said Father, "or you'll only be sorry you didn't later on." Mother felt she should not go because my father had not been well lately, but my father said to her, "Don't worry about me, Rachael, I feel better today than I've felt for years, so you go to the funeral, and wear your lovely black velvet gown that I like to see you in so much."

So to please my father, my mother went to the funeral. When they returned to the Robertsons' house from the funeral, there was a horse and cart waiting outside, a long, flat cart with sides all around it and seats inside. It was the parish cart, come to take the children to the workhouse. A man had been piling the Robertsons' screaming children into this cart, and he was only waiting for the eldest boy, a lad of fourteen, to come back from his mother's funeral before setting off. My mother was about to go into the house with Mr. Robertson when the fourteen-year-old clung to her, crying, "Oh, Mrs. Bowen, don't let them take me!" The poor boy had just witnessed the burial of his mother, and before he could gather his wits about him, he was bundled into the cart, still screaming, "Oh, Mrs. Bowen, don't let them take me, don't let them take me." They were trying to restrain him in the the cart, and his father was too grief-stricken to be of any help to him.

My mother begged the man to let her keep the boy. "Please, please let me keep him," she pleaded. "I can give him a good home." But the man was cruel, he had no pity for these poor children and he was deaf to my mother's pleading. He told her, "They are the property of the parish now," and ordered the driver to whip up the horse. I stood, holding my mother's hand, watching those poor children driven off down the street; we were crying, as was everyone else in the street. It was heart-breaking and pitiful to see, and to hear the children screaming and boy still crying out "Don't let them take me!" My mother told my father all about it, and said, "Oh John, I would have taken them all if I could have, and especially that oldest little boy. We haven't got much, but he wouldn't have starved. Still, it wasn't to be, though it nearly broke my heart to see them going like that."

SIX

At three o'clock the next morning I was awakened by my brothers and sisters crying. I sat up in bed and asked what was wrong, to hear them all say, "Daddy is dying." I jumped out of bed and ran into my father's bedroom, shouting as I ran, "Daddy, Daddy," and pulled up sharp in horror at the foot of my father's bed, to see my beloved father white-faced and exhausted, lying on a pillow stained with his life blood, and his bed a pool of blood. He tried to raise his hand to touch me, but he was too weak, and it fell back on his bed. There was a man standing by his bed, and I heard my father saying, in a very weak voice, like a drowning man, "Take care of my little ones." Then the man threw a coat over my head, and carried me out of the room. I could not scream or shout, I was too shocked by the scene I had just witnessed of my beloved daddy dying in his blood-stained bed.

The man put me down in our next door neighbour's house, where Mrs. Brown and her husband and three sons were trying to restrain my mother, who was crying out, "Let me go, John needs me." She was struggling to get away; they thought they were being kind in restraining her, but really it was cruel, because she wanted to be with him, her beloved John, at the last. My poor brother Benny, only twelve years old, had run out into the bitterly cold October morning wearing only his night-shirt, to go to Aunt Margaret's. No-one had sent him, he had gone on his own, all through those dark and lonely fields to Pwllyglas. He thought that if he could get Aunt Margaret to come, Daddy wouldn't die; and only love and fear for his father's safety could have made him take that walk in the dead of night. When he reached Aunt Margaret's house, he banged on the door until Uncle Charles opened the window and asked what was wrong.

"Come quick, Daddy is dying," Benny said, but he was speaking in Welsh and Uncle Charles could not understand him.

Aunt Margaret came to the window, but she too was unable to understand him. Still, she knew it was John, so she ran through the fields with Benny. But it was too late, Daddy was dead. Aunt Margaret laid my father out before going home to dress; she had hurriedly thrown a coat over her night clothes when Ben fetched her.

After my father had been laid out, they brought my mother and me back into the house. When we came in I was holding tightly to my mother's skirt, and we went into the parlour where my father had been laid out; the room was all draped in white. Then, when my mother went back into the living room, I wouldn't go with her, because I did not want to leave my father. I held on to his dead hand and said, "I can't leave Daddy, I've got to stay with him for ever and ever;" each time I was forcibly removed from the room, I would sit on the stairs and wait for a chance to go in again. So my mother, out of pity, said, "Leave her alone, if it is giving Ritty comfort to stay with John, put a chair there for her and let her stay with him."

My father died at three o'clock in the morning of October 14th, 1913, and at precisely five minutes to eight on the same morning the Senghenydd explosion occurred. It shook the street and broke many of the windows in the houses, and four hundred and thirty-nine men and boys lost their lives in the disaster. I did not leave my father's side until I fell asleep and was carried to bed. I held his hand and looked into his face, and said to him, "I'm never going to forget you, Daddy, and I'm never going to let you go." Then they put him into his coffin, and that was terrible.

Sadly we had visitors from America just then, my Great Aunt Ann's son, Lewis, and his German bride, a baroness; they had come over hoping to see my father, but they were too late, he had just died. They came into the parlour to see my father's body, and the baroness said to me, "Child, why are you sitting here in the cold? You are frozen."

"I'm being like Daddy," I told her. "He's cold and I want to be cold, I don't want to sit by the fire. I am minding my daddy so that no-one will take him away."

My father's body had to be kept in the house for a week, because of the 439 victims of the Senghenydd explosion who had to be buried before anyone else. From our house we could see the road from Pengam to Fleur-de-Lys, and horse-drawn pit carts and anything else that could carry men's bodies were passing down the road with the victims' bodies piled on top of each other just like sacks of coal, to be handed out to grieving families – 'your son', 'your sons', 'your husband' – like things of no consequence. It was a sad day for Pengam and the surrounding valleys.

On the morning of my father's death, when we had come in from the neighbours house, the postman handed my mother a letter. She did not feel inclined to read it at the time, so she put it on the mantelpiece, though she realised that it was from the school authorities. Later my mother was telling Uncle Lewis and the baroness the things that my father had told us children just a few days before his death when she told them about the letter, and said she didn't have the heart to read it. Uncle Lewis said to her, "Let me read it, Rachael. You will have to read it some time or other and it may need a reply, so let me open it and read it to you." The letter was to confirm that my father was now the headmaster of the largest school in Monmouthshire, and it said that his credentials had been of the highest standard received. So Uncle Lewis had the sad task of replying to the authorities that their new headmaster had passed away.

Although it could not come near the loss that my mother had suffered in losing Father, the loss of the headmaster's post and the security it would have meant was a serious blow, and now Mother suffered a third. Father was no longer a 'surviving child' and so his family could no longer expect to benefit from his parents' estate. And so my poor mother, who had had such high hopes for her family, was now only a penniless widow with five fatherless children to bring up alone. The only financial help that such a widow could expect was a pauper's pittance from the parish, and if my mother *did* apply to them for help, then the cart would rumble up our street again and take us children and our mother to the Workhouse as it had the little Robertson children. When this possibility was put before my mother I heard her say, "There is nobody who will take my children from me while my eyes are open. God is good, and if He does not come Himself, He sends someone. Something will turn up, and it will not be my children going to the Workhouse."

All the same, I was old enough to realise that if they could come and take the Robertson children by force, then they might come and force my mother to give us up. When my mother had asked if she could keep the little Robertson boy, the cruel man had said, "I've got to take them all," and now I began to think that if I held tightly to Daddy's hand, they wouldn't be able to take either me or the other children away; but it was a terrible thought.

Uncle Lewis and the baroness were staying at a hotel because there was no room for them in our house, but they wanted to be there in time for the service. They told my mother they had a proposal to put to her after the funeral. Meanwhile my father's eldest sister came to see my mother and told her that since only the best was good enough for my father, all the funeral costs would be borne by herself. It was the custom in those days that when there was a bereavement in the house, the bereaved husband or wife would not show him or herself outside the front door from the time of the death until after the funeral, and everyone concerned would have to wear deep black mourning; not even a white handkerchief was allowed unless it had a black border. After that there would be a twelve-months period of second mourning when only black and white could be worn. Aunt Rachael took all our measurements, and said the clothes that she bought would have to be good and substantial to last for the whole period of mourning; she paid for all our mourning.

Violet and I were dressed alike, in good quality black serge pleated kilts, with black satin half-sleeved tops to hold the skirts because we were too small for waistbands, and black jerseys, while our hats were black velour with a big rosette in front on a buckram base. (I was told that the hat cost ten shillings, a whole week's wages for a man.) Emily's outfit was suited to her age, but her hat was like mine except that she had two rosettes on the front of hers. We wore everything to match, according to Aunt Rachael's good taste. I don't remember how the boys were dressed, but Aunt Rachael attended to it all, and I heard later that she had also given my mother a useful sum of money to see her through.

The man who had been standing by my father's bedside that morning was my mother's first cousin, David Charles Thomas, a professional singer and the son of Richard Thomas, my mother's uncle. He came each day to be with us throughout that first week of mourning and to help my mother in her sorrow; like Uncle Lewis and his wife, he had been staying at a hotel each night. It was my mother's wish that her five children should follow my father's body to Bedwellty Cemetery, several miles from where we lived, where he was to be buried, but owing to the fact that so many men had to be buried as a result of the Senghenydd explosion, it was impossible to hire cabs for the funeral. Because she was a florist in Blackwood, Aunt Margaret had been successful in procuring a hearse and two black horses with high black plumes, the necessary sign of dignity at a funeral, but nothing else was available. (In fact we only managed to get the hearse and horses because Aunt Margaret was also a much-loved doctor in the village, and no-one wanted to let her down.) Only Ben and Emily would be able to walk the distance – everyone would have to walk behind the coffin. (All this was actually planned out of my hearing, but I was told about it later.)

The one problem remaining now was how to get me out of the parlour. Mother knew this would mean a considerable upset, but I had already heard someone say that the body had been calling for the grave for a long time now, and on the morning of the funeral our house smelled heavily of eau-de-cologne. My mother thought that if I was dressed in my mourning, it would induce me to come out of the parlour so that the undertaker could come in and get to the coffin, but though I put my new kilt and jersey on, and my new hat and shoes, I would not come out of the parlour. Mother now had a problem on her hands, since she did not want to have me forcibly removed. Then my little friend Dolly Parry's father came to the rescue (though I suspect my mother helped to arrange this.) I was dressed in my mourning, but still holding Daddy's hand and telling him that I would never leave him, when Mr. Parry came into the parlour looking very worried.

"Ritty," he said, "I've come to ask you a big favour. Mrs. Parry had a new baby yesterday and we don't know whether it's a boy or a girl, so I want you to come down and tell us what you think it is."

"I'm sorry, Mr. Parry," I told him. "I can't leave my daddy."

"You remember when we had a new baby before, don't you, Ritty?"

"Yes," I agreed.

"Well, you came down to see it, and you said it was a lovely baby boy. Now Mrs. Parry is very ill in bed, and she won't eat her gruel because she doesn't know if she's got a boy or a girl," he said.

"You are very rich, aren't you, Mr. Parry?" I remarked. "You can afford to buy a lot of babies. We can't afford to buy one, my mammy said so."

"Then you will come, Ritty?" he asked.

"No," I said. "I can't leave my daddy."

"Oh, I don't know what to do," he told me. "Mrs. Parry hasn't had anything to eat since yesterday. She won't take her gruel, and if she doesn't take it, she will be too weak to look after the baby. You wouldn't let anything happen to that little baby, would you, Ritty?" Mr. Parry urged.

I thought for a moment before answering him. What a great responsibility I had – I was responsible for my daddy, but I was also responsible for telling Mrs. Parry whether she had a baby girl or a baby boy. So I got up off my chair and let go of Daddy's hand, and asked his permission to leave him for a minute. I said, "I can't let Mrs. Parry and her baby die, so if you'll let me go to them, I'll come straight back and hold your hand again." Then I left my hat in the parlour, because I did not need it to go down to Mrs. Parry's house, took Mr. Parry's hand and went with him, unaware that this was the day of the funeral and that the minister and the undertaker were in the living room waiting for me to leave.

Mr. Parry held my hand tightly as we walked through a crowd of people, all dressed in black, but my mind was too full of the big responsibility I had to let the fact sink in that these were mourners come for a funeral. Mr. Parry lived quite a long way down the street on the opposite side, and when we got there we went into his house and up the stairs to the bedroom. Mrs. Parry said, "Oh, I'm so glad you've come, Ritty," and drew the bedclothes back, lifting the baby up for me to see. (Young babies then had to be kept right down underneath all the bedclothes.) Immediately I saw the little pink bundle, with its pink flannelette nightie and pink flannelette headsquare, I exclaimed excitedly, "Oh, Mrs. Parry, you've got a baby girl!"

"Oh, Ritty, aren't you clever, how did you know?" she said.

"Well," I explained, "the last baby you had, had a blue nightie and a blue headsquare on, that's blue for a boy and pink for a girl. So you'll know next time you have a baby. May I go home now, to my daddy, please?"

47

"Ritty," said Mr. Parry, "Mrs. Parry hasn't had her gruel yet, and she won't drink it unless you are with her and taste it for her, will you, Mrs. Parry?"

"Oh no," said Mrs. Parry, "Ritty must stay and taste it for me."

Mr. Parry brought up a large pudding basin full of lovely gruel, and two dessert spoons, then he picked me up and sat me on the bed beside Mrs. Parry. I tasted a spoonful and said to her, "It's delicious, Mrs. Parry." "Then you will help me eat it, Ritty," she said, and spoon for spoon we ate the basinful between us; I had not realised how hungry I was while I was sitting by my daddy. Then I got down from the bed and said, "Please take me home now, Mr. Parry. I must get home to my daddy."

Mr. Parry took me down the two flights of stairs, round the garden and down the lane, making the walk as long as possible to give the mourners time to get out of sight. I had wanted to run home by myself, but he held me back until he saw that the street was empty, then he let me go, and I ran straight home and into the parlour, only to find that the room was empty. I don't remember anything more until I woke up sometime later, when the mourners had all come back from the funeral. When I woke I found that I was lying in my father's armchair, which had been tilted up against the wall by the fire, and propped by two bricks under the legs to prevent it from falling; I was covered with a blanket, and that was where I spent the next few days.

Once the funeral was over, my Aunt and Uncle Lewis put their proposition to my mother; they wanted to adopt me and take me back to America with them. My mother said to them, "If she is willing to go with you, I won't stand in her way." So Uncle Lewis asked me if I would like to go with him 'across the pond'. I thought it would be like the little duck pond we used to skate on in the winter, and so I said I would go. Then I overheard Benny and Emily talking about the funeral, and saying what a long journey it had been, and how they had walked all the way there and back through the slush and muck of melting snow on unsurfaced roads full of potholes and puddles. Emily and Ben had walked behind the coffin with Mother, and they said that it was a very big funeral and even Uncle Lewis and the baroness had walked every step of the way.

Now, however, Uncle Lewis and his wife were ready to go

home and take me with them, and Mother had gone with them to make the final arrangements, leaving Emily in charge of us; I was still asleep in my chair bed. Emily was saying how she had asked our aunt to take her to America instead of me – they were a wealthy, childless couple, and I would be their heiress; but Aunt had told Emily, "No, I want the little fair one, she is like a relative of mine whom I left in Germany."

Emily told Ben, "When Ritty is rich and riding in a motor car, we'll be walking to Bargoed in the rain, and she will ride past us and splash dirty water over us." While I listened, I thought of the many times when we had been walking together to Bargoed and a car, travelling at the terrific speed of five miles an hour, had splashed us with dirty water! I did not show then that I had heard them talking, but when my mother and uncle and aunt came back to the house, they were ready to take me with them to the hotel and were talking of fitting me out with all kinds of clothes to wear to go to America. Then I told them, "I'm not going, I've got to grow up to work and get money to give to Mammy." They told me that when I got to America I could send Mammy all the money I liked, but the idea did not seem to register; I could not see how I could help Mammy if I went away and left her. All they could get out of me, however hard they tried and however many questions they asked, was the same repeated answer, "I won't throw dust over Emily and Ben, and I won't splash them with dirty water as they are walking to Bargoed!"

Uncle Lewis and the baroness spent a few days trying to persuade me to go with them. They said that they would send me to the finest eye specialist in America, to make my eyes stronger, and that I would go to the best schools, and have my own pony to ride on, and a doll's pram with as many dolls as I would like to play with; but to everything they said, the answer was always the same. I couldn't tell them that Emily had said I was selfish to want to leave them and go to America, or that I would then throw dirty water over them. Eventually they left without me and I did not go to America. (Nor did Emily, who was sixteen then, and had begged them to take her instead.)

SEVEN

My mother used to go out in the morning and pick young nettles; then she would make small beer (a non-intoxicating soft drink) from them, and sell it for tuppence a bottle. Christmas was approaching and money was very short – there was none to make the usual Christmas cakes and puddings, and all the uncles who had come, laden with toys, in previous years, failed to appear this time, so it seemed as though it would be a very black season. Then my mother called us together and told us that all the money she had in the world would not buy one decent Christmas present, so we would have to share what we had. She said to Emily and Ben, "You take Ritty to Bargoed with you and see what you can get to suit each one of you out of the little money that I do have."

Emily, being sixteen, was given half a crown, and the other four of us were to have one and sixpence each. So off we set, Emily, Ben and I, with the enormous sum of six shillings between us.

It was cold, and the road was long and lonely; we had to dodge the puddles and keep in tightly to the side of the road to avoid being splashed with icy water from passing carts. As we went through Senghenydd we came to a parlour shop, brightly lit, with its window full of little toys, and Emily and Ben lifted me up on to the sill to see if there was anything I liked in the window. There in the centre I saw a beautiful doll's cradle, which was made of cardboard and measured just six inches; it was covered in pretty white lace paper, with blue bows of paper ribbon and a little black chocolate baby lying in the cradle. It cost just the exact amount of money that I had to spend, and I asked Emily, "Please, may I have that doll's cradle?" They lifted me down and we all went into the shop, with Emily and Ben looking for something to buy for the others.

Standing against the wall inside was a huge toy grocer's shop. We stopped to admire it, and saw that best of all it had a barrel of

50

flour with a scoop, a real one, to scoop it out, as well as a smaller barrel of sugar with a sugar scoop. It was the sort of toy that we used to have given to us in our better-off days, but it was way out of our reach now, and with a sigh I went to the lady behind the counter, and said, "Please may I have that beautiful doll's cradle in the window? It's only one and sixpence."

She wrapped it up and handed it to me, then, after thanking her, I turned to leave the shop. Standing behind me was a tall strange man who said to Emily, "Would the little girl like that toy shop?"

"Oh, yes," said Emily, and to our amazement he said to the lady, "Pack that toy up and give it to the little girl, and give the little boy whatever he wants."

So Ben was given a big box containing something that he had been admiring. Meanwhile the gentleman, after paying for the purchases, left the shop; Emily brought herself a sixpenny box of dates, and she and Ben found something suitable for the other children. Then we left the shop and made our way home, because there was no need to go further into Bargoed.

When we arrived home, Emily and Ben opened the big presents that the gentleman had bought, and Emily told my mother that the shop was for her; I was too absorbed in my new toy to notice what she had said. It was true that the gentleman had told the lady to pack the shop up and give it to the little girl, but Emily had had to carry it because it was too big for me, and now she had claimed it as her own. Still, I didn't mind, because I had my lovely cradle to play with, and Emily told me I could help her play with the shop. Mother said, "The gentleman who bought you these toys was Lord Maesryddyd."

The next day would be Christmas Day, so we gave our presents to my mother to put in our stockings for us. Later that night, Christmas Eve, there was a knock on our door, and on the doorstep Mother found a large box of groceries, with a note attached saying simply, 'Merry Christmas'. She looked up and down the street, but there was no-one in sight, and she had no idea who could have brought the box. It contained everything imaginable for Christmas, cake, pudding, fruit and so on, and a beautiful goose. She never knew who put it there, but, as she told us when we saw the enormous box of groceries, "I don't know who brought this box, but as I have always said, God is good and if He can't come Himself, He sends." As for me, that little cradle meant more to me than all the expensive presents I had been used to, and it helped to ease the heartache left by my father's death.

Soon after Christmas my Mother had to call the doctor in to me, because I was losing weight, and he told my mother, "The child is grieving, and you are going to have to take her away from this house if you want to keep her." I believed I had killed my father because I hadn't prayed to God hard enough to save him; I didn't realise just how ill he had been, because he had never been in bed, and I was haunted for many years by my failure to pray hard enough to make him better.

One morning in February 1914 my mother got us all up from bed before daylight and said, "Now children, I want you to dress yourselves as quickly as you can, and eat a good breakfast, because I am taking you away from Edward Street and we must catch the first train from Blackwood this morning. We have a long way to go."

Mother packed some sandwiches and a bottle of home-made pop, and we set off before daybreak. She told us that she had settled with the landlord about the rent, and he had arranged to have our furniture put on the station wagon and sent to us at the address given to him – though some of the things had been sold to the neighbours who would collect them after we had gone.

So off we set, we knew not where, on that cold bleak winter's morning; all my mother would say was, "I'll tell you when we get there, I don't want Uncle Dai to know where we are going."

Uncle Dai had been putting pressure on my mother to have us children put in the Workhouse because he wanted to marry her, but didn't want the responsibility of five children. ('Uncle Dai' was David Charles Thomas, my mother's first cousin; we were running away from him.) That morning we boarded the first train for the Rhondda, and when we arrived there, Mother said, "Come on children, this is as far as we can go now." We were the only passengers alighting from the train, and we sat on the seat for a moment while my mother said, "Now, children, listen to what I've got to say. I had hoped to take you up through the Rhondda on the tramcar" (this was a rail track which ran along the main roads right up through the Rhondda, one track down and one up. It had overhead electricity cables attached to the tramcars which were electrically driven, and you could go the whole way for a few coppers.)

52

"But unfortunately," Mother continued, "I have no money left after paying our trainfare, so I am afraid, children, that it will have to be Shanks's Pony. It's going to be a very long walk and we are all going to be very tired. We will take the back road and try to cut off a little of the distance, as I want to reach the foot of the mountain as quickly as possible. I want no talking, children, save your energy for walking, because we've got miles and miles to walk, and the little ones are going to need helping. We are going to climb right over these mountains. Now, put your hands together and we'll say a little prayer. We'll ask God to take us safely all the way to Ogmore Vale, and there you will all be safe and happy. Ogmore Vale is a lovely place for children to grow up in."

Violet was only three years old, and had to be carried most of the way, but Ben and Emily and my mother took it in turns to carry her. Garfield and I were like twins, although there were two and a half years between us, and we would help each other along. Thus we walked wearily mile after mile until, towards dusk, we came to the foot of the mountain, in those days a wild, trackless place. We sat to rest for a little while, ate our remaining sandwiches and drank the last of our pop.

Meanwhile Mother looked around to find the best sheep track leading in the right direction; she wanted to get her bearings before darkness descended. Then we started on what seemed an impossible task, to climb those bare mountains in a bitterly cold February night. My mother had only just turned forty-two, and had the responsibility of five children to look after, but her one big fear now was that the mist would come down over the mountains while we were on top of them – that would have made it impossible for us to go on, and it would have meant certain death if we had to spend the night on the mountain. Thankfully it was a clear, frosty night.

Mother said to us, "Now, come on children, we are going to walk like soldiers. The track is too narrow to walk abreast, so we will have to go in single file." She took the lead, Emily went next, then Ben, with Violet in between them, getting a piggy back from each in turn: next came Garfield, and I brought up the rear. Garfield wasn't very strong, and he kept saying, "Can I go to sleep, Rit?" I would put my arm around him, and he would lay his head on my shoulder and sleep as he walked. We were like mechanical toys walking along, and my mother would call

53

out to us, "Sing, children, sing." Then she would start to sing and we would join in. This helped to keep our spirits up and took our minds off the cold.

Distance on the mountains is deceiving, just as it is at sea; what looks like a short distance can be miles of walking, and added to that, by the time we reached the top of the mountain it was pitch dark, and we had no light to guide us. We were walking very slowly because it was rough going, but Mother said, "As long as I can keep the lights of the Rhondda in my sight, I know where I am." After a few more miles, though, she could no longer see the Rhondda.

It was quiet and lonely, and very cold. I called out to my mother, "I thought we were going to see sheep on the mountain, Mammy?"

"There are no sheep up here, my love," she told me, and I said, "Mammy, couldn't we shelter like the sheep? Garfield is very tired, and I'm very tired, and Violet is very tired too."

"There are no shelters, love," said Mother. "What I mean when I say the sheep have gone to shelter is that they go off the mountain top in winter, and they shelter below, behind the boulders jutting out of the breast of the mountain."

"Couldn't we do that, Mammy?" asked Garfield.

"Keep walking, children," Mother answered. "Don't talk to me any more, I've got to concentrate, to try and find our way."

My mother wore a long, black skirt, with a thick leather belt around her waist, and she said to Emily, "Now, Emily, you hold on tight to my belt, and Benny, you hold on tightly to Emily's coat, and if you feel me slipping, then pull with all your might. Leave Violet to Ritty and Garfield."

Mother knew that at any minute she could come to a quarry or a deep crevasse in the mountain, and sheep had often been known to fall into these crevasses. Mountain tops are treacherous, and although they look beautiful in daylight, they are very dangerous at night, so Mother feared that she might step into one of these crevasses, because we were travelling by instinct alone, with no lights to guide us. I knew she was praying all the time, asking for guidance. At the darkest hour, just before dawn, when we had been walking all night, Mother called out, "Halt! Look down, children, on your right hand side and see what you can see." We all looked down, and miles below us we could see little lights, stars below us instead of above; they were

54

the lights of Nantymoel. My mother said, "Thank God for that, He has brought us in the right direction."

We were very excited to see those lights – only someone who has been lost on the mountains can know the joy of seeing a sign of life, although the lights were miles below us. Then Ben called out, "Will we be passing the Devil's Pulpit and the Stinking Well?"

"I am hoping that we won't pass them," Mother told him, "but that our path will lie below them."

Ben asked then what these things were, and said he had read about them at school. The Devil's Pulpit was two huge boulders, perilously perched on top of each other; in a stong wind they moved, but never fell, and no-one knew how they got there. As for the Stinking Well, Ben told us (and Mother confirmed this), if you dropped a silver coin into the water and came back in a few days' time, it would have turned into a copper coin. The water smelled foul, but was reputed to have healing powers, and people came from as far as America to drink from it. Mother told us that father had come many times to drink from the well, and take a bottle home with him. She said, too, that many battles had been fought on these mountains and people still dug up pieces of armour at times, and added that we were now on the highest mountain in South Wales and when it was a little lighter she could show us a beacon, already built, that would be lit if war was declared, to let people know of the declaration. We would probably pass it later. (And we were soon to see that beacon lighted, because it was 1914.)

At last we started to go downwards, towards the valley of Nantymoel. It was wonderful to have our feet on firm ground again, and to know we were safely over the mountains. We walked on, with our arms around each other, sleeping in turn as we walked. Garfield was a sweet boy; he would wake up and say, "Your turn, Rit," and it was wonderful to sleep though still walking. We walked all through Nantymoel just as dawn was breaking, down through Price Town, and then on to Ogmore Vale, and right at the end of Ogmore Vale, Mother said, "We are here, children, thank God." Garfield and I were almost unconscious with tiredness when she spoke. Then she opened a little gate into a small green space and banged at the door of a cottage. Two heads appeared at the window, one a man's; he was wearing a tasselled cap and striped pyjamas, and said,

"Who's there ?"

"It's Rachael and the children," said Mother, and the man cried, "Oh, my God!" and the two rushed downstairs. The door was quickly thrown open, and a stout, bearded man threw his arms round my mother, and said, "My God, Rachael, where have you come from?"

"We've walked every step of the way from the Rhondda," she said.

"You've never walked all over these mountains with the children," he said, and he picked Garfield up in one mighty arm and me in the other; our heads fell on his shoulders, and all I can remember before I fell fast asleep is the feel of his beard against my face, while the warmth of his body and the safety of his strong arms was paradise. As we were being laid gently down on the couch in the warm room, I heard him say to my mother, "And you've been walking all night, Rachael?" and Mother said, "Yes, every step of the way."

"My God! I will never be able to thank Him enough for bringing you safely to us." (We were not related; these were my mother's good friends.)

Next morning my mother said to us children, "Now, children, this kind gentleman is Mr. Reggie Williams, and you are to call him Uncle Reggie. And this lovely lady is Bopa Reggie, and we are going to stay with them until our furniture comes and Mammy can get a little home together for us."

"You can all stay here for as long as you like," said Uncle Reggie.

EIGHT

Most of the Williamses' children were married, but they had a little girl of ten, and I vowed to her that she would be my best cousin for ever and ever. Meanwhile the Williamses sent my mother back to bed with orders that she was to stay there all day; she needed the rest after her ordeal. Violet went to bed with Mother, and we were settled down on the couch where we stayed all day. Bopa said we must rest too, in case we suffered from our exposure on the mountain, though Emily and Ben were none the worse for their adventure and had gone off exploring the valleys. We were spoiled and petted and overfed all day, then at bedtime Uncle Reggie said, "Bed time now, Who'll go to bed without supper for a penny?" and we all called out, "I will, I will." He gave a penny to each of us, including his own two children, and we all went to bed hugging a big penny.

Next morning Uncle Reggie got us all down, ready for breakfast, and the delicious smell of bacon and eggs cooking made us feel very hungry. Uncle said, "Who'll give me a penny for their breakfast?" and we all said, "Oh! ! !" and handed back our pennies – but we had that delicious breakfast. One day shortly afterwards my mother was offered a little cottage: it had one large room with a walk-in pantry downstairs, with the stairs running from the living room into a large bedroom divided into two. It was in Water Street, a street with six houses, but seven front doors because the first house had two doors, one leading into a beautiful garden. Our little cottage was situated in the garden, and the passageway was the means of access to it. At the bottom of the garden was a door which opened onto a football field. If you pulled this door shut behind you, you could not get back into the garden, because there was no latch outside the door, but I thought myself very clever when I discovered the secret of how to open it. There was a little hole in the door, big enough for me to put my finger through, whereby I could lift up the latch on the inside. After this discovery I purposely locked myself out every day just for the thrill of opening it this way.

By now our few pieces of furniture had arrived, and we settled in quite comfortably. Ben found a job as an errand boy for a grocer, earning a couple of shillings a week to help my mother; he was still in school, but worked after school hours. Emily found work too. Our landlady, Mrs. Terrington, lived at Number One, Water Street with her unmarried son (the garden in which our cottage was situated was hers.) She was a pretty, white-haired, but rather stout old lady and she paid Emily to go in every day to wash her hair and do other little personal jobs for her that she was not able to do herself because she was too stout. As for me, to my joy I found that Mr and Mrs. Palmer in No. 4 had a small baby, and Mrs. Palmer would give me sixpence a week to go in after school and on Saturday and Sunday to nurse the baby while she cooked the dinner. I had all my meals with them on Saturday and Sunday, and what with that and the sixpence, I felt I was really contributing to the family funds, and I was very proud to be helping my mother.

Our living room window was in the pine end of the cottage and it overlooked the garden of a house in another street. Mr and Mrs. Evans had a large family of small children, and we could open the window and talk to them in the garden. Their eldest girl, Agnes, who was eleven years old, became my lifelong friend. To celebrate the move into our new house my mother made some rhubarb tart, the rhubarb coming from Uncle Reggie's garden, and when the tart was cooked we could hear the little Evans children saying. "What a lovely smell from the Bowens' house!" Mother opened the window and said, "Who likes rhubarb tart?" "We do!" they said, so she told them to go and fetch a plate each. Then the eldest girl held up their plates in turn so that each child could have a share. From that day on, whenever my mother made broth or pea soup, she always made enough to be able to give some to the little Evans children when they came to the window with their basins.

Just about then Ben was missing from the house at breakfast time every morning; he would only come in in time to wash his hands and grab a quick bite of breakfast before dashing off to school. When we asked him why he was not there to have breakfast with us, he would just say, "Wait and see." On the morning of my tenth birthday everyone said "Happy birthday, Ritty" when I came downstairs, and I felt immensely proud.

There were no birthday cards or presents in those days, it was enough for everyone to wish you a happy birthday, and my mother celebrated each one by making a pile of pancakes for tea. This particular morning, Ben hadn't gone missing as usual, instead he was there with the others to wish me 'happy birthday'. He crept up silently behind me, put his two hands over my eyes, and said, "Shut your eyes and see what God will send you." Then he took his hands away and said, "Now open your eyes and see what God *has* sent you. Happy birthday, little sister!" And he put a little china kitten into each of my hands – blue china kittens with very bright blue eyes, about four inches high and four inches wide; on each was written 'Votes for Women'. They were beautiful. I was absolutely thrilled, and said to Ben, "Oh, Ben, where did you get these beautiful kittens?"

"Now I will tell you where Ben has been for the last two months," said Mother. "He saw these kittens with the rag and bone man, and asked him how many rags would he want for the two; the man wanted so many sacks of rags, bones and iron, and Ben has been getting up early every morning, rain, hail or snow, and going around the back lanes and tips collecting those things. Mr. James at the bottom of Water Street let him keep his sacks of rags there until he had enough to get you your kittens. You see, Ritty, you are a lucky little girl to have such a kind and thoughtful brother. Ben had to go out each morning early, before going to school, because he had his job to go to after school – and he's only twelve and a half!"

One day the optician came to the house to test my mother's eyes (they came to your house in those days, the optician and the dentist; they had to, to earn a living) and I heard him tell my mother her headaches were due to eyestrain, and she should have a pair of spectacles to relieve the pressure. They would cost ten shillings and sixpence. I did not show anything, but I was very worried because I had heard my mother tell the optician that she couldn't afford it right now and she would have to have spectacles later on when she *could* afford it. I ran upstairs and prayed, "Please God, don't let Mammy go blind until I can save up ten shillings and sixpence." Every evening when we went to bed my mother always waited while we said our prayers before tucking us in for the night; one night she asked me why I was taking so long, when all the others were tucked up in bed, but I

59

could not tell her of all the things that I had to ask God for, because the list was getting longer every day. It began with "Please God, bless Ben for giving me the kittens, he is so kind to me, and please God, don't let Violet run fast down the hill from school, in case she falls and hurts herself." And now I had to add on to that, "Please God, don't let Mammy go blind until I can save ten and sixpence."

We didn't have many halfpennies then, but every halfpenny that I *did* have given to me went under the lino in my bedroom towards Mammy's glasses. It took a long, long time, nearly a year, and I thought I would never save that vast amount of money, because halfpennies were few and far between in our house. But the great day did come, and I thanked God for not letting my mother go blind; I told Him I had enough now for her to have the glasses, and then I proudly presented my savings to my mother.

"What is this for, Ritty?" she asked.

"I saved it for you to buy the glasses that Mr. James said you must have," I told her.

My mother was surprised, and she said, "Oh, Ritty, I have always fancied a basket chair" (they were the newest design in easy chairs, made of wicker, with cushions on them, and were very comfortable) "would you mind if I bought myself a lovely basket chair instead of the spectacles? It costs the same amount, ten and sixpence." I couldn't say no, and gave her the money, hiding my tears of disappointment, then I went upstairs to tell God of all my troubles, and ask Him if He would not let my mother go blind until I could save up another ten and sixpence.

One night there was a great commotion out in the street and we went out to see what was happening. People were running in all directions, some crying, and all pointing up the mountain, because the valley was lit up by the glare of the huge bonfire that was lit on the highest point, to tell all the valleys that war had been declared.

We were living near the crossing gates, and on the other side of these, just across the square in Ogmore Vale, lived a family of German Jews, named Cohen. They immediately went to the police station to be naturalised as British subjects. The minute war was declared, there was an immediate call-up of men and boys, and every day the troop trains carrying these people off to war would come from Nantymoel down through Ogmore Vale.

As the trains passed through the crossing, Mr. and Mrs. Cohen and their family would be standing by the gates, waving a Union Jack fixed to the handle of a sweeping brush, and shouting "God Save the King"; they did that every time a troop train passed. But they had no need to fear anything from the people of Ogmore Vale, they were accepted as equals.

My schooldays in Ogmore Vale were very happy. I made a lot of nice friends, in particular a small group of girls, and our favourite playtime game was to have a wedding. I was accepted into the gang because I was Peggy Williams's cousin, but they were a snobbish group, and the same two girls had to be the bride and groom every playtime, while we were the bridesmaids. From our playground to the upper school playground was a steep flight of about twenty stone steps, and the two girls who played bride and groom knew they were not allowed to play on those steps. However, they knew that the headmistress was my aunt, and took advantage of that fact to act as bride and groom coming down those steps which they pretended were the steps of the church, so I guessed that that was the real reason that I was accepted as an extra bridesmaid. The others were an ill-fated gang of girls, because each died at an early age. The 'bridegroom', Annie, died before she was fourteen, of a blood disorder; Gladys, the 'bride', died of a broken heart because her brother was killed at the commencement of the 1914-18 war; Irene, the 'chief bridesmaid', married young, fell down the stairs and broke her neck when she was twenty-one, leaving two little children (and before she died, she told me that she was not happily married); Dorothy, the other 'bridesmaid', took her own life when she was in her thirties; and Agnes Evans, my best friend, threw herself over the rocks in Porthcawl later in life. I am the only one of that 'bridal party' to live to a mature age.

61

NINE

Just before my eleventh birthday David Charles Thomas turned up at our cottage doorstep, much to our dismay. He had found us after searching for a year. He told Mother that he had joined the Army, and he insisted that she should marry him because he had to keep his word to my dying father. He backed this up by saying that she owed it to him to marry him because he had sacrificed his whole career as a professional singer for our sakes. He had been on contract to tour the world, singing duets with Alice Maud, 'Madame Spencer-Lewis', the contralto (who had earned the title of 'the second Madame Patti' from his majesty the King); Alice was the daughter of my great-aunt Ann and Colonel William Lewis. However because David Charles had broken his contract with his manager in order to fulfil his promise to my father on his deathbed, Alice had had to tour on her own, singing solo. If my mother married him now, she would become entitled to his Army pay for herself and his step children.

Emily and Ben begged my mother not to marry him, and they planned a way to prevent her from doing so. David Charles left the house to spend the night with friends, and later that night, after dark, Emily and Ben came in from the garden, deathly pale and frightened. Our living room was dimly lit with an oil lamp on the table in the middle of the room, which left most of the room in semi-darkness, and they came into this darker part of the room, and said, "You can't marry Uncle Dai, Mammy, we've just seen Daddy, he came to us in the garden." My mother looked at their poor white faces and asked, "What did Daddy tell you?"

"He kept saying, Tell Mammy not to, tell Mammy not to," they said. "That's all he said, then he was gone."

"That was a good act, children," said Mother. "Now go and wash the flour off your faces, and come and have your supper ready to go to bed." For the moment she continued to resist

62

David Charles's arguments.

We were still in deep mourning for my father, and one day I asked my mother if I could wear my kilt and jersey to school just for once. (I wanted to impress a young boy of my own age who seemed to have taken a fancy to me.)

"Definitely not," said my mother. "These are your Sunday clothes."

"I only wanted to show the girls in school," I said, "because they don't go to church, to see me in them." But Mother was adamant. She told me I was being very vain and shouldn't ask to wear my best clothes to school, so I went out of the house very upset and vowed I would run away from home and never come back home. My mother was horrid, she loved Emily and Violet but she didn't love me. I didn't know where I was going, but I set off in the opposite direction to our house, determined never to go home again.

It was drizzling with rain, and I walked along with my head down, looking at the puddles and saying to myself, "I hope I have pneumonia and die, and then my mother will be sorry she was cross with me." Then to my surprise I saw a threepenny bit shining in the wet road. I picked it up and looked around. There wasn't a soul about, it was a lonely road and I had now walked about a mile away from my school in the wrong direction. I forgot about how much I wanted to hurt my mother; all I could think of was getting home and giving her the threepence, so I ran as fast as I could.

"Look what I've got, Mammy, I didn't steal it, I found it on the road, and there was no-one else about," I cried excitedly, as I got into the house.

My mother took the coin, put it to her lips, and said, "Thank God for that. I hadn't a bit of tea in the house, will you go to the grocer's, Ritty, and get me some things out of this threepence."

I ran to the shop, and asked the grocer, "Please can I have a penny packet of tea" (which was two and a half ounces), "a pennyworth of fresh bacon cuttings" (which was about half a pound or more), "and a pennyworth of fresh cheese cuttings" (which was a half pound). And so I had a nice parcel of groceries for my threepence.

My mother had never done any gardening in her life, but one day she decided that she was going to plant our part of the garden and so she began with potatoes. The man next door called out to her, "What are you planting, Mrs. Bowen?" and she said, "I am going to try to grow potatoes."

"What seed potatoes are you using?" he asked.

"Oh, I can't afford to put potatoes in," Mother said. "I'm going to try to grow them from potato peelings. Someone who has more money than I have can afford to peel their potatoes thick and throw the peels into the lane. I have picked up a bucketful of them, see?" and she held up the bucket for him to see.

The man roared with laughter, and said to her, "What do you expect to grow from those?"

"Well," said my Mother, "the ground is here, idle; I might as well take a chance, it won't cost me anything. If nothing comes up, there's nothing lost, and I will have had a try anyway."

In the course of time, when the man was digging up the potatoes grown from his expensive seed, my mother was digging up *her* garden; she called to him and asked, "What sort of crop have you got?" "Very poor," he replied, Then Mother showed him her crop of beautiful big potatoes grown from just peelings, and he said, "Well, Mrs. Bowen, I'll never laugh at a woman gardening again!"

Eventually David Charles persuaded my mother to marry him, and they went off together to Blackwood to be married in Llanfraith Church; then we moved back to Pengam to live, in the house Dai had prepared for us. (It was a lovely council house, in Garden City, Pengam.) And so we were back where we started from; this brought back the memories of the sadness of my father's death, and I became very ill again.

One day the young man from next door came into our house, and said he had something in his pocket for me. "Put your hand in my pocket, Ritty," he said, "and see what I've got for you." But I just wasn't interested, and said, "No, I don't want to."

"Well, put out your hand, then, and close your eyes," he said, "and see what God has sent you."

I did as he said, and he put a little live puppy in my hand. It was a miniature toy Yorkshire terrier.

"It's for your birthday, Ritty," he said. It was my eleventh birthday, and I lost my heart to the little puppy right away. I had something now to live for and from that day I started to get better – I might even say that I owed my life to that little dog.

My stepfather had joined up and gone off to war, and although the government did not pay out much for children, my mother now had a steady weekly wage coming into the house, and we were even able to have a penny pocket money occasionally. This went immediately into my savings, and now I was able to put away a penny a week towards the cost of my mother's spectacles; I still prayed each night, asking God not to let her go blind until I had saved ten and sixpence – though I had never heard my mother complain about her eyes.

One day Ben, who was now nearly fourteen, brought home a newly found friend, a young man in his twenties, and introduced him as Harry Baldwin, a music teacher.

"He teaches the pianoforte," said Ben. "Mam, Ritty wants to play the piano, couldn't she have lessons with Harry?" Mother explained to Harry that my father had promised me that I could learn to play the piano, but unfortunately we had no piano and couldn't afford lessons. So Harry asked my mother if he could give me a lesson free, just for him to see whether or not I was capable of learning. After I had had my first lesson, Harry told my mother, "Your daughter is born to be a musician, she should definitely be taught the piano. Her finger work is excellent. Please let her come to me twice a week to be taught, it is only sixpence a lesson."

I was in the seventh heaven then. All my dreams were coming true, I had my little dog, and now I was having music lessons. The days didn't go by quickly enough for me to get to my music lessons, and I loved playing the piano. One night, after I had been learning to play for some time, I went to my lesson, and Harry's mother said, "Come into the living room, Rachael, and have a warm, it is cold in the parlour." So I went out and warmed myself, and played with Harry's little sister. Harry had been gone now for about half an hour, and his mother seemed very anxious. She kept pacing the room back and fore, and saying, "Where is my boy, where can he be? It's not like Harry to leave his pupil." Then she asked me, "Did you see Harry when you came along, Rachael, because he had only just gone out as you came in. Are you sure you didn't pass him on the road?"

"Yes, Mrs. Baldwin," I said, "I saw Harry walking up the street with two men, one walking on each side of him."

She burst into tears and said, "Oh, my God, the Redcoats have taken him". Harry had been conscripted into the army straight off the streets – and conscripts in the 1914-18 war were sent immediately into the front line. A report came later, saying that Harry had been killed. His death put an end to my ambition of becoming a pianist, because I never had a second opportunity.

I was now a pupil at Fair View School, Pengam, the school to which my late father had been appointed as its first headmaster, and we were living near Pwllglas Blackwood, where my Aunt Margaret lived. (At the time of my father's death his briefcase, with all the papers and documents concerning my grandmother's inheritance had vanished, and though no accusations or denials had been made, the relationship between my mother and Aunt Margaret had become strained, since Mother knew that the only one interested in taking the briefcase from our house was my aunt.)

My cousin Margaret Ann Bird's children also attended Fair View School, and her daughter Maggie, who was my own age, and I were very close friends as well as cousins, and we always went to school together. We all loved Margaret Ann, but once something terrible happened. One evening when we were coming home from school, Maggie was in a quarrelsome mood because someone had upset her, and I asked, "Why are you in such a bad mood, Maggie? I haven't done anything to you." Maggie answered spitefully, "Oh, your father's dead and you've got a stepfather. I don't like you." I was shocked, because Maggie had never spoken to me like that before. I wanted to answer her back, but I could think of nothing to say. Then I blurted out, "Well, Maggie Bird, if I *have* got a stepfather, my mother doesn't sleep with the lodgers!

Maggie burst into tears and said, "Ritty Bowen, I am going home and I'll tell my mother you said she sleeps with the lodgers!"

I was very frightened, though I did not understand what I had said. When I got home my mother wasn't there, but there *was* a message for me, which said that my mother was at Margaret Ann's and I was to go up there, as she wanted me. So I went to Margaret Ann's house in Bedwellty Road, just a street away from our house, but I wouldn't go in, I was too shamefaced, and I waited outside. Then Margaret Ann came to the door and said, "Come in, Ritty, don't stand out there, we know what you've been saying." When I went in, there were Mother, Margaret

Ann and Maggie, all waiting in judgement on me. I was ashamed of what I had said, even though I did not know what it meant, and I told my cousin, "Oh Margaret, I'm truly sorry for what I said, but I only said it because Maggie called me 'old stepfather'."

"All right," said cousin Margaret, "we'll forgive you." And then my mother and Margaret Ann both burst out laughing, and after that I didn't feel so bad.

Shortly after that, Ben celebrated his fourteenth birthday, and on the Saturday after his birthday he hurried into his house, very excited, and shouted, "Mammy, get me a pair of long white duck trousers and a box and jack – I'm starting work in Oakdale Colliery on Monday."

At that my mother sat in her rocking chair, covered her face with her hands, and cried like a baby.

"Why are you crying, Mam, I thought you'd be pleased," said Ben.

Mother answered him, "I knew you'd have to go to work one day, Benny, but never did I think you'd want to go to the colliery. What would your father say if he was here now?"

Ben stood behind my mother's chair and put his hands on her shoulders, then he sang to her in his beautiful tenor voice:

Mother I love you, I can work for two,
Don't let the tears run down your cheeks,
I'll bring my wages to you every week.
Mother, I love you,
What more could a loving son do.
You have worked for me for a long, long time,
And now I will work for you.

He kissed Mother, and said, "I can't be a barrister, Mammy, but I am not afraid to work for you."

And so at five thirty on Monday morning our brave Ben, in his long white ducks, with his oval tommy box containing his lunch in one pocket, and a man's red flat cap on his head, set out to earn his living as a miner. I went out with my mother on to the road to wave him off, then Mother said, "You go back to bed now, Rit, I'll come up later." I went to bed, and when I got up again at eight o'clock, my mother was still standing on the road, following the route that Ben had taken with her eyes. I heard it said many times after that, that my mother did not go back into

67

the house again that day until she saw Ben coming back up the road again after his first shift down the mine. She said she could not go inside the house and lock the door on Ben.

A fortnight later Ben had his first pay. He came home very excited, and said to my mother, "Hold your apron out, Mam;" it was an old custom with the miners on payday for their wives and mothers to put on a clean white apron and take a kitchen chair out on to the doorstep. Then each woman would sit on her chair and wait for her colliers to come home; as the men passed, they would each drop their pay docket and pay into her lap. Now Mam was a collier's mother and must have the same respect paid to her.

After Ben had bathed and had his dinner, he set off for the sweet shop, to spend sixpence of his shilling pocket money to buy three tuppenny bars of Fry's Chocolate Cream. When he came back from the shop, he went upstairs and put a bar of chocolate under my pillow, Garfield's pillow and Violet's pillow. It had been my parent's practice all our lives, on every Saturday night when going to bed, to put a bar of chocolate under each pillow, so that when we woke on Sunday morning, we would put our hands under our pillows and find the bars there. That way my father and mother would have an extra half hour in bed while we ate our chocolate. We had missed this treat for a few years now, because of our poverty, but on Sunday morning Ben was too excited to wait for us to wake up by ourselves; he came to wake us and tell us to look under our pillows. When we showed our surprise, Ben said, "I'm a working man now, and I am going to take Daddy's place. You shall have your chocolate under the pillow every Sunday morning as you used to do," and he was as good as his word.

The manager of the colliery came to our house one day, and told my mother that it was a shame for Ben to be working underground, because he had the brain of a barrister, and he could not understand why such a brilliant boy had been allowed to come to the colliery to work. Mother told the manager, "My late husband was a barrister, and it was always our wish that Ben should follow in his father's footsteps, but Fate decreed otherwise."

"Well," said the manager, "all I can say is, it's a damn shame that a boy with his brain should not have the opportunity to do what he was definitely cut out for."

TEN

We didn't stay long in Pengam, because my mother's heart was in Ogmore Vale where she had many good friends and relations, and she went over there and found a house to rent in Lewistown, number twelve of a brand new row of houses. The row had been built by the owners of the Lewis Merthyr Colliery to house their colliers, but because of the war and because our stepfather was fighting overseas, we were able to rent one. This time we went by train.

By now it was coming up to Christmas and the council decided to give a Christmas party for the children of the men who were serving in the army. We had invitations to the party, which was held in the Leisure Hall; in the middle of the hall stood a big Christmas tree, and after the party we all lined up to receive our gifts from Father Christmas. Violet had a box with a doll dressed in a beautiful blue dress, and I had a beautiful doll, the same size, dressed in pink; as well as these gifts, each girl was given a pink flannelette nightdress, while the boys were given flannelette pyjamas. When we went to bed on Christmas Eve, we put on our new pink nightdresses and Garfield wore his blue pyjamas. As for me, all my life I had had to have a doll dressed in blue, and now at last I had one dressed in pink, something I had always wanted!

We lived in that house until I was thirteen, then my mother got restless again, and decided that she wanted to live in Abergwynfi, to be near a friend whose husband was also away in the army, leaving her with a baby girl, Gwenny and a little crippled boy of four. This friend wrote to my mother saying that she was very lonely and suggesting that it would be nice if Mother could come to Abergwynfi to be near her. My mother felt very sorry for her friend, and she decided that we would go to Abergwynfi to be near her; so we packed up and set off by train, having sent our furniture ahead by rail. Our little Yorkshire terrier, who was our pride and joy, travelled with us;

we all adored him, but he was especially my own. We stayed with Louise Price, my mother's friend, for a few days until my mother found a beautiful flat in the last house of a terraced row in High Street, Abergwynfi. Our landlady, Mrs. Salmon, lived in a detached house next door to us.

Our house was the last of a group of four three-storeyed houses, and all the gardens together were like one large play area; the side entrance to the garden was through one common side door opening off the hill going down through High Street. Coming in from the hill we passed the first three houses, then, before coming to our house we passed an alleyway, with steps to take us up to the main road. Our flat was the basement of a three-storey house; a bedroom went out over the alleyway. At the bottom end of our play space, which was walled-in all round, were four toilets, each toilet being for the use of either two bottom or two top flats; we used to let our little dog out into that area, and someone would see that he did not go up into the main road.

One day my mother asked me if I would go to the shoe-maker with a pair of shoes to be soled and heeled for her, and she suggested that I should take little Dai, our dog, on the lead because a walk would do him good. I took the shoes into the cobbler, and was coming back into our house through the side gate when I saw a man come out of the toilet and walk up towards the alleyway. He lived next door to us, in the top flat, but I had only seen him once before, when I nursed the baby for his wife in their house, while she did her ironing, and I did not know what work he did. I had never seen him in his working clothes, but this day, as he was coming up the garden, he was in collier's pit clothes, with his tommy box filling one pocket of his coat and his tin water jack standing upright in his other pocket. He wore a red muffler knotted around his neck and flat cap on his head. He smiled at me, and I thought he was going to ask me if I would mind the baby for them again, so I stood on the pavement and waited until he came up close to me. Then, as he lifted one foot on to the pavement, just half a yard away from me, smiling all the time, he turned into a ball of fire, then into smoke, and disappeared.

I was rooted to the spot and could neither speak nor move. My mother had seen me standing there, through the window, and so she came out and asked me why I was standing there.

70

When she saw my face, she said, "My God, Rit, what is the matter? You're as white as a sheet!" I told her what I had seen, but she thought I must have imagined it, and so she took me into the house, gave me a cup of hot tea and told me I was suffering from shock. She soon convinced me that I had imagined it, though I knew she believed that I had seen something. At this time Ben was working with Mr. Garfield Thomas, delivering milk, because Mother had not allowed him to work in the colliery at Abergwynfi, and he was in the house when I came in with my mother. "Mammy," he said, "Rit has never seen Mr. Reynolds in his working clothes, and yet she has described him exactly as I saw him going to work this morning. And he is in work at the moment, so she couldn't have seen him clean-faced a while ago, unless she has had a premonition."

My mother, like all Welsh people, was very superstitious, and she said, "It could be, Ben but I hope to God that nothing has happened to that young man in the colliery, for the sake of his little wife and child."

Then Garfield came home with our comics, 'Puck' and 'Rainbow' and 'Chips', our weekly treat, and I soon forgot about Mr. Reynolds. On the next day, I had been shopping for my mother and was coming in through the side entrance when exactly the same thing happened again. This time I stopped in fear because I knew what was going to happen, and as before, just as he raised his foot to step on the pavement, there was fire and smoke and he was gone. My mother took me in again, and asked Ben to fetch Louise Price.

"Tell her to bring the two children and come up, I want to see her," said my mother. When Louise came up, Mother told her what I had seen, and asked her what she thought it meant. Louise said, "I would send for the doctor if I were you, Rachael, that child has seen something or she wouldn't be looking like that. She's as white as a ghost, and Ritty is not a child to imagine something like that."

My mother asked her if she would call into the doctor's on her way home and ask him to come up, but I begged, "Don't send for the doctor, Mammy, please don't send for him. How can I tell him I saw a man who wasn't there turn into a ball of fire? He'll think I'm crazy, and they'll want to put me in a mental home. I'll never go out of this house again, Mammy, please don't ask me to, then I can't see anything."

71

On the following day she gave me money and told me to go to the shoe-maker and fetch her shoes. I was shaking with fear at the very thought of it, and I said, "No, Mammy, I can't go, I can't go." My mother made light of it, "Oh, you won't see it again," she said. "I'll tell you what we'll do, take little Dai with you on the lead, and go and fetch my shoes. Then, when you come back to the gate, take little Dai off the lead and he'll run into the house. When I see him, I'll come out and fetch you, you stay by the gate."

I brought the shoes, let the little dog off the lead at the gate, and my mother came down to fetch me as she had promised.

"There you are, Rit," my mother said, as we went into the house. "Nothing has happened; you won't see it again, forget it now, you must have imagined it."

"Yes, I expect I did, Mammy," I said, but I knew in my heart that I really *had* seen what I told them I had.

My mother was hanging up a piece of wallpaper by the door when suddenly there was a knock at the door. Mother called out, "Half a minute, don't open the door, I'm standing on a chair behind the door, wait until I come down." Then she said to me, "Rit, come and open the door."

I opened the door, screamed, and backed away, almost fainting with fright! Mother went to the door, then, and when she got there she said, "Oh, my God!" and she too nearly fainted with shock. Mr. Reynolds was standing there, exactly as I had seen him, with red muffler, flat cap and so on. He looked at us in surprise, and he must have wondered what on earth was wrong with us. My mother half expected him to turn into a ball of fire, for she thought she was seeing an apparition.

"What do you want?" Mother asked him.

Mr. Reynolds said, "Is your little dog in, Mrs. Thomas?"

"Yes, he's here," said Mother, and she called out, "Little Dai, where are you?" but there was no answer.

"He must be there," I said. "I brought him in."

Then my mother asked Mr. Reynolds why he wanted to know that.

"Well," he said, "there's a little dog dead up on the road, and I think it's your little dog. Two alsatians were fighting, and your little dog got in the middle of them. I think he choked, there isn't a mark on him."

And so it was clear that there had been a reason for the

72

apparition, another tragedy in our lives. Mr. Reynolds went and brought our little dog indoors, and said that he had been on his way to work when he saw it happen, so he came back to tell us. I sat up all that night nursing my little dead dog in my arms. I had never gone to bed without him since he had been given to me, and now I sat on the stairs holding his little body. My mother tried to find a taxidermist to have him stuffed, because we thought in that way we could have our pet with us always, but there was not one west of Cardiff. It was nearing Christmas, and we had to have our little dog buried up on the mountian but we were broken-hearted at the loss of our pet.

On 'pension day' we found that something had gone wrong with my mother's money; her army pay was several shillings short and had been so for a few weeks.

"I thought this was going to be a nice Christmas," she told us. She had made Christmas cakes and puddings, with all of us joining in to help, and it should have been a good Christmas for us, but now, with the shortage of money in her army pension, things were looking bleak. "We'll be all right for food," said my mother, "but I've got no money for coal."

The coal house was bare, and it was just a few days before Christmas. (If Ben had still been working in the colliery, we would have been having concessionary coal, of course.)

Emily had joined the army before we went to live in Abergwynfi; she had seen one advert in the paper asking for a Welsh girl, a Scottish girl, an English girl and an Irish girl to help form a women's army, and she had been the first Welsh girl to join. After fitting them out with khakhi uniforms, exactly like the men's except that the girls wore skirts, the army sent each one back to her own country with three rail warrants and orders to bring three more girls back with them. That was how the first army of women soldiers started. They called them the Women's Army Auxiliary Corps, WAAC for short.

However there was no money coming from Emily, and Ben's wages were small, so my mother said, "I don't know what we are going to do for fire from now on. I've swept the coal house clean, and I've burned all the old boots we had, so have a good warm now before you go to bed, because God knows how we'll keep warm tomorrow."

The next morning I got up from bed as soon as it was light. I hadn't been able to sleep all night, I was so full of the sorrow of my little dog's death; it had been snowing all night, and I had been thinking of him sleeping under the snow. Now I dressed and put my coat on, then put an old coat belonging to our Violet over my head, wrapping the sleeves round my ears to keep them warm. Next I put an old pair of gloves on, took two buckets out of the coal shed, and crept quietly out of the house without waking anyone. I went out on to the pavement, and turned left towards the mountain where my little dog was buried (I didn't know exactly where the grave was, but I felt it was close by); then I went down to the ash tip, and pushed the snow away with a stick to uncover the cinders – or ashes, as we called them – that had been tipped there, and filled my two buckets with them.

When I got back to the house, my mother was just getting up, and she asked me, "Where have you been, Ritty?"

"You can light a fire now," I told her, "I've got plenty of cokes."

"You can't go out in this, Ritty," she said, "it's too cold."

"No, it isn't," I said. "I'm enjoying myself. Light the fire, and make some tea by the time I come back."

I went to get another two buckets of coke, and it was lovely then to come back to a nice warm fire and a hot cup of tea. After that I spent the entire day going backwards and forwards to the tip, and when there were no cokes left to collect, I brought back old boots. In my anxiety to keep the coal shed full, the sorrow of the loss of my little dog was put aside, and by night time our shed *was* full. When my mother saw it, she said, "Thank God, we are right now until after Christmas. I've got a bucket of hot water ready for you, so come and have a bath now."

We had no bathroom, so my mother sent Violet and Garfield on an errand, just to get them out of the house, and Ben said, "I am going down to Louise." He did this every day after work, and he would take Louise's little crippled boy out for a breath of fresh air. With all of them out of the way I was able to have my wash in our tin bath in front of the fire. Meanwhile, before he went down to Louise, my mother told Ben, "When you come home, ask Louise to come up and see me. I would like to have a talk with her." Then, when the children came home from their errand, Mother said to them, "You haven't been carol singing since we lost little Dai, so how about you taking them out tonight, Rit, you'd like that, wouldn't you?" My mother's idea was to stop me grieving about my little dog.

74

It was the night before Christmas Eve, so I took Violet and Garfield and we went around the houses we hadn't already been to. Abergwynfi was a very Welsh valley; nearly all the men were miners, a very kindly lot, and if they had known we had no coal in our coal house, they would have filled it from their own cellars. Every householder was given a concessionary ton of coal every month, free of charge, but there was a stipulation that any miner caught giving away or selling his concessionary coal would forfeit his allowance of free coal for the rest of his mining life. So my mother said, "What the people don't know, they can't worry about, so we won't let anyone know we have no coal. We can't let anyone take that risk for us."

Before knocking on any door during our carol singing, we would sing all the well known and loved carols; we knew them all in English *and* Welsh, and we knew all the people. We had good voices, Violet in particular, and we wouldn't knock on the door until we had sung all the carols. Mostly people would deliberately not answer our first knock because they loved to hear the little verse we said when we were going away:

Christmas is coming, the goose is getting fat,
Please put a penny in the old man's hat.
If you haven't got a penny, a ha'penny will do,
If you haven't got a ha'penny, then God bless you!

Then the doors would always open, a smiling face would greet us and thank us for our lovely singing, and sometimes we were given a penny each.

While we were out singing, Louise had come up, and was having a serious discussion with my mother, who told her about our little dog and about Mr. Reynolds coming to the door.

"What do you make of it, Louise?" asked Mother. "There must be a reason for this thing to happen. Remember, she twice saw him turn into a ball of fire. It seems that tragedies follow Ritty around – it was she who saw her father dying when he burst a blood vessel and was soaked in his own blood. We had to leave Pengam because of that shock. And I didn't tell you, did I, Louise, the reason why we left Lewistown to come here." And then my mother started to relate the tragedy that had happened in Ogmore Vale.

There was a family named Brookes living near us at the time;

they were elderly people, and Mr. Brookes had an artificial leg. Their daughter was in her twenties and worked away from home, while the elder of their two sons was mentally retarded; the younger, though, was an intelligent, good-looking boy of thirteen, called David. David Brookes had started working in the colliery just after his thirteenth birthday. (Normally boys started work after their fourteenth birthday, but David had been favoured bcause his father had lost his leg in the colliery and was now only able to do light work and earn small wages.) I was teased a lot at school because David Brookes told the children he loved me and was going to marry me when he grew up; I would retort angrily, "I wouldn't marry you, David Brookes, if you were the last man on earth!"

That morning, when I set off on my mile and a half walk to school, Emily gave me money to buy chocolate for her. I was to bring them home at dinner time, and put the money in my desk at school. That day, instead of having play at playtime, our teacher took us for a walk up Rhiw-Glyn Mountain. There was a farm on the top of the mountain, and all the schoolchildren who went on walks up there were given a glass of fresh milk and shown round the farm. In the spring the fields surrounding the farm would be yellow with daffodils, and then, in their season, blue with bluebells; it was a beautiful sight and our walk would really be a nature ramble. It was wonderful, too, to look down on the road coming from Ogmore Vale past our house, just like a white ribbon spread across the green fields and see the traffic like toy horses and carts. The cemetery was beside the road, and from where we stood we could see young trees that had been grown and trimmed to form the name of the place, 'Pwll y Pant Cemetery.'

It was so beautiful that we were lost in the wonder of it all – houses looked no bigger than little dolls' houses. Teacher looked at her watch and said, "Oh, my goodness, it's past twelve o'clock, you'll be late for school this afternoon!" We were then above the colliery, part of which was on the mountain and part down in the valley, and to get to our homes we would have to go down the mountain and along a track that the miners used which would take us down an embankment and across a busy railway line with its warnings of 'No Trespassing'. From there we would cross a plank over the river, then go up another steep embankment on to the road that we had looked at from the mountain top, and finally make another climb up a steep hill to the side of the mountain where my home stood. The track was a short cut made by the miners to get them to the colliery. Now, though, the mine owners were having an iron bridge built from one mountain to the other crossing over the gorge, but so far they had only built the iron frame; the floor had not yet been put down, only the girders that would eventually support it, which were about a yard apart from each other.

Teacher said,"You Lewistown children had better dismiss here. How many of you are there?" There were only two of us, since the rest all lived near the school, so she asked, "Are you two girls sure you can find your way home from here?"

"Yes, Teacher," we said, "we can find our way down," and we started to go down the mountain near the colliery.

We were walking through the top of the colliery to the path that would take us across the railway line and the river when we heard a voice. It was David Brookes, teasingly shouting, "Pssst, girls" to draw our attention. It was the colliers's lunch time, and Davy had been sent to get a bottle of water for his workmate; he was now on his way back over the screens. The 'screens' was a bridge going from one part of the colliery to another, and in its centre was a square hole containing a machine which controlled the drams. The drams had two thick chains, one coming from the hole, which pulled the loaded dram of coal from the colliery, and the other chain taking the empty dram back again.

Davy Brookes was walking backwards along this bridge while he called out, teasing Muriel Woods and myself, and I shouted out to him, "Davy Brookes, turn around and look where you are going, and don't show off!" The chains had not been working when he had crossed earlier to fetch the water, but now they were back in motion, and I realised the danger. Davy turned, but too late; the chain had caught his feet, and with a terrible scream he fell and was dragged down into the hole. Muriel Woods was screaming and screaming, but I couldn't utter a sound, nor could I move, I was rooted to the spot, paralysed with fright.

The machinery was quickly stopped and ladders were put up. Men were running in all directions, and one of them ran up the ladder, to where we could see Davy's legs hanging out of the hole. I wanted to shout or move, but still I could do nothing. A man passed us, on his way to the telephone, and as he passed,

Muriel asked him, "Is he hurt much?" "We don't know yet," the man shouted back, "we can't find his head." Then I saw a man supporting Davy's little body; his back was one big, bloody hole, and the man said, "He's gone, poor little chap." At last something snapped inside me, my legs were released, and I ran and ran, like one possessed, until I got onto the frame of the bridge, and jumped from girder to girder. The men looked up in horror, open-mouthed at the dangerous way I jumped, but fear had lent wings to my feet, and I did not stop running until I reached home.

It was a boiling hot day, but I felt neither hot nor cold, I was numb. I ran through the open door of our house and did not stop until I collapsed on the living room floor. My mother got down on her knees beside me, and said, "My God, Rit, what's the matter?" But I could not speak. People had seen the terror on my face as I ran past them, and had called after me, "Ritty, what's wrong? What's happened?" but I couldn't answer and just kept on running. Now these people were coming to the house to see what had happened.

The doctor lived two miles away and there were no telephones, but when my mother called out, "Someone fetch a doctor," a man's voice said, "I'll go, missus," and he ran the two miles there and back. Mother was trying to get me to speak, but all I could say was "Dai, Dai, Dai." She could see that I was in a terrible state of shock, so she did not attempt to move me off the floor, but looked around for our little dog, and said, "It's not little Dai. Is it Uncle Dai?" Still all I could say was "Dai, Dai." When they looked up from our street, they had seen us on the mountain, and now my mother asked, "Did you go for a walk with the school?" But she could tell by the expression on my face and in my eyes that I could not speak, and she went on, "Did you come down by the colliery?" Then she knew. "It's little Davy Brookes, isn't it?" she said.

My mother asked one of the women to stay with me until the doctor came, because there was nothing more that she could do for me at that point, and she told the woman, "I must go down to Mrs. Brookes." When she reached the house, she could see four men coming down, the street, carrying the little body on a board, covered with bradish (brattice – a heavily oiled piece of cloth used for water-proofing). My mother was just in time to stop them knocking at the door, and she told them, "For God's

78

sake, stay back a bit, let me go in and prepare the mother." – If she had not stopped them, they would have presented that poor mangled body to the mother and said, "Here is your son. He is dead and we have brought him home."

Mother went into the house and, taking the woman gently in her arms, said to her, "Come and sit down, my dear, I have some bad news for you." Then she began to break the news to her as gently as she could; but Mrs. Brookes knew; she could tell by the look on my mother's face, and even before Mother started to speak, Mrs. Brookes said, "It's my little Davy, isn't it?"

My mother attended to Davy next. His whole body had been smashed, but she washed him and put all his working clothes in a sack, asking one of the men to bury them. Then she laid the little boy out and covered him before letting his mother into the room, so that Mrs. Brookes would not see his battered body.

Meanwhile Dr. Anderson came to our house as quickly as he could. He didn't move me but said that my mother had done the right thing in leaving me on the floor, and they were to leave me there until I could get up on my own. "Leave her there, and when she is ready to move, put her to bed. She has had a terrible shock."

"Will she ever speak again, doctor?" asked my mother.

"She may," he answered, "but it will be a long time."

Mother knew what I was trying to tell her then, and she said to the doctor, "She doesn't want to go to bed, she wants to go to school."

"Well," he replied, "let her do whatever she wants when she gets up, don't force her in any way. If she wants to go back to school, then don't stop her. I can't do anything for her now, we'll just have to let nature take its course."

Muriel Woods had gone back to school and told the teacher what had happened; she was none the worse for the ordeal. Now I went too, but as I walked up the street, I could smell the oil from the cloth that covered Davy's body, and I vomited all the way to school. I just went in and got the money I had put under the desk and went home. I never went back to that school again.

It was this story that my mother related to Louise Price while we were carol singing. "You can see why we had to get away from there," she told Louise. "The doctor advised me to get Rit away as soon as possible, and now I don't know what to do. We'll just have to wait and see how she'll be after Christmas."

While this was going on, we had returned from our carol singing, counted the money we had collected, and given it to my mother. But she said, "No, you children have earned it, go and buy something for yourselves, for Christmas."

So late on Christmas Eve, when it was dark and all the shops were lit up, we pooled our money and started out to walk to Blaengwynfi where the best shops were. Violet and Garfield chose what they wanted, and then we bought a present for my mother, and a present for Ben because he was a good brother. That left us with one and sixpence, the price of something I had always wanted – a box of paints; and so we all went home happy with our purchases. (I was delighted with my paints because I had only had crayons before.)

It snowed heavily that night, and next day, after dinner, when we were settling down by a nice fire (me with my paints!), Ben asked Garfield if he would go for a walk with him, up on the mountain in the snow.

"Isn't it too cold to take Garfield out?" said Mother. "Stay by the fire nice and warm." But Ben was sixteen and wanted a bit of excitement, so off they went.

They had been gone for quite a while, and snow was falling, when Mother began to worry. It was Christmas and the days were short, so it was already getting dusk; my mother got up and paced about restlessly. She said that she hoped they had not gone over the mountain and got lost, and so after a while I put my coat over my head and Mother and I went to look for them; by then they had been gone for hours. We followed their tracks for some way, but then the snow flakes covered the marks. I had been praying quietly, and I knew my mother had been doing the same, though neither of us had spoken a word. 'Please, God, turn them back, don't let them get lost on the mountain,' I prayed. Then, when we were beginning to despair of ever seeing them again, we heard Ben whistling higher up on the mountain. The sound came nearer to us until at last they came safely back.

When they came home, Ben told us that they had wanted to walk to Ogmore Vale, but they had got lost and so they had turned around and come back. If it had not been for the death of our little dog and the fear that the boys were lost on the mountain, it would have been a perfect Christmas Day, but now that they were safe and we were all snug inside our home, we were able to relax and enjoy the Christmas atmosphere. It brought to mind my father's frequent saying, "In a cottage there is joy, when there's love at home", and that night as we sat around the fire, thankful that God had heard our prayers and turned the boys back when they had been tempted to go on, we sang a song my father used to love to hear us sing:

> Love at home, love at home,
> Hate and envy ne'er annoy when there's love at home,
> Love at home, love at home,
> In a cottage there is joy when there's love at home.

Ben and Emily had a better knowledge than I did of our better-off days when we had servants to wait upon us; now they had the experience of our poverty and the lack of things that they had once been used to having, but they still knew the joy of love at home. Once Ben searched the ash tips for rags and bones, to pay for a present for my birthday, and now I had searched an ash tip for the means of warming my family, and felt no shame in doing so, because it was one of those things that made the loving home of which my father had spoken.

ELEVEN

Once Christmas was past, my mother's thoughts turned to the problem of our future. Should we stay here in Abergwynfi and wait until the war reached us? Or should we go back to Ogmore Vale? She talked it over with Louise, and I heard her say, "Ben and Garfield must be very homesick for their friends in Ogmore Vale for them to want to risk walking over the mountains through all that snow on Christmas morning. I think I'd better take the children back there, or Ben might possibly try that walk again, and I could so easily lose my two boys to the mountain.

And so my mother packed up, and we went back to Ogmore Vale, where we had another nice house, Number 19 Pentre Bailey Terrace. At number 18 lived Mr. and Mrs. Davies who had a large family of children, including a daughter of my own age named Ethel, with whom I became very good friends. In fact we liked all the Davies children especially the youngest, Islwyn, aged four, and Ernie, aged three. Ernie called Islwyn 'Dical-wyn', and they were devoted to each other. I loved best of all to watch those two little ones playing, and to listen to them chatting together; their favourite game was 'Choo choo trains,' where little Ernie was the engine, and Islwyn would hold on to the end of his jersey and be the train.

Ben was now seventeen, and he came home one day with the news that he had joined the army. My mother had not wanted him to go back to the colliery, but she had not wanted him to go into the army either, and she told him, "You can't join the army, Ben, you are too young, you have to be eighteen."

"Too late, Mam," he said, "I've taken the King's Shilling, and I've signed myself as eighteen. I'll make an allowance to you."

And so he went off, quite happy to be a soldier, but had his illusions shattered very very soon. He was terribly homesick.

Mrs. Davies was a stout woman, and a very nice neighbour, but she was a terrible borrower; she did not have anything in her house for domestic use, and was forever borrowing – buckets, bowls and so on. On one particular morning I was out in the street watching the two little boys playing their favourite game of 'Choo choo trains'; they were coming up from the bottom of the street, their little faces aglow with happiness, and the thought came to me, 'I wish I was an artist, so that I could paint a picture of those two, and the rapture on Ernie's face as he drove Islwyn (who was his train) along.'

Mrs. Davies came out of her house and went into ours, saying to me, "Come and help me, Rit, I'm going to borrow your mother's two tubs and her washing board. Come and help me carry them."

I went into the house behind her, and she told my mother, "I was taking the boiler off the fire just now, and I remembered I hadn't asked you for a loan of your two tubs." Suddenly we heard a terrible scream, coming from Mrs. Davies's house. She had taken the big iron boiler off the fire, then, remembering she hadn't borrowed the tubs, she had put the boiler down on the floor before coming into our house. It seemed that the train, Islwyn, had broken away from the little driver, Ernie, who had run, chasing the 'engine' into the house, and had fallen into the boiling water. My mother was first into the house and he died in her arms.

I felt that somehow, in some way, I was responsible for all these deaths, and once again I withdrew into my shell. It seemed as if I was never to love without bringing disaster, and I vowed to myself never to love anything or anyone again. One day my mother sent me to fetch her army pension for her, because she had a bad head and didn't feel like a long walk that day. I went to Ogmore Vale, but as the man was handing me my mother's pension, he looked at me and asked, "Are you Rachael Ann Bowen?"

"I am," I said.

"How old are you?" he asked.

"I am fourteen today, it's my birthday," I told him.

"Just a minute," he said to me. "Give me that money back," and he crossed my name off my mother's 'ring book' (that was what the pension book was called) and deducted two shillings, the amount the government allowed each child per week.

"Here you are," he told me, "tell your mother it will be this much less from now on. You are not entitled to it now."

I did not know how to break the news to my mother that now she would have no more to keep me, because I was fourteen, but my mother said, "Well, I expected this. We'll manage some-how."

I had been having instruction in dressmaking from Mrs. Cinderby in our street, on the understanding that I would become apprenticed to her when I was fourteen, and so my mother said, "How would you like to work full time with Mrs. Cinderby? I have spoken to her and you are to start on Monday." In fact all this had been arranged and my first quarter's tuition paid for before my mother knew that my part of the pension was being stopped, so I said to my mother, "You won't be able to send me to Mrs. Cinderby's now, you'll have no money to keep me and I'll have to look for work."

Mother said, "No, you must have your chance to be a dressmaker, because I know that's what you want." My mother's headache had reminded me of her need for glasses, so I went up to my bedroom and got down my savings from their hiding-place in the chimney. I found that I had the full amount of ten and sixpence, and I gave it to Mother and said, "Now you can have your glasses, Mam, I've saved this money, and now you won't have any more headaches."

Mother was very touched and pleased, but she told me that I was not to save any more. Mr. James had told her that she didn't need glasses, so she bought herself a rolled gold wristwatch and strap with the money.

Ben had been in the army for a few months now, and one day he arrived on the doorstep, exhausted. He told Mother that he and the two boys who had joined up with him, had run away from the army, because they did not want to be soldiers; they had walked all the way from London. My mother got Ben off to bed, but shortly afterwards Sgt. Savage, who lived just behind us, came down to our house.

"Mrs. Bowen," he said, "Ben has deserted from the army, and I have instructions to pick him up. Is he home?" My mother took the policeman indoors, and told him that Ben had walked every step of the way from London. He was very tired, and was asleep in bed, and she asked if the sergeant could pick him up in the morning instead.

Sgt. Savage said, "Leave him there, Mrs. Bowen, I haven't seen him yet. I'll come and look for him in the morning." Ben went back quietly the next morning with the sergeant. The penalty for deserting was death by shooting, but because Ben

84

was not of military age, they could not punish him. So instead they shipped him straight out to India, to the Punjab. He was not allowed to notify his mother or anyone else as to where he was going, but on the train on the way to the troopship, he wrote a note to Mother telling her not to worry; he was quite happy, and had had no punishment, and he would write as soon as he could to let her know where he was stationed. He put my mother's name and address on the envelope and wrote on it, 'Will whoever finds this letter please post it to my mother;' he had no stamp, but someone found it, put a stamp on it, and posted it to her.

By now I had done my first quarter with Mrs. Cinderby, and enjoyed every moment of it, but then my mother told me that Dr. Anderson had been to see her and told her I must not do any more sewing. He said that too much sewing on a treadle sewing machine would be too much of strain on my heart, so there was to be no more dressmaking for me. I was very upset about this, but I asked my mother if she would come with me to see the Matron at the training school for nurses in Blackmill Hospital, because I wanted to be a nurse, and I wished to know if there was a vacancy there for me.

Matron Phillips and Sister Silverside were spinsters, two ladies who had just come down from Bournemouth to take charge of Blackmill Hospital. I asked Matron if I could learn to be a nurse, and she said, "Oh, my dear, how old are you?"

"Fourteen," I said, and she explained, "But you have to be eighteen before coming to work in an Isolation Hospital."

Then I told the matron that they had stopped my pay and my mother was not having any money to keep me, but I didn't want to stay at home and eat all that food for nothing.

"Please, I'll do anything," I begged her. "I'll scrub floors, and clean, and do anything. Oh, please, Matron, give me some work."

I pleaded so hard that Matron told me, "If you were sixteen, I could give you work as a ward maid, but you are too tiny, and you're only fourteen." She took me down and showed me the wards, saying, "Look, this is what a ward maid has to do, scrub all these wards every day. Could you do that?"

There were two very large wards, with twelve beds in each, a big hall and a large kitchen where the nurses prepared the patients' food, all of them areas of bare boards that had to be scrubbed every day. Again Matron said, "Could you do that?" I swallowed very hard, and said, "Please, Matron, let me try."

Matron said, "But look at your little hands. They are hardly big enough to hold a flannel."

"But I know how to scrub with the grain," I said. "I have been taught."

Finally Matron turned to Sister, and asked, "What shall we do with her, Sister?" Sister Silverside looked at me, then back at Matron, and said, "Let's keep her." That started two years of happiness with them.

They did not make it any easier for me than for anyone else. They put my hair up in pins, and made a little uniform to fit me, then told me what I had to do when the committee men came, which they did, often and without warning. I had to pretend I was a patient, take off my cap, let down my curls and discard my uniform; but if they were to catch me unawares, I was to say that I was dressing up like the grown-ups! They trained me to be a nurse, but I also had to do any chore that I was asked to do, and I worked very hard and certainly earned my two pounds a month and keep.

I gave my wages to my mother; I had no need of money as there was nowhere to go, and when I was off duty, I just walked home. In the summer Matron and Sister Silverside mowed the lawns themselves, and they would call for 'Tiny' (the nickname they gave me) to come and have a ride in the wheelbarrow. They would fill it with the cut grass and put me to sit on top if it, and wheel me around the grounds. Then every night they would both come into my room and rub my chest with camphorated oil, because they said I had a bad chest. Although I did not have an easy time, and the work was hard, I could easily have become spoilt by the way they showed their affection for me.

We had a little girl called Phoebe Triggs, from Pontycymmer, in the Typhoid Block. She was the only typhoid patient at that time, six years old, but looking just like a six month old baby, she had been ill so long. There was no hope of a recovery, she was, as they said, just waiting her time, and Sister Silverside asked me if I would like to nurse the child. It meant nursing her in a shawl because her bones were sore after lying in bed for so long; but if I nursed Phoebe, it would relieve the nurse who usually cared for her, so that the woman would be free to work in the other wards which were so very busy.

One day I was nursing Phoebe in the Welsh shawl, cradle fashion, walking up and down the ward and singing softly to her, when she put up her little hand and touched my face, and said, "Nursy, I wished you was my mummy." Then, when I was settling her down for the night in her cot, she put her little arms around my neck and drew my face down to hers – a thing that we were forbidden to allow with a fever patient – and said, "Kiss me, nursy, kiss me night night, and joking you are my mummy." What could I do? The child was dying of enteric fever, the worst form of typhoid; she was dying and she wanted to feel the warmth of her mother's arms around her, something she had not felt for many months. How could I refuse her dying wish?

She asked me again, "Please, Nursy, kiss me night night." I couldn't let her die without 'pretending' to be her mummy, so I kissed her and said, "Goodnight, my little darling," hoping that that was what her mummy would have said. She settled down to sleep, and I sat down at her side until the night nurse came to relieve me. I did not feel afraid of having kissed her, but my conscience couldn't let her go without showing her I loved her, and I prayed to God not to let Phoebe die. Three weeks later I collapsed with typhoid fever myself; but by the time I collapsed, Phoebe was well on the road to recovery and soon went home. I was nursed in the nurses' home, up in my own bedroom, isolated and cared for by Matron and Sister alone.

Emily had now come home and brought her Australian fiancé with her; she was going to be married, and I was to be bridesmaid. It would be a military wedding. Meanwhile, Sister Silverside and Matron took it in turns to be with me. I was very ill and delirious and as Matron was coming into my room one day, I said to her, "You are my mother, aren't you?"

"No, dear," she said, "I'm not your mother."

"You are, you are," I said, "Say you are my mother."

"Yes, dear, I am your mother," she agreed. I felt comforted and fell asleep; but that night I had put a thought into her mind.

My cousin Sammy had come over from the Rhondda; he was on leave from the Royal Navy and had come for Emily's wedding. When he got to our house, he asked where I was, and my mother told him that I was in hospital and she did not think that I would be coming to the wedding because I had been very ill with typhoid fever and no-one had been allowed to see me. So Sammy said, "I'm going down to see her."

When he arrived at the hospital, Matron told him, "If she had been ill in the ward, you could have seen her, but she is being nursed in the home because of the seriousness of her illness and it is highly dangerous for anyone to see her. That is why we have had to keep her family away."

"Well, will you show me her bedroom window?" asked Sammy.

The matron showed him my window, which was in the middle of an ivy-covered wall – and before you could blink he had climbed the ivy and was shouting through the window. "How are you. lovely girl? Are you coming to the wedding?" Then Sammy, Matron and Sister had a long chat underneath my window, and after he had gone, Matron came into my room and asked, "Would you be very disappointed if you didn't go to the wedding? Your cousin said your bridesmaid's clothes are all ready for you."

I told her that I would like to go, but I would rather stay away than endanger anyone else's life. Early the next day, Matron woke me up and said, "Come on, you are going to have a disinfectant bath this morning." After that bath I was also bathed in scented water, because, Matron said, "We can't have you going to the wedding smelling of the hospital." I got excited then, and asked, "Am I going to the wedding?" "Yes," said Matron. "Sam is coming down to fetch you in a taxi."

When the taxi came, Matron saw me off, saying, "Now, remember, only to the house to see the wedding, then you must come back." When I got to the house, I was dressed like the other bridesmaids in a white dress with a big khakhi sash; the men were dressed in uniform. I forgot all about my promise to Matron just to stay in the house and look at the wedding, and instead I went off to the church.

Emily and her fiancé were married in the old Llangeinor church. (There were no houses in Llangeinor, only the church and churchyard, a pub and a farm, and yet on the Sabbath day that church would be full; people came from all around to attend service there, some on horseback, some walking miles from their homes.) When we came back from the wedding, Matron and Sister were sitting waiting for me – but they did not give me the row that I expected. Instead they took me straight back to the hospital .

Emily decided that she wouldn't go back to the army, and she stayed with Mother while her husband went back. The war was nearing its end now, and Emily claimed her discharge on compassionate grounds. Shortly afterwards we heard from the War Office that Richard Bird, Cousin Margaret Ann's eldest son, had been killed in action. Dick had lived with us while his mother was carrying out her singing engagements, and we had looked on him as a brother (calling him affectionately 'Dickiebird'), which was why the message came to us and not to his mother. He was only nineteen when he was killed.

TWELVE

At last the great news came: the war was over. By then we only had one child patient left in the hospital, and the entire staff, including the domestics, were given the evening off to go out and celebrate. Matron and Sister Silverside asked me if I would stay with the little girl, who was better, but still convalescent, because they both wanted to go and join in the festivities that night; I was quite well now, but not strong enough yet to walk the mile to my home. Matron gave me some harmless fireworks which I could set off in the ward to amuse the two of us while the rest were away. I pinned Catherine wheels to the locker and set them off, but after they had burnt themselves out, I found, to my horror, that they had left scorch marks on the locker. I confessed to Matron when she returned and showed her the marks, but she laughed and said, "Well, we'll leave them there, so that we have something to remind us of the wonderful day when the war ended."

We had a probationer nurse then, Edie Herford, who lived in Ogmore Vale. Every day the fever nurses were given two hours off to go up into the mountains and breathe fresh pure air as a precaution against the diseases they nursed in the hospital, and Edie used to walk the two and half miles to her mother's house in that time. Then she walked back, and every day, on her way back, she would call in at my mother's house, tell her all the news, and have a cup of tea.

I was fifteen now, and Emily had been married almost a year, but I had no suspicion that Emily was expecting a baby, so it was a great surprise to me when Nurse Herford told me to ask Matron for an hour off to go up and see Emily because she had a baby girl! I was so excited! I ran to Matron and asked, "Oh please, Matron, may I have an hour off to go home and see my sister? She has a baby girl!"

I was so breathless with excitement that Matron smiled, and said, "All right, off you go – and come back in an hour and tell me about this wonderful baby."

I had one and sixpence saved, and I took my savings and hurried away from the hospital. There was a Fete and Gala in Blackmill that day, and I knew there would be stalls there where I could buy some little gift for Emily. It was a mile to Blackmill, and I thought that if I could run down and buy a present and run back again, then I could hurry the other mile up to my mother's, to see the baby, and that would leave me just enough time to get back to the hospital. So I went to Blackmill and bought a beautiful brand new golliwog off one of the stalls for a shilling, as well as a big bar of Cadbury's chocolate; then I went home as fast as I could to see the new baby.

"Where's the baby, where's the baby?" I gasped.

"She's up in the back bedroom," said my mother. So I ran, still gasping, up the stairs to the bedroom where Emily showed me her wonderful baby girl. I dumped the golliwog and the bar of chocolate in the arms of that tiny baby, barely a few hours old, and said, "These are for you." Emily looked up at her husband, who was standing at the bedside, and smiled. Then I asked the baby's name, but I didn't have time to hold it. Instead I went quickly down the stairs and dashed back to the hospital, where I went to Matron's room and told her that my sister had the most wonderful, beautiful baby in the whole world. Then, all in one breath, I rushed on, "She's beautiful and I didn't go home straight away I went to Blackmill and I bought her a golliwog and a bar of chocolate then I rushed home and put them in her arms!" Matron and Sister roared with laughter. "A golliwog and a bar of chocolate for a new baby!" they said, and they looked at my face – I was quite astonished because I had not been laughed at before. "Well, that was very nice of you, 'Tiny'," they said, at last.

Some time later they sent for me to come to their room, because they wanted to speak to me. I went along, and Sister Silverside said, "Sit down, Matron and I have something to tell you."

So I sat down, and Matron explained, "Tiny, Sister Silverside and I are leaving this hospital now that the war is over. We are going back to London."

I was absolutely shattered at the news, for since my father's death no-one had shown me as much love and kindness as these two ladies had done. I ran out of Matron's room, up the stairs to my own room, threw myself face downwards on the bed, and cried as if my heart would break. But the two came upstairs after me, and Matron said, "Listen, Tiny, to what we have to say. We want you to come with us, and we are going to ask your mother if we can take you."

We all went up to Lewistown then, to ask if my mother would give permission for me to go with them, and they told Mother that I was a born children's nurse.

"Does Ritty want to go with you?" asked Mother.

"Oh yes," I said. "I would love to go and be trained in Guy's Hospital."

"But I can't afford the fees for her training," said Mother.

Then Matron and Sister said, "If you will allow us to adopt your daughter, all her expenses will be paid, and it won't cost you a penny. That will be our privilege and pleasure."

"Well," said my Mother, "if that's what you think Ritty is cut out for, then I won't stand in her way. But I'll miss her money, especially when Emily goes out to Australia. I don't know what I'll do without it."

If my mother had not said those words, I would have been the happiest girl in the world, but that dashed all my hopes. I had made a promise when my father died, that I would grow up to work for her, and I couldn't go away and leave her short of the help my money would give her. The ladies begged me to go with them, but I could only say that I had to stay behind and help my mother, and I let them go away believing that I didn't care. They did not know of the nights when I cried myself to sleep. I hadn't cried after my uncle Lewis and the baroness had left, with all their wealth, but I hadn't loved them as I loved these two wonderful ladies.

We had a new Matron now, Matron Fry, a short, fat, kindly lady. There was a big tomcat in the hospital, and Matron Phillips had been fond of it, but to Matron Fry it was just another animal, so she told the caretaker to lock it in the discharge block overnight because the place was over-run with rats. Next morning the cat came up to the Home in a terrible state; the rats had bitten big lumps out of his head, and he seemed to be in dreadful pain, though no-one took any notice because it was only an animal. However, the cat aroused my pity, partly because of its suffering, and partly because it was a link with Matron Phillips and Sister Silverside. I filled some bowls with

92

tepid water, and put a little iodine in the water, then took some towels, covered my arms with old woollen jerseys, and struggled with the cat until it let me bathe its wounds.

It was a big, powerful cat, but I think it was weakened by loss of blood, because after a time I was able to pin its legs down. The blood had congealed, and I had to bathe the cat's head, neck and shoulders to soften this crust, but at last I managed to wash away the mess, while the iodine would help to kill the poison. Then I covered the holes with a healing ointment and let the cat go. It did not seem to suffer so much after that treatment, and I did the same every night and morning, noticing that the cat fought me less every time I treated him. After a while he ceased to be terrified and followed me, miaowing as if asking me to bathe him. At first Matron had forbidden me to treat the cat, in case he hurt me, but by now she was looking on in admiration as he followed me around. He was never put back in the discharge block again, but before I left the hospital he had been fully restored to being a normal healthy cat and had taken up residence in Matron's room again.

THIRTEEN

At the end of my two years' training I left the hospital; Matron Phillips had once advised me to go to another hospital once my training was over, and I took her advice. By now I was sixteen, but although I was trained, I would still have another two years to wait – until I was eighteen – before I could go to another hospital as a probationer, so I applied for a place as a Land Army girl, and was sent to Abergarw Farm in Brynmenin. The farmer, Jenkin Morgan, had grown up on the farm, and his sister acted as his housekeeper. Her husband, a white collar worker, and her daughter, who was twenty-one and taught at Brynmenin School, shared the house with them. Jenkin Morgan himself, who was in his late fifties, had been courting a Miss Thomas, a farmer's daughter of the same age, who was one of three spinster sisters who lived with their elderly bachelor brother on Pant-yr-Awel, a large training farm between Blackmill and Ogmore Vale.

By the time I was posted there, Jenkin Morgan had married his bride and they had settled into Abergarw Farm, while Mr. Morgan's sister was about to move out to a detached house nearby. I had to wait until she moved into her new house before I could move into her bedroom because it was only a small farmhouse, and this was just about to occur when a tragedy happened. The young schoolteacher had taken her pupils down to the field by the side of the river to play ball, when the ball was kicked into the river and a little boy went into the water to save it. At this point the Ogmore and Garw rivers had joined on their way to Brynmenin, and they ran very deep and powerful at the spot where the ball had gone in, so the little boy was soon in difficulty. The young teacher jumped in to rescue him, and got him safely back to the bank, but then the strong current washed her out to her death. (Her statue, in bronze, was erected in the school grounds, and the story of her heroism can be read by anyone going by the school, while the cemetery where she is buried, near the school, has a large commemorative angel which can be clearly seen by anyone passing.) Thus I took up my position at the farm at a very sad time, and my bedroom - and the bed I slept in - were the places that had been hers, from that day she had been born until she died; when I saw them, I felt honoured that I was going to sleep in the bed of such a brave and wonderful girl.

Mr. and Mrs. Morgan had difficulty in conversing in English, being Welsh speakers, and I, being Welsh, was expected to speak in that language only; if I spoke in English they turned a deaf ear. My first introduction to farm work, was learning to milk a cow. To begin with, though, the smell of the milk and of the warm bodies of the cows made me feel very heady and sick, while several of the cows were very aggressive and Jenkin Morgan had to give them a tap before even he could milk with them. I was taught on Daisy, a very old, very patient cow. I took to milking quite well, and my next task was mucking out; but if the smell of the milking shed had made me feel sick, you can imagine what *this* job did to me! While I was mucking out the shed, up over my ankles in slurry, I thought of the snowy white walls of the hospital, and compared them with this shed; the comparison was so funny that I leaned on my sweeping brush and roared with laughter. Then I started to sing 'The Farmer's Boy,' which brought Mr. Morgan out of the house to see what was happening. He too started laughing, and said, "I can see you are going to be better than any farmer's boy!"

The river divided us from the fields where I had to turn the cows out to pasture, and I had to drive them around the front of the house, on to the main road, over the water by way of a hump-backed bridge, through a gate, and into the field on the other side of the river. When I was bringing the cows back for milking in the evening, I decided to take a short cut and drive the cows through the water, which was shallow at this point, before the other river joined it, so I knew it would be quite safe for the cow and myself. The only snag was that I got wet feet following the cows, and after a few journeys I decided I would have to find an easier way of crossing. I selected one of the younger, stronger cows and whispered in her ear, "You are going to give me a piggy back," then threw myself across her back like a sack of potatoes and let her carry me across the river. Mr. Morgan saw me coming back like this one day, riding on the cow's back, and

95

said, "Oh, merch i, you're a caution!"

I soon taught myself to ride bareback, and the only snag to that was that it was a mountain farm, and I had to walk up to Cae-pen-cindda ('Field behind the wood') over very uneven and trackless ground. I would have to hold on to the horse's mane and try to get my two feet to meet under her belly, but my legs weren't long enough to give me the grip I wanted, and I would glance down to the ground in places where it was particularly rough and think to myself, "I hope she doesn't throw me off here."

Friday afternoons saw me plucking chickens, ready for market on Saturday morning when Mr. and Mrs. Morgan would take the chickens, as well as fresh eggs and cream, to the market to sell. One Saturday morning Mrs. Morgan wasn't well enough to go to the market with her husband, so he asked me, saying, "Come on, bach, you are going to ride into market instead of Mrs. Morgan." Ladies rode side-saddle in those days, and I had never ridden on a saddle, so it was my most terrifying experience on the farm, that ride from Brynmenin into Bridgend market.

The hardest part was trying to keep the horse straight, but I had a trial run in the back yard before going out on to the main road, and I completed that safely.

Jenkin Morgan taught me to saw and mow, to reap, to top and tail swedes, turnips and mangolds; farming in those days was very primitive. We had great fun hay-making. It was hard work, for we had to cut the corn with scythes, tie it into sheaves and then stack them in bundles of three to dry, with the ears of corn facing upwards. We used to have helpers in for harvesting, and Mrs. Morgan woud bring up buckets of food for us to eat; we would sit in the shade, enjoying the delicious food. Once the corn was dry, we would stack it in the barn, ready for threshing.

We had one large special clover field, high up on the mountain, and for this Jenkin Morgan would take the horse-drawn gambo, and I would follow behind, carrying the sickle. This task of carrying the sickle was the only aspect of farm life that I did not enjoy, though it was a job that had to be done. Unlike a scythe, the sickle was a six foot razor-sharp blade, wide at the handle and narrowing towards the top of the blade till it reached a fine point. It had a long wooden handle, with hand grips, left hand and right hand, for holding, placed at different angles of the blade. Jenkin Morgan had to teach me how to carry

96

it before I could be trusted with such a dangerous weapon; to carry a sickle safely, the handle had to rest against the right hip, the right hand holds the right hand grip, and the second grip, nearest the blade is held with the left hand, while the blade goes over the left shoulder, coming down over the back towards the right leg. As I was so short, the blade almost touched the ground, and I had to stoop forward a little to prevent this happening. When I got to the field Mr. Morgan would take the sickle from me, carefully, and then encircle the grass with it. This was a very skilled and specialised job, not entrusted to anyone but himself.

Next day we would be given wooden rakes to turn the grass over on the ground to dry. Then the time would come to gather the hay. Jenkin Morgan would bring the gambo and the two horses, and I would stand in the gambo, pitchfork in hand, while Mr. Morgan passed me up a pitchfork full of hay, which I took from him and spread out in the gambo. One hot summer's day we had worked all day long; Mrs. Morgan had sent up food for us, and we had rested for a short while to eat our food. We looked about us as we ate, for the air was sweet with the scent of clover and the mountain air especially was pure and lovely. It was a beautiful day, and I felt very happy. We were both very tired, but we wanted to finish the field before nightfall, and in due course the gambo was piled high with the sweet hay, and I was standing on top of it, still holding my pitchfork in my hand. The horses were tired and anxious to get back to the stable, and when Jenkin Morgan called up to me, "We're finished now, bach," the horses thought it was their command, and started to move off, taking me unawares. I pitched forward from the top of the hay, on to the hard ground, and lay there for a moment, stunned. Mr. Morgan was very frightened; he thought I had broken my neck, so I got up quickly to assure him that I was all right. But I must have been a little concussed, because that night I tossed and turned with pain – though when Mr. and Mrs. Morgan came into my room to see if I was all right, I pretended I had just been dreaming.

I loved both Mr. and Mrs. Morgan, and I adored farm life, but the food was terrible. Each morning Mrs. Morgan would say the same thing to her husband, in Welsh, "How many eggs, Jenkin?" and he would say, "One." But only he would get one, for her breakfast and mine would be a doorstep of stale home-made bread and a scraping of rancid butter. Dinner would be potatoes and a slice of home-cured boiled Welsh bacon (which was solid fat, without a streak of lean), and sometimes we would have a little cabbage with it, while for a sweet we would have a slice of cold, thick rice pudding. We had the same meal every day of the week except Sundays, when we would have a little of something else with gravy.

Mrs. Morgan had a baking day once a fortnight, when she would bake enough loaves of bread to last for the next two weeks. In the farm kitchen was a big open fireplace; the wall surrounding the fireplace was four feet thick, and in it, by the side of the chimney, were a few loose bricks which Mrs. Morgan would take away. Inside the wall was a square iron oven, in which she could cook two large four pound loaves at a time. While the bread was in the oven, she would line some trays with pastry, put in some boiled rhubarb for a filling, cover this with a pastry lid, and cook them after the bread had finished cooking. Then, when all the cooking was finished, the stuff was put on the shelf in the dairy, to wait until all the stale bread and cakes had been eaten up.

Every teatime our meal consisted of more doorsteps of bread and a piece of stale rhubarb tart, but long before we had consumed the last of the bread and tart, the whole lot would have become mildewed. When I complained about this, Mrs. Morgan said, "Eat it up, it's good for you," and by supper time I was so hungry I would eat anything, however revolting it might be. Supper was usually one thick slice of stale bread, no butter and a piece of cheese, the same every day. My first supper at the farm had looked so tempting after a hard day's work on the farm, and I had looked forward to some nice home-made bread and cheese. I was really happy and prepared to attack my meal with gusto; I broke off a piece of bread and put it in my mouth, then picked up the cheese to take a bite out of it; underneath the cheese, on the top of my bread, was a pile of wriggling maggots. I screamed and threw down the bread, but the Morgans laughed, and Mrs. Morgan said, "Eat it up, Rachael, it's good for you, it's only cheese maggots." So I ate up the edges of the bread, round the maggots, leaving them on my plate. But the same dish was served up to me every evening of the whole year I was there on the farm. So then I asked Jenkin Morgan if I could have a raw swede for my supper instead.

Mr. Morgan and I made a pact. Every night he would bring me a raw swede; Mrs. Morgan would peel it, and then I would sit on the old Welsh settle in front of the fire and eat it. Meanwhile Mrs. Morgan would read the paper, and Mr. Morgan would go across the hump-back bridge to a little inn on the other side of the river for a pint. Then, after I had finished eating my swede, I would go to the pub to fetch Jenkin Morgan home; if he wanted to spend a longer time in the pub, he would bring me a larger swede, so I always knew how long he wanted to stay by the size of my supper. Mrs. Morgan would say to him, "Don't be long now, Jenkin," and he would reply. "As soon as Rachael finishes her swede, she'll come and fetch me." I would go to the pub and just show my face round the door, then Mr. Morgan would say, "Right, merch i," and come out with me. One night he gave me an extra large swede, so that he was out longer than usual, and that time he said to me, "Did you eat your swede, Rachael?"

"Yes," I said. "All of it?" "Yes." "Well, well," he said, "Such a little tummy, such a large swede! Where do you put it?"

It was a very happy year, and the Morgans told me I was better than any man they had had, and they hoped I would stay with them always. I had every intention of doing so, but then I had a message from my mother telling me that I was to go to Brynmenin railway station and book a return ticket to Bridgend. My mother would be on the train, and we were to see Emily, Jim and baby Beryl off to Australia. I went to the station, where my mother was looking out for me, but no-one spoke; we were too full of emotion to speak to one another. But as the train was leaving Bridgend Station for London, Emily shouted out something from the carriage window. We could not hear what she said, but my mother ran to catch those last words of Emily's as the train moved off, and I had to use all my strength to hold my mother back from jumping on the train. That night I didn't feel like a swede; I went straight up to my room and cried as if my heart would break, right through the night. Several times the Morgans called out from their bedroom, "Are you all right, Rachael?" but I was too upset to answer them.

A few weeks later I was called to come home because my mother was very ill; the doctor said she was dying of a broken heart. I had to say goodbye to the happiest year of my life, and to two of the nicest people I have ever known. I went home to nurse my mother and look after our home; and if I thought work on the farm was hard, looking after my mother and the house was much harder.

FOURTEEN

It was sad at home. Emily had been my mother's seventh child, but the first she managed to rear, and now she had gone to a strange country, with a man we knew little about, taking the baby we loved so much with her. Jim had hoped to be demobilized in Britain, because then he would have stayed in Wales, but all Australian servicemen had to return to their native land, taking their families with them. He had assured my mother that he owned a beautiful farm in Western Australia, where Emily would have a life of ease in a land of plenty, but in fact his 'farm' was a smallholding, left in his father's care. When they arrived at the bush, they found that Jim's father had sold the smallholding and spent the money on drink, so that the old man was now a hobo without a home, and had nothing to give Emily and Jim. However Emily let us believe that everything was as Jim had said it would be.

It was near Christmas one day when I went to Ogmore Vale to do the weekly shopping, and all the shops were brightly lit and decorated with Christmas fare. The year was 1919, and this was the first Christmas after the end of the war. It was lovely to see everything looking so bright and gay, after the dull years of the war, and I lingered by the shops, looking around happily. In the window of a toy shop I saw a French doll, dressed in pink and blue silk, the most beautiful doll I had seen in years; but the price was tremendous – three and sixpence a week for twenty four weeks. I would like to have bought it for Emily's baby and sent it out to her for Christmas, but it was too late to start paying on a weekly card for that year. (Though after shopping I went home and told my mother all about the doll.) Even though I had no money to buy it or to pay into a club, I could not get that doll out of my mind. I knew that by hook or by crook I would have to get it for baby Beryl.

Lewistown was built on the breast of the mountain just below Pentre Bailey Farm, and in the evenings, to have a break from the house, I would climb the rest of the mountain to the farm and sit with Mrs. James while her husband went to the local pub. (She led a very lonely life, because the farm was so isolated, and also her daughter, who had been Emily's bosom pal, had married Lady Blandy Jenkins's nephew and left home.) One evening, while I was sitting in Mrs. James's big farm kitchen, keeping her company as usual, I told her about the lovely doll I had seen in the shop window and how I longed to buy it for Beryl. "But it's three and six a week, and I am not earning any money now I'm home," I said. "So I can't afford to buy it."

"Would you like to do some washing?" asked Mrs. James.

"I'll do anything if I can get three and six a week," I said.

"We've got three men working here," said Mrs. James, "and they are lodging at Tŷ Bach (little house) on the farm, but they only wear Welsh flannel clothes and, being bachelors, have no idea how to wash them. Do you know how to wash those things?"

"Yes," I said. "You have to put a little ammonia in the water to keep the flannel soft and prevent it from shrinking. I would love to do the washing for them."

"I'll tell them," said Mrs. James. "You want three and six for doing the work – will that be all right?" And so it was agreed. I would wash their three big flannel shirts, three pairs of long flannel drawers, and six pairs of long woollen stockings. (Drawers were similar to trousers, but tied with string under the knees and over the tops of their long woollen stockings, to keep the stockings up and the drawers down; these were worn underneath their trousers.) I had to wash and air their clothes, darn the woollen stockings when needed, and patch the other flannel garments as necessary, all for three and six a week. Then each week, after returning the washing and collecting my three and six, I would go straight to the shop in Ogmore Vale and put the money on a card, until at last the great day arrived when I was able to bring the doll home and we could send it out to Australia.

My mother was better now, and I was seeking a position in a hospital. I was seventeen and a half and anxious to start earning money again. My friend, Ethel Davies, who lived next door, came into our house one day very excited, carrying a newspaper in her hand, and read out, 'Maesteg Isolation Hospital has vacancies for a probationer nurse and a ward maid.'

"Wouldn't it be lovely, Rit," she said, "if we could both go to that hospital. You could be the nurse and I could be the ward maid. What work does a ward maid do, Ritty?"

I told her that they lit fires and scrubbed out wards.

"Oh, I could scrub floors," Ethel said, as we showed the advert to my mother and told her that we would like to try for the jobs.

"Right," said Mother. "We'll go in the morning. I'll come with you."

"Which way shall we go?"

"Well, we haven't got any money, have we, so we'll go by Shanks's pony over the mountains."

Next morning we started our long walk from Ogmore Vale over the mountains into Maesteg. We walked for hours, and were very weary and hungry as we arrived at the Cross Inn in Maesteg; we could smell the fresh bread coming out of the ovens of Tucker's bakery nearby.

"Empty your pockets," said Mother. "Let's see how much money we've got between us." She collected all the money we had, and found it amounted to fourpence, the price of a loaf of bread. "Now, you girls, you sit on the grass while I go in for a loaf of bread."

The lovely smell wafting towards us from the bakery made us feel hungrier than ever. My mother came out of the bakehouse smiling and carrying a loaf of bread; she broke it into three portions with her bare hands, and we had a portion each. To me it was the most enjoyable meal I have ever tasted, but unfortunately, being so hot and fresh, it gave me the hiccoughs. When our 'meal' was ended, we started our long trek down a narrow lane to the hospital, right at the top of the Bryn mountain. As we neared the hospital my mother said to me, "As you are hiccoughing so badly, you'd better let me do the talking." Mother and Ethel had both been trying hard to stop my hiccoughs, but to no avail; but fortunately, when we walked through the big iron gates of the hospital the shock of going into a strange building stopped the hiccoughs at once, and I was able to explain to Matron that we had come in answer to the advertisement for a nurse and ward maid.

"Which one of you wants to be nurse, and which one ward maid?" she asked.

I told her that my friend would like to be a ward maid because since her family was large and she had always had to stay at home, she had no references. Then I told her that I had spent two years at the nurses' training school in the hospital at Blackmill, and the matron of Blackmill Hospital would give me a verbal reference if she rang her. So the matron of Maesteg Hospital phoned Blackmill, and was very pleased with the reference my previous matron gave her; I was engaged on the spot. Ethel was told to stand by, then Matron would send for her as soon as she required a ward maid. Then Matron rang for the maid, and told her to take us to the dining room where we were given tea, after which we walked back over the mountains again and arrived home weary and footsore – though I was very happy as I got my things together, ready to start work the next day.

A week later the matron, who had quarrelled with her ward maid, sent for Ethel and she started her duties as ward maid. We soon discovered that Matron was bad-tempered, and an alcoholic; she was removed very shortly after we took up our duties, and was replaced by a very nice woman who was courting the minister of one of the chapels in Maesteg. (She eventually married him.)

My first task after arriving at the hospital was a very embarrassing one; I was told to give a blanket bath to a young man in his twenties (who was later to tell me that he had fallen in love with me!) He was a very nice-looking young man, Albert Vincent by name, and he and Patsy M'Carthy, a fine young Irishman, were patients suffering from scarlet fever. They were the life and soul of the ward, and kept us happy in our work. Every morning when I went on duty Patsy would greet me by saying, very quickly, in his strong Irish accent, "Good morning, Nurse Bowen, good morning, nice morning, nicest morning we've had for many a morning, good morning, Nurse Bowen, good morning!"

After the men patients left hospital, it was the practice that if they met any member of the hospital staff at night, they would escort them home, because it was such a lonely walk. The police also had an arrangement with the hospital that any member of the staff, if unescorted, could call at the police station to obtain an escort back to the hospital as it was situated at the top of a very lonely mountain. However, it was seldom necessary to call at the police station because there were always some ex-patients about, waiting for an opportunity to take us home. After I had been at the hospital for some time, and had been escorted back many times by Albert Vincent, he asked me if I could consider him my sweetheart. But although to me he was a perfect gentleman, I knew he was also a tearaway, who could use foul language and, by his own admission, liked visiting public houses.

I had been religiously brought up, and although we had fallen on bad times, this had not altered my moral outlook, and so I told Albert that although I liked him very much, I would never become involved with anyone who visited pubs and used bad language. Then I thanked him for the many times he had brought me home to the hospital, but pointed out that there could never be anything between us. It was a Saturday night, and we had to be back in the hospital before the gates shut at nine o'clock, so Albert saw me in through the gates, then hurried back down to Maesteg, where the Salvation Army were holding their open air meeting. Instead of going into the public house as was his usual custom, he broke ranks, went into the centre of the Salvation Army circle and, in full view of the crowds gathered around, he renounced all his bad habits and gave himself to Jesus. From that day until the day he died, in his late seventies, he was a true Christian, and was a pentecostal minister with his own church in Maesteg for many years.

I stayed at the hospital for two years. The money was small – two pounds a month was all I earned – and times were so bad in the valley that all my money was going home to help the family, which meant that I was unable to buy the things I wanted for myself; so I took a job at Bridgend, at the Angelton Mental Hospital, where I could earn one pound, six and sixpence a week (£1.32½p).

That year Good Friday came while I was working my month's notice at Maesteg Isolation Hospital, and Matron gave Ethel the day off to go home and see her mother who was ill. I asked Matron if I could have the day off to go with Ethel, because there were no trains that day and she would have to walk over the mountains alone; Matron agreed, and also gave her maid the day off. None of us had any money, and though we were prepared to walk home, we knew we could not come over the mountains at night and be back within a day, so we decided to see if the pawn shop at the bottom of West Street was open. It was, and I pawned my wrist watch, which was rolled gold, and my locket and chain. All the man gave me was half a crown for the lot, which was only enough to get us back. We decided to walk home along the P.T.R. railway line, thinking that it would be quicker, and to pass the time we recited the old song:

> In the shade of old Freeman's pawn shop
> My watch and chain I did 'pop' (pawn)
> To pay the fine for walking the line,
> Or else down to Cardiff I'd go.
> I was tried in Bridgend yesterday
> And the judge said I would have to pay.
> If money don't pay, then you go far away,
> In the shade of old Freeman's pawn shop.

When we arrived, my mother was surprised that I had walked home; she asked me if I had been to chapel, and I said, no, I had had the day off to come home with Ethel because her mother was ill.

"Well, she has got better very quickly then," said my mother. "This morning James Pentre Bailey Farm came down to tell us that a sheep had been killed on the railway line, and if we would like to carry it up with him, he would cut it up for us and we could have it. Mrs. Davies went down to carry her share up, and she was all right then. Now, go into the pantry and see all the meat we've got!"

There was more meat on the shelf than I had seen in years. There was a pile of hot cross buns there too – unfortunately they were as hard as bricks, but in spite of that I enjoyed them. In our home Good Friday was a very sacred day, when no work was done at all, and that day we sat reminiscing over past Easters when my mother had all her five children at home. Throughout the war years food was very scarce, and white bread was a luxury, since the only bread easily available was what we called 'black bread'; our breakfast consisted of half an egg, except on Easter Sunday mornings. On that morning each year it was our custom for Emily, Ben and myself to take Garfield and Violet for a long walk down the railway line to pick primroses. (There was no traffic on the line on a Sunday.) The biggest and most abundant patches of primroses were along the line between Blackmill and Tondu. Then we would go home, tired but happy, each of us with a posy of primroses to give to my mother, to wish her a happy Easter; and the thing that helped our weary footsteps on this homeward journey was the promise of a whole egg each for breakfast, a treat that would be awaiting us when we arrived home. We looked forward to those Easter Sunday mornings for months before, just as we did to Christmas.

Buses had only just begun running at this time in my life, but we were fortunate enough to have a bus which would take us down almost into Tondu, from which we hoped to bus into Maesteg. Ethel did not go back with us that night – she said she was taking another day off – so it was just Augusta (matron's maid) and I who found ourselves stranded in Tondu with a long lonely seven mile walk to the Cross Inn, Maesteg, facing us. When we arrived at the Cross Inn we hoped, desperately, to see someone who would accompany us on the even lonelier walk through country lanes, up to the Isolation Hospital on top of the mountain, but there was not a soul in sight. We hesitated for a little while, in case someone came along, but no-one appeared, and there was nothing for it but to start off on our journey.

We did not speak during the whole of the two mile journey, because it was so lonely on that road that we were afraid of the sound of our own voices. Fortunately, when we arrived at the main gates of the hospital, we found that the caretaker had left them unlocked for us; but we were all supposed to be indoors by nine o'clock, and it was now eleven and we did not know *how* we were going to get in without drawing Matron's attention. Finally the only thing we could think of was for me to climb up the drainpipe and in through the bathroom window; then I would come down and open the back door for Augusta. But when I was half-way up the drainpipe, I found I could go no further, neither up nor down! Evidently I was not the only one who had got in by way of the drainpipe because Sister Price was waiting in the bathroom, and when she realised my plight, she hurried out and helped me back down again. Then she asked why I had tried to get in through the bathroom instead of ringing the doorbell. We told her that we had had to walk from Tondu as there were no buses, and this had made us so late that we did not want to disturb Matron.

"Get to bed quickly," said Sister Price, "and report to Matron in the morning."

Next morning, looking like two scared rabbits, we reported to Matron. Augusta May held back, and I found myself elected spokesman, so I stammered, "I'm very sorry, Matron, for any inconvenience." (I really didn't know what to say!) Matron looked up, and burst out laughing. She must have thought of the picture I made stuck up the drainpipe, because she laughed so much that she had to dismiss us.

Then, as I was leaving the room, she called me back and said, "Come here, I've got something to say to you. No wonder you were too weak to finish climbing the drainpipe – you hadn't been to bed the night before, had you?"

I didn't answer, and she said, "Come on, speak up, I know the truth, Nurse Miles has confessed."

Nurse Miles was a new probationer, doing night duty, and as there was only one patient on the whole of the diphtheria block, she had been too frightened to stay on her own, so I had stayed with her for two nights.

Matron said, "You foolish girl, how long did you think you could keep that up, working all day in your own ward and then sitting up all night with Nurse Miller? She can do it, she is in bed all day while you are on duty."

"I did sleep a little, on one of the open beds," I told Matron.

"Carry on then," she said, "and don't do it again."

FIFTEEN

I started work in Angelton on Wards Five and Six. It was totally different to fever nursing. Although the money was small in the isolation hospital, the food was excellent, plentiful and beautifully served, whereas the food at Angelton was rationed; we were given a daily portion of bread and were allowed a mid-day dinner. The dinner for the staff of Wards Five and Six was cooked by two of the inmates in a kitchen which smelled greasy, and I didn't have the stomach for it. We even had to eat in the kitchen, and since I could not bear the smell, I took a little gravy, nothing else, and ate my portion of bread with it. Every Monday we lined up for weekly rations, which we kept in a locker in our bedrooms, and which consisted of one rasher of streaky bacon, one egg preserved in waterglass, half a pound of cheese, and a saucer of jam.

Our bedrooms were cubicles off a very large dormitory, and since the inner wall of each bedroom was open at the top, just like the inner walls of the dormitory, we were actually on duty day and night. There was always a very heavy smell coming from the dormitories, because some of the patients were incontinent. We were given two and a half days off duty each week, the days to run consecutively, and we had one pound, six shillings and sixpence a week wages. On my first day out each week, with my wages in my pocket, I would leave the grounds of the hospital through the back entrance, and walk a mile to the Meter House on the Bridgend Road, which was a stop for the buses travelling up through the valleys to my home.

However, after a few days working in the mental hospital, I didn't wait for a bus; I preferred to walk the nine miles home to clear my mind. I would give my mother one pound, five and sixpence, and keep a shilling (5p) for myself; times were very hard in the valleys in those days and that was a godsend to my mother.

I would arrive home just as my mother and stepfather were

sitting down to breakfast, and enjoy breakfast with them. The boiler would be on the fire waiting for me, and after I had eaten, I would do the week's wash for the family, using just the old-fashioned tub and washing board and a bar of soap. There were no detergents in those days, of course, just soda to boil the clothes, and this played havoc with the hands. I had to wash for four men – my stepfather, my two brothers and a boy my mother had adopted – and three women, my mother, my sister Violet, and little Nancy (my cousin's motherless baby who had come to us at six months old and was now five.) That task would take me practically the whole day, and left me with just enough time to clear up and get back into my uniform and then catch the bus at the bottom of our street to take me back to the Meter House. That bus trip would take sixpence of my shilling pocket money, and the other sixpence I would keep for my second visit home, on my next day off that week, when I would give my mother's house a good clean right through, again leaving myself with just enough time to get back into my uniform.

From the Meter House I had over a mile to walk to the hospital, and though I didn't mind this walk in the day, at night I was very frightened. There was only one building after Bryn Cethin, a half mile away from the Meter House, and after that one walked on to the hospital where I worked, through a path with marshes on either side and a mental hospital at both ends, Parc Gwyllt on my left and Angelton to the right, with about two miles between them. I had to use a torch on dark nights, so that I could see where I was putting my feet, or else I could easily have walked off the path into the marsh. On the journey back at night I would sometimes stop and hold my breath, straining my ears to hear if there was anyone around. I consoled myself with the fact that I was a good runner, and could out-distance anyone if I was in danger – but luckily I always got back safely, and I was happy in the knowledge that I had eased my mother's burden, both moneywise and by sharing her work load. Then, on my half day off each week I would take my half-pound ration of cheese and go to bed with my book.

On Sundays I would take my patients to the hospital church, crocodile style, with me at the head and another nurse at the rear. After church, as a treat, we would take them for a stroll around the great park. Each nurse carried a whistle in case of emergency if a patient attempted to break away or became

110

violent, and each member of staff carried their own heavy key, attached to a leather thong looped through a wide leather belt buckled round the waist. The key hung down to the knees, on the right-hand side of the body, and was concealed by a stiff white apron.

That was the year that Elizabeth Bowes Lyon married Prince George (later George VI), and an epidemic of smallpox broke out. Every patient and member of staff had to be innoculated; the doctors attending the hospital saw to the patients, but the staff were told they could go to their own doctors if they wished, in their off-duty time. The innoculations were carried out in alphabetical order, and as my turn, under the 'B's, came on my day off, I decided to go to my own doctor in Ogmore Vale, although I would have to be in Dr. Anderson's surgery by eleven o'clock, and I had eleven miles to walk to get there.

Next morning I set off on my long trek, leaving the hospital soon after 6 a.m. and walking along the river bank until I came to the footbridge, a peaceful, pleasant walk through woodland, with the birds singing. After I had crossed the bridge I had to walk back along the other side of the river for a little way until I came to a tunnel which ran under the railway line. I had to walk through this in order to come out on the other side of the track, where there was a copse full of wild flowers. It was a beautiful walk so early on a summer's morning – though a very frightening journey on a dark night, especially when one went through the tunnel and the copse. After leaving the track I had another mile to walk to the Meter House where I would reach the road from Bridgend to the valleys, and I had to keep my wits about me on that journey because some of the male patients worked in the grounds of the hospital; staff were advised to use the main gate and not the back entrance, but that would have taken me a lot out of my way. Once I was up on the main road I could relax, for the marshland journey was over. That morning there was not a sound, no living person in sight for miles; it was as if I were the only one in the world.

Buses had started running from Bridgend to the valleys, but there was only one up and one down each day, and as I did not know their running times, I had no option but to walk, rather than wait. As I walked, I reminisced, to pass the time away, and to make the journey seem less hazardous. It was good then to know that the war was behind us, and the world was at peace.

111

My friend Ethel had stayed on at Maesteg Hospital when I left, and my thoughts turned to her father and his return from soldiering in France. He was a small, pleasant man who liked his drink, and his favourite drinking song was:

I'm lazy, lazy, awfully, frightfully lazy,
One day from night 'till morn,
I do nothing but yawn;
All I want is to go hush a bye,
For I'm too lazy to live,
And too lazy to die!

Hence very few people knew him as Tom Davies, but rather as 'Twm Lazy', and the whole family were known as 'Davies Lazy'. News had come that 'Twm Lazy' was coming home on leave from France, and Mrs. Davies received a letter stating that he wanted no-one to meet him at the railway station except Ethel and myself. Although he had a family of ten children altogether, the others were instructed to stay at home and wait for him there, and on that important day Ethel and I, all dressed up in our best clothes, walked the mile and half to the station. We waited on the platform, surrounded by the Ogmore Vale brass band as the train pulled into the station, the band struck up. I felt so proud and excited that day that I didn't even remember what they played – all I know is that it was a welcome home song to the returning hero – possibly 'Land of My Fathers'. This sort of hero's welcome was given to every soldier returning from the trenches. After the musical welcome, Ethel and I were lifted on to a gaily decorated horse-drawn colliery cart, where we sat one on each side of Twm Lazy; then, with the colliery band playing loudly, we drove off, waving gaily to the crowds who had lined the streets to welcome the hero. I felt like a princess, sitting next to a king, and it was like this all the way home to Lewistown. (Every soldier coming home to Lewistown would bring with him some hard, dark brown chocolate, and it was a treat we all looked forward to enjoying.)

Remembering this and other stories, I walked along until at last I arrived at Dr. Anderson's surgery, at the top end of Ogmore Vale; I told the doctor that I was supposed to be innoculated, and asked him if he could do it for me. Dr. Anderson told me that he had not done a vaccination or an

112

innoculation for many, many years, but then he said, "If you will go to my house and ask my wife for my case, I'll do it for you." So I went – but when I saw the thirty steps that I would have to walk up to get to his house, which was high on the breast of the mountain, I didn't think my legs would carry me up them, not after the eleven miles I had just walked to the surgery! Eventually I made it; when his wife handed me the doctor's case she said, "He hasn't done a vaccination for years and years! Still, if he wants it, here it is." I already had four scars on the muscle of my left arm from a childhood vaccination, and now, I knew, I would have another four below them. Dr. Anderson scraped four places on my arm until they bled, using a little instrument that had four needle points attached; it was unpleasant, but not unbearably painful.

After this I still had two miles to walk back to my mother's house, which made thirteen miles I had walked that morning. Fortunately it was house-cleaning day, not washing day. Little Nancy, who had been watching out for me, ran up the street to meet me, saying, "Where have you been, Gigga? I've been waiting for you." (When my mother had adopted her at six months old, she could not say either 'Rachael' or 'Ritty', so she called me 'Gigga', and though now, at six years old, she *could* say 'Rachael', she still called me 'Gigga' when she was nervous or excited). I had to tell Nancy all about my vaccination, and when we came near our house she ran in shouting, "Our Gigga's been 'waccinated', don't anyone touch her 'waccination'. I had to show my arm to them all, and explain what had happened and why I was late. Then, out of the blue, Nancy came out with the words, "Oh!, Poor Ritty's 'waccinated' arm, the one what done it ought to be punished, oh, poor Ritty's waccinated arm!"

I wasn't able to do a lot of housework that day, but I did what I could, and it was soon time for me to catch the bus back to the hospital. I got on the small, very shaky bus at the foot of our hill. As we were going through Blackmill, we had to go up a steep 'S bend' road, with a hump-backed bridge before we reached the Bridgend road, and we had got part way up the steep slope when suddenly the bus broke down because it was unable to take the hill. We all got off and started pushing. The bus had stopped in a dangerous position on the bridge, where there was just a low fence on either side, with a long drop down to the railway and the river. The driver kept on shouting instructions to us, and we had great difficulty in preventing the vehicle from running into the sides of the bridge and toppling over into the river. Then we pushed and strained to get the bus up the steep hill, but it kept running back down on us, so that we were in danger of being thrown against the sides of the bridge and over the top and into the river. When the driver put the brake on, we could not move the bus, and when he released it, the bus ran back, and altogether we were in a terrible predicament. Eventually, after what seemed like hours, we managed the job, and all got back into the bus, very much relieved to get that dangerous manoeuvre completed.

On the left hand side of the Bridgend road there was a grass verge which ran parallel with the Rallt wood, with a high hedge between the verge and the wood. Very often horse-drawn gipsy caravans parked there, but there were no gipsies on this particular day because the police had moved them on. The roads were not sealed or surfaced in those days, and the bus driver drove on to the grassy verge; the wheels sank into the soft ground and the bus tipped right over on its side so that we were all thrown around, and many of the passengers were cut by broken glass because the windows were broken. Those of us who could, had to scramble out and help the driver to push the bus back up on to its four wheels. There were not many male passengers, so women and children all had to push. There was no other traffic on the road to ask for help, but eventually we were able to start off again, and pretty soon I began to feel very sick what with the long walk I had had in the morning, my vaccination and the trouble with the bus, which were now beginning to take their toll. As each mile brought me nearer to the Meter House, knowing that I would be the only one to alight, I began to dread the thought of the bus reaching there.

The lovely summer's day (in reality early autumn) had now become a cold dark night, and I even found myself wishing that something would happen to the bus again or that I would have an accident, so that I would have to be taken to the Bridgend Hospital, and wouldn't have to face the terrifying ordeal of that walk back to the Angelton hospital. No such thing happened, and I had used up my sixpennyworth of bus ride and had to get out. My one fear now, since I was feeling so ill, was that I wouldn't be able to run away from danger. I had always depended on my fleetness of foot to carry me safely out of trouble, but now I knew I was defenceless. However prayer is always a great comforter, and I kept repeating all through that journey, "Stay by me, God, don't leave me."

I got back to Angelton and went up to the dormitory to my bed, one of those in a small cubicle that was cheerless and drab. The bed had a horsehair mattress with a pillow of the same horsehair, which was very hard, and the blankets were of very tough material; there was nothing cosy or soft about them, but at least they were warm – there was no central heating then. The dormitory walls were so low that every sound could be heard coming from the wards, and my head ached, so that I could not sleep. I did not feel like going back on duty in the morning, but I had no choice, because though the vaccinations did not seem to affect the patients, the nurses were badly affected, and many of those who slept out did not come back. We were very short staffed for weeks.

The mental hospital was a sad place to work in, for me at least, because I would put myself in the patient's place and say, "There, but for the grace of God, go I." There was one patient, Anne Cummings, who was considered to be a violent patient, and I had been advised by the nurses to leave her to herself as she was better on her own. Some time previously, as I came in from the airing court where I had been on duty, the charge nurse had called out to me, "Come in here, nurse, and give me a hand quickly." I hurried to her aid, but pulled up sharply when I realised why I was needed. Anne Cummings was being forcibly held against a wall while a charge nurse was punching her, and my pity for the poor young woman made me forget that my duty was to obey the charge nurse. I called out to her, "I will help you in any way except that, you are ill-treating that girl and I will not be party to it."

"I'll report you for this," she said, "and it will be the sack for you."

"It can't be part of hospital treatment for two of you to hold that girl while another one ill-treats her," I told her. "I will not help you to do it, and if it means the sack, well, so be it." She did not report me though – I think if she had, she herself would have been sacked, because ill-treatment was not allowed, and her own behaviour to patients would have come out if she had reported me.

I came down on duty the day after being vaccinated, but

115

because the other nurses were busy about their own duties, no-one noticed how badly swollen my arm had become. However there *was* one who noticed – Anne Cummings. She came to see me and said, "You are not well, nurse, are you? Let me see your arm." My uniform sleeve was a leg o' mutton shape, wide at the top and tapering down to fit very tightly at the wrist, and Anne asked me for a pair of scissors so that she could open the sleeve. (Each nurse carried a pair of scissors, but patients were not allowed to have them.) Then she said to me, "You are to take it easy with this arm, and I'll do your work, don't you worry about it." I handed her my scissors, and she cut the seam open and folded the sleeve back, then put the scissors back on the little chain which I wore under my belt. From that moment on Anne became my shadow and proved to be an angel of mercy; without her I could never have stayed on duty. There were so many patients to be innoculated that it took several weeks before the job was completed, and we were very short staffed because some nurses were off duty for weeks.

Now it was Christmas, and there were just two nurses on duty in a ward with fifty patients; I was one of the nurses. Mrs. Richards, the charge nurse, was seldom in Ward Six, and she told me that if I needed help I was to blow my whistle, but until then I would have to struggle along as best I could. On Christmas Day itself the nurse who was helping me on Ward Six was taken to help out on Ward Five, leaving me alone with fifty patients, except at meal-times. Patients' meals were supplied from the main building and brought through the airing courts. Dinner was the only meal where knives and forks were supplied, and it was then that Anne Cummings was her true worth. She laid the tables and guarded the knives and forks, and woe betide anyone who tried to take anything from Anne! It would not have surprised me if someone had told me that Anne had been a nurse on those wards, for she knew everything that had to be done, and where everything had to go.

I could trust Anne with anything; she would put out the knives and forks in front of the patients, though it was the nurse's job to see that every piece of cutlery was counted and returned after the meal. The carving knife and fork had to be hidden under my apron until the meal came, but as it had to be set out on two large tables, it would have been impossible for me to keep my eye on every piece of cutlery. If Anne had used the cunning that the

116

insane are supposed to have, she could easily have overpowered me and taken my key and whistle from me; I would have been powerless in her hands. But Anne had told me that I could trust her, and so I did; and in trusting her, I felt safe with her. If a knife, or any other piece of cutlery, was missing, Anne would walk round each table counting while we were waiting for the meal to be brought; then the whistle would have to be blown. Help would come at once and each nurse would hunt for the missing piece until it was found, because the meal would not be brought in until every piece of cutlery had been accounted for. Pieces were taken from time to time, but none went during the period that I worked there.

Wards Five and Six were away from the main building of the hospital, but as so many nurses, from all parts of the hospital, were off sick, there was a re-allocation of staff, and Mrs. Richards transferred me 'on Loan' to the main building. My key would fit any of the locks, and so I was able to enter without ringing the doorbell. I only opened the door wide enough to squeeze my body into the passage, but as I went in a woman was coming towards me, who said, "Oh, thank you, nurse, for opening the door for me." She was fully dressed, complete with hat and coat, and so I had no reason to suspect that she was anything but a nurse going off duty. However, though I had only been at the hospital for a matter of months and this was the first time I had gone into the main building, some instinct warned me of danger, I thought that if this woman had been a nurse, she would have had her own key, and wouldn't have been waiting inside the door to be let out; if she had been a visitor to the hospital, she would have used the main entrance.

In a flash I realised that this was not a time for standing about, wondering who she might be, or she would be out of the door like a shot. I wedged her against the door, and hoped that someone would come quickly, for she was bigger than me, and, being a patient, had the strength of three. I couldn't get at my key because I was holding her tightly, and if I had released my hand to get at my whistle, she would have gone through the door. We were in the back corridor of the hospital, standing in a passage way with doors on either side, all locked, and it was highly likely that we would be standing there for hours waiting for someone to come out of one of the wards into the passage way, so I did what I always did in times of trouble, and prayed for help. By now the patient had realised that I knew she was escaping, and she began to offer me money to let her go. "I'm a rich woman," she said. "Help me to escape and I'll reward you richly." And she kept raising her offer until it was thousands of pounds if I would let her escape.

After what seemed like hours, a nurse appeared in the passage way, and between us we managed to get the patient safely back to the ward. It was a very strange experience for me, and one I was very glad to know was over. One of the nurses on the ward was very lame, and she told me that as all her patients were bedridden, she had been darning her stockings during a quiet moment (although it was an offence for a nurse to bring any kind of needle onto the wards). Then she had been called to assist another nurse who had to go into a padded cell – nurses were not allowed to go into padded cells or strong rooms by themselves they had to be accompanied by another nurse. She quickly concealed her darning neeedle on her person, then, as they entered the padded cell, the patient jumped at her, tearing the darning needle from its hiding place and ramming it deep into the nurse's legs. Although they operated on her immediately, she had been told that she would always walk with a limp.

I was back in Ward Six for Christmas Day. It was a very large room, well furnished and sleeping fifty patients, with a large, heavily guarded fire at both ends of the ward, and an abundance of beautiful padded reclining chairs. In the centre there was a pillar which was decorated to resemble a horse chestnut tree, and encircling the 'tree' was a wide, padded divan; no cost was spared to ensure the comfort of the inmates.

On this particular Christmas Day, because so many nurses were still off duty, I was alone on the ward except at mealtimes and in the morning when I would have help. There was a dance for the inmates over in the main building, but those in Ward Six who were fit to go didn't want to do so, and in the evening Mrs. Richards came to tell me that she could not send any help, but I would have to manage alone, and use my whistle in case of trouble. So now I had to find a way of keeping fifty patients happy. A bowl of oranges and apples had been brought in to me so that I could give one orange and one apple to each patient as a Christmas treat, and I asked Anne Cummings to make up the fires for me. Then I put as many chairs as I could round the fires and told the patients that we were going to sit around them, all

118

nice and warm, and have a cosy evening. I kept talking to them all the time, trying to hold their interest; they had to be spoken to as though they were children and many could not even think for themselves, so they had to be directed into a chair.

I told them that we would put the chairs close to each other, to make room for everyone to sit down together – which was not easy when there were fifty unstable people to settle – and then I told them that when they were all settled down we would play a game. They all entered into the spirit of the thing, and helped each other to get into the chairs where normally they would have been pushing each other out of the way. The patients in my ward were aged from about thirty to sixty five, and those who were not likely to fall asleep, I settled on the divan around the tree. Then I gave individual attention to each patient in turn, so that each one would feel important. This would lessen any possibility of jealousy or temper arising. All this I achieved with the assistance of Anne Cummings, and I knew that I was completely safe and protected with her, although she too was a patient and considered to be very dangerous.

With Anne's help a small card table was arranged in a position where it could be seen by all the patients, and I took some babies' building blocks from a cupboard. Then I put a few chairs around the table, and the ward was so silent you could hear a pin drop. I said to them, "Do you know what we are going to do now? We are going to build these blocks one on top of the other until they are right up high." When that was done, I stood in front of them and clapped my hands, and said, "Now we are going to huff and puff till we blow the house down." Then those sitting round the table actually blew the blocks down, but the whole ward, those sitting round the fires and those sitting on the divan, all blew too, and when the blocks fell they thought they had blown them down. They had great fun, and kept clapping and shouting, "Do it again, nurse! Do it again, nurse!" so that I had to keep building the blocks up for them to blow down, over and over again.

After a while Anne Cummings, who was standing behind my chair, whispered to me, "Get up quick, nurse, the committtee are coming," and in through the door walked the Matron, eight committee men and a charge nurse. (It was an offense, punishable with dismissal, for a nurse to be caught sitting in the ward while on duty). I stood up quickly by the side of my chair, feeling rather guilty, but one of the committee men called out, "Carry on, nurse, you are doing fine," and Matron added her commendations. They came up to see what we were doing at the table, and once again I built the blocks up and all the patients huffed and puffed and blew them down for the visitors. Matron told them that they were very good, and she and Mrs. Richards looked very pleased; one of the committee asked how many patients were in my charge, and Mrs. Richards said there were fifty in that ward. They turned to go, then, turning in the doorway, Matron said, "Well done, nurse, this is the most peaceful and happy ward we've seen today."

After Christmas the nurses started to return to work, and we were soon back to normal. I went on duty one morning, helped to get the patients out of bed, got the beds made, and took the patients down to the day ward, but then the strain of the last few weeks and the after-effects of my innoculation finally took their toll, and I collapsed on the ward. I was put to bed and told that I must stay there until I was given permission to get up, because I was suffering from strain and exhaustion. The staff were all preparing for the New Year's Ball, which had been postponed because most of the staff had been off sick; it was to be a costume ball. The charge nurse ordered a fire to be lit in the nurses' rest room, and I was to convalesce there; the nurses brought me some green and yellow tissue paper when they went off duty, and I made several costumes for the girls, who were to be dressed as flowers. The costumes I made were roses, and I went to the dance myself as a daffodil.

I went back on duty for a few weeks, but the doctor was not satisfied with my health, so they put me back to bed and sent for my mother. When she arrived at the hospital they told her that six doctors had failed to cure me, and they felt it would be better if I was taken home and put in a general hospital.

"She has been vaccinated with impure lymph," they said, "and the poison has gone all through her system. We strongly advise you to remove her from this hospital to somewhere where she can receive the right care and treatment. It is our opinion that she will never be strong enough to nurse again, and we will arrange a disablement grant for her."

My mother said she would speak to her doctor about it, and see what he advised. I was now completely confined to bed, and at night the noise from the wards was making my head pains very hard to bear. Then, early one morning, on what would have been my day off, I set off with my suitcase, to walk home. As I was walking along the road, a bus came along; I had intended to hail it, but by now I was staggering along the road like a drunken man. I was afraid to stop the bus, because the pain in my head was so bad that I felt I couldn't stand the jostling, and so I kept on walking. The driver slowed down and shouted at me, "What the h... do you think you are trying to do, commit suicide?" Eventually I reached home, and my mother and stepfather were very surprised to see me, but agreed that I had done the best thing in coming home.

The hospital authorities sent a report on my condition to Dr. Anderson, but he did not advise me to go into hospital, since he felt he could get me back on my feet himself. Next a letter came to our house from the hospital, telling me that as Dr. Anderson had innoculated me with impure lymph and had, as a result, so reduced my health as to prevent me from taking up nursing again, they recommended that I engage a good solicitor and sue my doctor. They added that I was not entitled to a disablement grant, because I was one stamp short of a twelve-month. I read the letter and put it on the fire, without letting my mother or stepfather read it. I didn't want to cause any trouble for Dr. Anderson, who had attended us so faithfully, and who was a good doctor, and since I had lost the disablement grant, I saw no point in dragging our doctor through the courts for monetary gain. I never mentioned it to Dr. Anderson, but I know that the hospital had informed him of their advice to me.

SIXTEEN

Dr. Anderson visited me every day and advised me that the best thing for me to do, when I felt well enough, was not to nurse my weakness, but to find a light job somewhere where I would have a change of scenery and faces. I studied the advertisements for job vacancies, and when I saw an advert for the post of head chambermaid in a large hotel in Kensington, in London, I thought it would be the next best thing to nursing. I felt fit and well enough now to apply for the position. The advertisement stated that any applicant must be of good appearance, and that a photograph must be enclosed with the written application, so I applied, enclosing my photograph and a reference from Maesteg Hospital. (My stepfather had been hinting that it was time I earned some money, so I waited anxiously for a reply to my letter.)

In fact I received a reply almost immediately, saying that I was to come on Monday, arriving at Paddington at four o'clock; I would be met there and escorted to the hotel. I was asked to wear a white buttonhole. When I arrived at Paddington, a young lady put a hand on my shoulder and asked, "Are you Miss Rachael Bowen?" Then she raised her hand, and a man came, and put my little tin box in a waiting cab. As I got into the cab myself, I noticed that the windows were darkened, but though I felt that that was strange, I made no comment. After I was helped into the cab I can remember nothing more until I woke up in a strange, grubby, cell-like bedroom in the basement of a little boarding house.

I looked all around the room and saw that the walls and floor were of bare stone; the bed was a narrow camp bed and the only window in the room was heavily barred and thick with dirt on the inside. The room was about five feet wide and fourteen feet long, but there was no other furniture except for another camp bed at the lower end of the room on which a young girl, of about my own age, but dirty and untidy, was sitting. I said to her,

"Who are you?"

"The bleeding cops picked me up off the streets and brought me here," she answered, in a strong Cockney accent.

"How did I get here?" I asked her, "I remember getting into a taxi and that's all."

"You'll know soon enough," she answered with a shrug.

Just then a woman came into the room and said she was Madam Lehman. She was a big, strong, masculine woman, with huge arms, a double chin and a very heavy bosom. She said to me, "Oh, you are awake, Rachael."

"Yes," I said, "but how did I get here and why am I locked in this cell? Is this a prison, what have I done? Why have you locked me up? I came to London to be a chambermaid in a large hotel."

"It's all right, you are in my hotel. I am Madam Lehman, and this is Rose," said the woman, indicating the girl on the bed. "She was picked up by the police and brought here under my care. Take your nice dress off, Rachael, and I'll put it with your other clothes. Here, put this on," she added, handing me a uniform dress which she must have taken out of my trunk.

"Madam," I said, "what have you done with all my clothes?"

"It's all right," she said. "I've locked them safely away."

"Where is my bedroom, Madam?" I asked. "If my clothes are in there, tell me where it is, so that I can leave this horrible cell."

"This is your bedroom," Madam said, "and that single bed is yours, and the camp bed belongs to Rose. I've got a nice treat for you tomorrow. I'm going to take you to Lyons Corner House tea shop for tea, at four o'clock. I always give my head chambermaid a treat on her first day." Then she left the room.

"She's a bleedin' German," said Rose. "*And* her bleedin' son."

"Who is the young lady who picked me up at the station?" I asked Rose. "She said her name was Eileen."

"She finks she's madam's daughter," Rose told me. "But she ain't no bleedin' German. And don't ask no more questions, I ain't yer to tell yer anyfink."

That night I knelt down, terrified, at my bedside to say my prayers. "Dear God," I prayed, "I came to this place with such faith and such hope, but I feel as if I have fallen into a den of thieves. Dear Lord, watch over me and protect me from the evil I feel is around me, help me to get away from this place."

123

Rose, who had been watching me, said, "You've got a bleedin' hope of getting out of this place!"

The next morning Rose showed me what my duties were. First we carried large enamel jugs of hot water to the bedrooms. Only two were occupied by guests, one by a Major Marriott and one by Mr. and Mrs. Cummings, all of whom were long-term residents. There were no bathrooms in the hotel and the guests washed themselves in their bedrooms, each of which had a marble-topped washstand on which stood a large china jug-and-basin set. They were supplied with fresh towels once a week. Then we went down to breakfast in the basement kitchen. The cook came in daily, and I discovered that I was not simply the chambermaid, but the *only* maid, apart from the cook. The kitchen was dark, with no window or outside door, and the only light came from a low-powered bulb which hung naked from the ceiling, and showed up the stone walls and flagged floor. There was a big open grate over which the cook, a slatternly, middle aged woman, was bending, frying some kippers. The only furniture in the kitchen was a scrubbed table, with two or three kitchen chairs. The room had been divided in half, one part being the kitchen, and the other being sealed off with steel walls which covered the back door and kitchen window so that all the light went into that half and none came into the kitchen.

Our breakfast consisted of one bread roll and a quarter of a kipper per person. We were just about to sit down to this when a young man came and sat down at the table with us. He was about thirty years old, clean and well-spoken, with an educated accent. He usually only appeared at meals in the kitchen, for he did not sleep in, and I never saw him do any work, though he said he was a porter; but as there were no guests coming or leaving, I didn't see what work there *was* for him to do at that boarding house.

There were only two entrances to the place, through the main door, which I never saw open in all the times I passed it, and which was always locked, and through a door under the front steps, in the area. That door too was always kept locked and bolted, and the key was always kept in Madam's possession. The back door and window that should have been part of the kitchen were behind the steel walls, so there was no way anyone could escape from that place.

Next morning, at precisely two thirty a.m., I was awakened

from my sleep by a tremendous noise, coming from above my head. It was the sound of four pairs of heavy feet coming up the front steps of the house, and it sounded as if the owners of the feet were carrying a heavy weight or burden. There were a lot of gutteral voices speaking in German, and more German voices coming from behind the locked door. Then there was the sound of heavy bolts being drawn and a key turned in a stiff lock, then the door opening, after which there was a clanging of chains and the sound of thuds, as if several heavy objects were being dropped on to the floor. Finally there was a lot of heavy chatter in German, then the front door was shut, locked and bolted again. I felt my hair standing on end, and the top of my head felt frozen. I asked Rose if she knew what it could be, but she said, "Go to sleep, and if you know what's good for you, you'll not let on you heard anyfink. You'll get used to it, you'll hear this every morning at this time."

Some time the following morning Madam said to me, "You sleep a funny way, Rachael."

"Do I, Madam," I asked.

"Yes," said Madam. "You lay on your tummy with your arms above your head, and your head resting on your arms. Aren't you afraid you'll smother?"

"How do you know this Madam?" I asked. "Did you come into my bedroom last night while I was asleep? Did you want something, Madam?"

"Oh, only to ask how you were, and to see if you were all right," said Madam. I decided that as the room was only a few inches wider than my bed, in future I would pull my bed across the doorway so that she couldn't come into my room while I slept.

At half past three Madam told me to get ready, as she was taking me to the tea house, and we would take Rose with us for company. She brought me the clothes she wanted me to wear, the suit I had worn to come up to London, together with the same hat and shoes, and then we set off for the tea shop, with Madam on one side of me and Rose on the other. When we arrived, Madam smiled and nodded to several men sitting at one of the tables. She also pointed me out to them, and put me to stand in a position where they could inspect me – though I did not realise that at the time; it was only later that it became obvious to me that I had been put on show for the benefit of the

125

men. Then she got me to sit on the other side of the table, where I would have my back to the men. Rose kept me occupied in conversation while Madam signalled to the men behind my back, (like a tick-tack man at the races!)

That night, in our bedroom, I said to Rose, "Madam seemed to be very popular in that tea shop today. She was waving and smiling at so many people."

"There's more to that than meets the eye," said Rose. "She was pointing you out to those men."

"Why should she do that?" I asked. "She's not the only person in London who's got a servant."

"She's put another advert in the paper," said Rose, "advertising her hotel, with a Welsh chambermaid."

"That's silly," I replied. "What's the difference between having a Welsh chambermaid and an English one?"

Next morning the young man was again sitting at the breakfast table, but he did not arrive at the servants' entrance, and I wondered how he had got in, and what he was really doing there. That evening I was feeling very hungry; the food was very inadequate for the amount of work I had to do. I asked Rose, "Is there a shop around here where I could buy a packet of biscuits? I have a few coppers left, do you think you could let me out so that I can buy some?"

"You've got a bleedin' hope if you think they'll let you out. But I'll get some for you, if you're hungry," said Rose. She took my money and went upstairs, and told Madam she wanted to go to the shop, so Madam came down and opened the door for her.

"Could I go with Rose, Madam?" I asked. "I'd love to have a breath of fresh air." She did not answer me, but just slammed the door and waited for Rose to come back. She pulled Rose inside quickly when she returned, so I had no chance to slip out. I went down the basement stairs, through the kitchen and the passage to my 'cell' as I called my room, and there, standing in the passage way as if waiting for me, stood the young 'porter'. "My name is Jack Long," he said to me. "What is a lovely girl like you doing in a place like this?"

"I thought I was going to be head chambermaid in a large hotel," I told him. "But this is what I found, a grotty, run-down boarding house. There are no other maids here, and as for being head chambermaid, I'm just the maid of all work. But I could ask you the same question; what are you doing here?"

"I quarrelled with my father," he said, "and I left home in anger. My father is John Long, the famous film producer. – You should be on the screen, you know. I would like my father to see you. Have you ever had any wish to be a film actress?"

"Yes," I told him. "When I was eighteen, a new company opened up in Cardiff. It was called 'The Star Cinema Company' and they held auditions for boys and girls; they even laid on a special train for the youngsters. It was on my half-day off from the hospital where I was working, and I joined them on the train. But though I was successful in the audition, I knew that I could never afford the two guineas weekly that was required for my two sessions a week training, let alone the train fare; I only earned two pounds per calendar month as a nurse, so it was out of the question."

Jack Long listened to what I had to say, then he commented, "That settles it, you've got to come and meet my father."

"Sorry," I said, "I've got work to do," and I walked away from him.

(I had reason to remember that audition in Cardiff in later years. In the same compartment as myself on the train were a man and woman and little boy of about eight or ten years old. The boy was dressed in a dark brown velvet knicker-bocker suit with a round straw hat with a turned-up brim, and his parents seemed to be very proud of their little son whom they called Stanley; their entire conversation centred around Stanley's future. On the way back from Cardiff that evening I once again found myself in the same compartment as these people. Little Stanley sat between his father and mother as he had on the earlier journey, and his father kept patting the boy's hand, while every now and then the mother would hug the child; I could see they were just bursting to tell me their good news. I was sitting facing Stanley, and I leaned forward and said to him, "Were you successful in the auditions, Stanley?" He seemed a sweet little boy, much loved, but unspoilt, and his father and mother said simultaneously, "Of all the boys that went down on the train with us, only our Stanley passed the test. And some day, you see, our little boy will be Stanley Baker, famous film star! No-one else, except for one girl, passed the test."

I surprised them by telling them that I was that girl, but when I showed them the literature I was taking home, and they saw that it was the same as Stanley's, they were convinced.)

Jack Long kept continually waylaying me in his 'pantry' and pestering me to go with him to meet his father. Then one day he stopped me and said, "My father is getting impatient to meet you, I've told him so much about you; so will you come with me to meet him now?" I told him that he must stop bothering me, because I had no talent for acting, I never had, and I never would; and if his father was so anxious to make me a film star, and could do such wonders, why had he not made his son a star too, if he was indeed 'the famous John Long, film producer'?

"My father told me I was a ne'er-do-well," said Jack Long, "and that's why I've come here, to show him that I can earn my living."

I looked at him them, and said, "If you want to do something for me, then help me to get away from this place. You are free to come and go as you please, but I am a prisoner here, because all the doors and windows are locked and barred. I have cousins here in London who are professional men, if only I could get out and find them. But even my box, with all my clothes, is locked away, and when I want a change of clothes, Madam brings them to me without even giving me a choice of what I want to wear."

On Sunday it was the cook's day off and a real old hag of a woman took her place; she only needed a broomstick and witch's hat to be a perfect witch. I kept out of her way as much as possible, because I didn't like her at all. She told me she was over eighty; she only came to cook the Sunday dinner. After dinner she came to tell me she was ready to leave, and she held out her hand and asked me. "What are you going to give me before I go?"

"I've got nothing to give you," I told her. "I have no money."

"You hide from me, don't you?" she said. "All the other girls give me money, and I haven't got time to come looking for you; my rat is waiting for me."

"Did you say 'rat'?" I asked.

"Yes. He is my pet rat, and he's all the company I've got in my garret."

"Well, you get paid for coming here on a Sunday," I told her. "Madam gives me nothing, I haven't been paid since I've been here."

Mr. and Mrs. Cummings were the same. They used to search behind doors and in cupboards, convinced that I was hiding from them (which in truth I was), and when they found me, they would say, "Oh, there you are, Rachael. We've been looking everywhere for you, were you hiding from us?"

"No," I would answer. "I was just doing my shoe-lace up, did you want me for anything?"

"No," they answered, "We just wanted to say hello, and we have decided we will give you half a crown a week. We will leave it for you in our bedroom." But I never found any money there. In fact I seldom went into their room, because Rose had warned me that I should always make sure that there was no-one there before I entered; so I would first knock on their door, and if anyone called out "Come in", I would apologise and say, "I'll come back later." One day I knocked, and when there was no reply, thought it safe to enter. I went in, and found Mr. Cummings sitting on his bed. I turned around, saying, "Sorry, I'll come back later," and made to leave the room. Mr. Cummings jumped off the bed and caught hold of me; we scuffled, but I managed to get away. When I was safely outside the door, I called back to him, "I will never come into your bedroom again."

That night I told Rose what had happened. Rose often questioned me, but she never gave me any information in return. She would ask whether I had any friends or family in London, and it was as if they were trying to find out whether or not anyone would miss me. I told Rose that no-one knew where I was in London, as I had answered the advertisement to a P.O. Box number. Meanwhile I could not easily write to anyone; I had to ask for paper and pen if I wanted to write home, and I had to give my letter to Rose, or Madam, or Jack Long to post for me, because I could not go out. Since I never received any replies to my letters, I suspected that they were not being posted. I was also very suspicious that someone was trying to get into my bedroom at night because Madam would often say to me, "What is behind your door? It can't be opened at night." I would repeat, as often before, "Do you want to come into my room for anything, Madam?" Also the noises I had heard before continued every morning at two thirty – the footsteps, the voices, the chains; it happened at exactly the same hour every day.

After much persuasion Madam finally allowed me to go out one Sunday afternoon. She gave me the clothes that she had chosen from my box for me to wear, and then I asked her for my handbag and some of the money that she owed me from my wages. She gave me a few coppers and said, "This is enough for you to go to Hyde Park Corner, as well as your return fare back here." I got on the bus and told the conductor how much money I had, asking if he had any suggestions as to where I could go on that amount of money. He gave me a return ticket to Marble Arch, and gave me the number of the bus and the time that is would be leaving, so that I would be sure to catch it and be back at the boarding house by the time appointed.

At Hyde Park Corner I found myself standing in a crowd, listening to a speaker who was standing on a box. There was a young girl standing by me who was also on her own, and we got into conversation; she told me that her mother was French and her father English. As we walked around, I saw Mr. and Mrs. Cummings watching me from the crowd, and I told the girl about them. "Let us go somewhere where they can't see us," she said, "and we'll see if they are following you."

Several times we tried to get away from them, but they always appeared again, so it was obvious that they were following me. The girl asked me, "Why don't you run away from that place now you're out of it?" I told her that I had no money, and in any case no trains travelled to the Valleys on a Sunday. I would have to wait for a better opportunity. "How far do you think I could go with these people watching me?" I asked. "If I don't see you, will you try to remember this address?" (We had no pen or paper to write it down.)

I returned to the hotel, but the Cummings did not travel on the bus with me. That night Rose told me that the Cummings never went out on a Sunday – but this day they had, so they were certainly following me. Madam said I was a good girl to come back in time, and if I continued to be good she would let me go out again in a fortnight. (Rose went out on alternate Sundays.) So a fortnight later Madam gave me the same amount of money, and told me to go to Marble Arch, as I would enjoy myself there; but I went to Hyde Park instead. There I found a secluded spot, and sat down on a bench, reading a newspaper that someone had left behind. After a little while I got up and walked across the grass to some beautiful floral bushes, where I lay down on my tummy with my hands under my head and read my newspaper. I had been reading for some time, feeling very safe, and happy to be free, when I looked up and saw two faces watching me over the bushes. It was Mr. and Mrs. Cummings.

I pretended that I had not seen them, then, after a little while, I got up and walked slowly away to where there were more people. Eventually I went back at nine o'clock, to see if my suspicions were correct. I asked Rose if the Cummingses were in their room, and she said, "No, they went out just after you left." They came back just after I got in.

Later I said to Rose, "Madam and Eileen quarrel a lot, don't they? Who are they quarrelling over?"

"What do you mean?" asked Rose, "who are they quarelling over?"

"I don't always hear what Madam says," I explained, "but often I hear Miss Eileen screaming at her mother, "Don't you dare touch her, I'm warning you, don't you dare lay a hand on her.""

Rose only giggled, and said, "Miss Eileen likes you. Don't say I told you, but don't let the Cummingses get near to you or that will be the last time you'll be seen by anyone." I knew then that all my suspicions had been correct.

Jack Long started to waylay me again, with talk of finding work in France. He told me that he was fed up with working in this place, because the money was no good and the food was bad.

"I think I'll go back to France," he said. "If you'll come with me, that is." He had been trying to make me believe that he was the only trustworthy friend I had in that place, and by now he had gained my confidence. I began to tell him of my fears and suspicions, and I even felt very tempted when he said, "We'll get work in a hotel in France. I'll be a waiter and you can be a chambermaid. We'll have more money then."

Though his persistence had almost convinced me, something inside me still kept warning me to beware, and that night I put all my doubts and fears into my prayers; my faith told me to have nothing to do with Jack Long and his talk of freedom. He was extremely good-looking, well-mannered and well educated and he always appeared immaculate, but he never seemed to be working. This didn't ring true; he didn't even live at the hotel. So I told him I couldn't go to a strange country with a strange man. At that he said, "I can't leave you here, I've got a suspicion that there's white slave traffic going on."

One day he told me, "I'm going tonight, Rachael. I've packed up my bags. This is your last chance – will you come with me?"

He showed me two heavy suitcases and said, "See, they are packed, ready to go." But I wondered how he had got these two packed suitcases with him when he didn't even live in the hotel.

"I'll get your wages," he said, "and your box of clothes, and get you out of here tonight. Just say you'll come. I can't go and leave you."

"Well," I said, "If you can get me out of here, let me go to the police station and see what they can do for me."

"No," he said, "you stay here, I'll go to the police station. I won't be a minute, it's just around the corner," and he disappeared, leaving me standing in the hall. Of course I guessed that he had not been to the police station at all when he got back, he had been so quick; he could not have got there and had the long conversation that he claimed, and then got back to the hotel in the short space of time he was gone.

"It's all right, Rachael," he said to me when he got back. "There's nothing to worry about, the police know what's going on here. They've had the place under observation for a long time, and I told them that you were being followed by two people from the hotel when you go out, and that I fear you might be taken away for the white slave traffic. Don't worry if you see those people following you again, because the police will be following them and you'll be quite safe. But make up your mind now, are you going to come with me and get away from all this?"

"No," I told him. A tall Frenchman had come in with Jack Long, and now Jack turned to him as he said to me, "Well, if I can't persuade you to come with me, do me a favour before I go. Take the gentleman up to his room for me."

So I took the Frenchman's weekend case and led him up the two flights of carpeted stairs and across the two landings. To my surprise the number on his key was that of the bare attic at the top of the house, so we next went up a narrow flight of wooden stairs and along a bare, dimly lit corridor until we came to a door in a recess. I unlocked the door and stood back to allow him to enter, but he said, "You go inside first." At that I took another step backwards, away from him, but he threw his arms around me, and pulled me to him, as if he wanted to kiss me. I surprised him by pulling my arm free and slapping him across the face with all the force I could muster, which made him put his hand up to rub his sore face. At that I broke away from him, and though he tried to grab me, I was too quick and ran across the corridor and

132

down the stairs, taking them two or three at a time; then across the landing and down one flight of carpeted stairs, until I came to a door, slightly ajar. The Frenchman was hot in pursuit, but I thought I could evade him by hiding in an unoccupied room.

Across the room, to my surprise, was a large French window, draped with light curtains, which opened onto a small verandah. (It was the first and only unbarred window I had seen in that house.) I ran towards the window, intending to climb over the railing and lower myself down into the street, but in my haste to escape I had failed to notice two frail old ladies sitting one each side of the fireplace. They forgot their frailty when they grabbed me, just as I was putting my foot out on to the balcony, and pulled me back into the room.

"You can't go out there," they said. "You are not allowed to be seen."

They were assisted by two men who had been sitting on the other side of the room and whom I had also failed to notice in my haste. I was pushed outside again, into the corridor, at the mercy of the Frenchman, but I ran swiftly along the corridor and down the other flight of stairs, until I reached Madam's door and banged furiously. I was very frightened and very upset.

Madam opened the door just a little way, and behind her I could see her daughter Eileen. "Madam," I told them, "I want to get away from this place, open the door and let me out. I don't want to stay here."

"What is the matter, Rachael?" asked madam.

"Leave this to me," said Eileen. "I'll handle it."

"It's that Frenchman, Miss Eileen," I said. "I showed him up to the attic, and he had the audacity to try to kiss me! How dare he think that because I am a servant girl I would be flattered by his attentions. If this is the sort of guest you have in this hotel, then I'm not staying. I demand that you let me out."

Miss Eileen came out into the deserted hall. The front door was locked and barred as usual, although it was early evening. "I'm very sorry about this, Rachael," she told me. "I shall speak to the monsieur, and see that this doesn't happen to you again. You know I work very hard here, Rachael, don't you? and if you leave, all the work you do will be added to mine. So please Rachael, for my sake, don't leave."

The next morning I saw the Frenchman leaving Madam's bedroom in the early hours; they were both laughing. I did not see him again after that.

Meanwhile, I still heard the strange noises at the hotel at night; certainly all the activity happened in the early hours. All through the day I would not see a living soul come or go, and the atmosphere in that place seemed to create fear, even at meal times in the kitchen. The cook did not speak to us or sit with us at meals, but was continually bent over her stove, and there was no conversation at any time. After the episode with the Frenchman, Madam said to me, "I have been in your bedroom Rachael, and put a packet of sweets under your pillow. I shall put a packet there every week, as a little present, because you are such a good chambermaid."

"Thank you, Madam," I said, and I hurried to see my treat (I hadn't tasted a sweet since I left Wales). Under my pillow I found a paper cone containing a pennyworth of the cheapest sweets, the boiled variety, costing about tuppence a quarter.

One day Madam summoned me to her room and told me that she had received a very nasty letter from my mother. "Your mother threatens that unless I send you home immediately, with all your clothes and all the money owing to you, your cousin Jack Jones, who is a barrister and lives in London, will come here, and she will sue me for keeping you locked in this hotel against your will. I have called a taxi for you, and here are your clothes, so you'd better get ready right away. And here's your money for the four months you've been here. I was only keeping it for you, you know – after all, you had nothing to spend it on, did you? I have sent a wire to your mother, telling her what time you are leaving London today, so that someone can meet you."

I dressed hurriedly, then Madam unlocked the front door, and even walked up to the taxi with me. She put me in the taxi and said, "Are you comfortable Rachael? I have paid your taxi fare and tipped the driver, so you've got nothing to do except get on your train and go home."

She said to the taxi-driver, "Take her to Paddington, and see that she is put safely on the train for Wales."

When I arrived at Blackmill Station, my brother Ben and my adopted brother, James Price Bird, were there to meet me. They were very excited to see me, and carried my little tin box for me. Then, when we arrived at home, my mother said, "Thank God that letter did the trick. You can thank Dr. Anderson for his work in getting you home when we heard how

134

you were being treated. He'll be coming to see you tomorrow."

When Dr. Anderson did come to see me the next day, he told me I was a very lucky girl to get away from that place; but now I must put it completely out of my mind.

"I think it would be a good idea," he told my mother, "if Rachael had a nice long holiday somewhere, where she can relax and forget these last few months and the strain she's been under."

SEVENTEEN

One day my brother Garfield brought home three young friends of his who had just moved to Pant-ye-Awel from Birmingham. They were brothers, and Fred, the eldest, was a Methodist minister; their sister had married a Welshman and lived in Ogmore Vale. They came up every day, and Fred and I became very friendly.

I had come home so quickly (seeing nothing of London) that I had not been able to buy any presents for Violet and Nancy. Violet and I had always wanted a bicycle, but we had never been able to afford one, so we went into Ogmore Vale where I bought a bike, for both Violet and myself to use; Fred said he would teach us both how to ride it. One or two lessons were enough for Violet, then she could ride it with ease, but I was a slow learner. As long as I thought Fred was holding the back of the bike, I rode quite well, but the minute he let go of it, I would fall off. One day, full of confidence, I decided to master this bicycle myself, so that I could go home and boast that I could ride a bike, so I took it out and managed, with the aid of an embankment and a hedgerow, to mount the machine. I started off at the top of the hill, and the only way I could keep my balance was by pedalling as fast as I could.

I flew down the hill – fortunately there was no traffic on the road at the time – and kept up my speed, up hill and down dale, flying like the wind. It was exhilarating and very thrilling, the first time I had ever gone flying through the air! The trouble was that I didn't know how to stop and at last I encountered my first sign of traffic, a small car coming towards me from Blackmill. I didn't know what to do, and I could not stop the bike, so I directed myself into the hedge, where I fell off. Then I turned the bike around and walked it home.

The next day my mother had a visitor, Dr. Anderson. He came down to tell her that he had seen me on a bike, and I was never to ride it again; I did not have enough sight to ride a bicycle, and the shock of any accident, however slight, could cause me to black out completely and become totally blind. So the bike was handed over to Violet to be her very own property.

Several times I went to the cinema with Fred, and several times we went to chapel together; then after chapel we would go to his sister Edith's, for supper. But we were just good friends, nothing more. In the meantime my brother Ben had brought his sweetheart home from Dorset, and said they wanted to be married from my mother's house. They wanted the ceremony to be held at the old parish church in Llangeinor, where Emily and Jim were married. Maud Thick was a very nice girl, quiet but not shy, and we all took to her very quickly. They wanted to stay with my mother while they decided whether to live in Dorset or Wales, so my mother gave them the parlour to live in, so that they could start out on their own.

It was a very pretty wedding, and I was the chief bridesmaid. Maud had no idea how to cook, and she asked my mother to teach her how to do this and how to look after a home. She had earned her living in Dorset by lace-making and gloving, and had had no time to learn how to be a housewife. One day Ben came out to the kitchen, very excited and proud of his wife, bearing a plate of Welsh cakes. "I want everyone of you to try these," he said. "My wife made them." It was fortunate for us that we had strong teeth; we had to eat them while Ben watched us, and we took a chance on suffering from indigestion rather than wipe that proud look from his face by telling him they were awful. Garfield whispered to me, "I bet our Maud put cement in these cakes instead of flour!"

Then Maud told my mother that *her* mother would be pleased to have me stay up in Dorset with her until I was well again; so I went there, and was met at the station by Maud's two sisters, Ella and Alice. Gillingham was a quiet, sleepy village, with just a little village shop, and we didn't meet a living soul as we passed through the village. It seemed quite deserted, with not even a dog or cat in sight. I remarked on the peace and tranquility of the place, and Alice and Ella told me that the men were all at work, some as farm labourers, others as quarry workers; they took their lunch with them, and were away all day. Meanwhile all the female members of each family would be at home at that time of the day, either gloving or lace-making. The men's wages were very, very low – the maximum wage for quarrymen or farm labourers was one pound ten shillings (£1.50), so it was necessary for the women to work at home; often they could earn more money than their husbands. The girls showed me where they worked, in a flat over an empty lock-up shop. They repaired lace, and at the end of their working day they would take the lace home with them and work on it, sometimes until late at night. They travelled to and from work by bicycle, carrying the lace in a big black bag, and so they were able to earn quite a bit.

We came to the end of the village and turned into a lane. On the opposite side of the road there was a high wall, and I noticed an acrid smell coming from that direction; it made me feel sick, and affected my head and stomach. I asked the girls if it was a prison, and what was the awful smell coming from it; they laughed at my ignorance and seemed unaffected by the smell themselves. They said it was a brewery and the smell was the smell of hops; I would get used to it. The girls had come to meet me from work, and had their sack of lace on the bar of their bikes, as they walked beside me. I learned that every man, woman and child had a bike, because that was the only way they could get anywhere - the houses were very scattered and some of the people had many miles to travel to and from their work-place.

We had a very long walk, through pretty country houses; the Dorset countryside was very beautiful. It was farming country, and whichever lane you walked would lead to a farm or a farm cottage. I was amazed at the beauty and the cleanliness about me, and as I walked along the lanes, I could see beautiful fruit trees, apples, cherries, pears and plums, all in full blossom; the scent of the blossom was heavenly. The cottages were quaint and old, and often the only indication that a cottage was there was the smoke coming from chimneys in the thatched roofs. After walking for about a mile, we came out into an open space and there, facing us, was a little country inn, 'The Meads', with its sign swinging in the breeze; it had a privet hedge on either side, and was not much bigger than a double fronted house. On its left, on the other side of the hedge, in a large, beautiful flower garden, was Mrs. Thick's cottage, where she and Ella and Alice lived.

I had never seen anything more beautiful in my life. Holly-hocks stood majestically against the white-washed walls at the front of the cottage, and as we opened the wicket gate and walked down the garden path, between the hollyhocks, it was like walking through a welcoming guard of honour.

Mrs. Thick welcomed me. She was a small woman, with snowy white hair, but she was not as old as her silvery hair suggested. Mr. Thick was a quarry worker, and when he came home from work. I took an immediate liking to him. He was a very nice old man – indeed, he was a perfect gentleman, and though he looked younger than Mrs. Thick, he was actually older. He had been married before, and had a family from his first marriage as well as the four girls from his second.

To my joy I found a pigsty at the back of the cottage, with a plump sow in it which they were fattening for market. It didn't take me long, with my love for all animals, to become acquainted with the sow. I was spending a very happy time here in the country, and a particular source of joy was getting myself lost in the lanes and finding my way out again. Ella was an unmarried mother with a little six-year-old boy. (She was still courting the boy's father, and eventually, when the boy was about ten, they married.) Timmy was a lovely boy, unspoilt and the apple of his grandparents' eyes. Each evening I looked forward to seeing the girls coming home from work with their packs of lace. Their tea would be waiting for them, and immediately afterwards they would take their work out to the front door, and the only sound to be heard would be the click, click of their fingers as they flew back and foward through the lace. To please them, I would have to pull up a chair and sit beside them to try to learn from watching them; but their fingers moved too quickly, and the flashing of the needles made me close my eyes because it made my head ache. Their sister Maud had told them of a song I used to sing (about an unmarried mother), which had many verses, and every night they would ask me to sing it to them, saying it soothed their nerves.

I saw no-one apart from Mr. and Mrs. Thick and the girls; at night, when their work was done, they would all go to the little inn for a drink of beer. When daylight faded, there was not sufficient light for the girls to work, because there was no electricity and the only means of light was a small oil lamp in the living room. The cottage had only two rooms, one large livng room downstairs, and one large room upstairs which was partitioned off to make two rooms. Mr. and Mrs. Thick and

139

Timmy shared the main bedroom while I shared a double bed with Ella and Alice, under the eaves behind the partition. Since it was a thatched cottage, we were lulled to sleep by the sound of the mice playing football in the thatch; I didn't mind the mice, but I did object to being wakened early in the morning by spiders tickling my face as they dangled on silken cords from the roof. Earwigs were also something of a bother; but that was life in the country, and it did wonders for my health.

One Saturday, soon after my arrival in Dorset, Mrs. Thick took Ella and me on a little train journey to Salisbury market; I have never enjoyed a day as much, before or since, as I did that one. It was an open market, and we bought freshly picked strawberries which were delicious, quite unlike any other strawberries I had ever tasted. As we left Salisbury by train, we saw the white horse cut out of the chalk mountain by Australian soldiers during the First World War, and I hoped I would be able to see it again before I went home; unfortunately I saw it only that once.

During my stay in Dorset there were many fêtes and galas, and we did not miss one, however far we had to go, because we enjoyed them so much; I didn't have a bike, so the girls had to walk with me. Every night we had bread and cheese and a glass of cider for our supper, but I didn't like cider, so I had a cup of tea. (If Mr. and Mrs. Thick could not get out to the inn, they would have their cider sent in for them.) Strangely enough, a nice young man started to call on Mrs. Thick in the evenings; I assumed he was a relative. Mrs. Thick introduced him to me, explaining that his father was a gentleman farmer, the landlord of all the farms for miles around. The son was handsome, tall, well-groomed and well dressed, well educated – altogether a real gentleman. Mrs. Thick suggested that James, as he was called, should take me for a walk through his father's estate; after that he became a regular visitor to the Thicks' cottage, and walks around the farms became a regular occurence. It was very interesting for me, because he would point out different things and explain them.

After I had been in Dorset for three weeks, I decided that if our doctor back home had suggested that I stay there for three months, then I would have to find work and pay my way; though Mrs. Thick had assured me that I could stay there for as long as I liked, and there was no question of payment because they enjoyed having me there – after all, I was her daughter's sister-in-law. However I asked Ella and Alice if they would speak to the manager of their factory for me, which they did, and soon I was going out to work every day with the girls, though I had to leave the house about half an hour before them, because they rode their bikes but I had to walk.

I had learned a little from Ella and Alice about the art of lace-making, and now the supervisor showed me the rest of the job. There were six of us working there – seven including the supervisor. In the centre of the room was a long black table, like a billiard table but with a polished top. The supervisor took a roll of unbleached bridal veiling and pulled the ends of it across the table; as it had come straight from the mill it was full of machine flaws, with broken threads making holes in the lace. The supervisor picked up each flawed part with her two fingers and tied it in a knot, so that each flaw made a knot, according to its size, in the lace. Then, when she had completed all the knots, which could range from thirty to a hundred or more, she would pull the roll back across the table, counting all the knots, after which she would tie on a label which bore my name and number of knots; that was my work. All the knots had to be opened and repaired until the whole roll had been completed. The supervisor gave me a black velvet thumb pad, which I put on the thumb of my left hand, then I would sit down and draw the veil towards me, open each knot, lay it across the velvet pad, and repair the damage with a needle and silk thread.

The supervisor told me that I was very quick to learn, and she was pleased with my work. But no matter how hard I worked, I couldn't get my needles to click as fast as Ella's and Alice's, and although I took my bag home at night and worked on it in the house, I was still very slow.

We were paid by the number of knots, and I could never manage to earn more than about ten shillings a week. The girls went home to dinner each day on their bikes, but I took a dry lunch to work; then on the mid-day break I would have to leave the premises, so I would come down the fire-escape and go for a walk, eating my lunch as I went, and admiring the beauty of the country. It was a joy to open my lunch packet because Mrs. Thick made her own bread which was delicious. Her loaves were long bottom loaves, baked on the bottom of

141

the oven, without a tin, and they were crisp and crusty all round. She would cut the bread longways, to make long sandwiches, which were filled with cold meat; I always ate my whole lunch pack, because eating as I walked gave me a good appetite. I would dream dreams as I walked along the winding lanes, trying to make up my mind which cottage I would like, one day, to be mine. I didn't ever want to leave Dorset.

Ella and Alice paid their mother ten shillings a week for board and lodging, and my third Saturday I presented Mrs. Thick with my own first ten shillings; I had sixpence left for myself, to save towards the next fête and gala. There was only one thing I didn't like in Dorset, and that was the taste of the potatoes. They were freshly dug up from the garden, but they were cooked in a net, which was placed in the saucepan, and I thought this gave their taste a tang like the smell of earwigs. After the potatoes had been turned out of the net, the net was placed across the fence to dry, ready for the next time it was needed, but I thought of the ants and earwigs that crawled over the net while it was on the fence, and I wished they wouldn't boil the potatoes in it!

Now I found another young man was visiting the house, a Mr. Jack Sutton, a butcher's son. he too was very nice looking, and spoke with a cultured English voice, unlike the Dorset accent. Mrs. Thick would suggest that I go walking with Jack, and I would protest 'but what about my lace' to which she would reply, "Oh, never mind your lace, you are here on holiday. Go out with Jack, he can show you the countryside." So, not wanting to offend her, I would go out with whichever of the young men turned up at the cottage. This went on for some time, and Jack and James would compete with each other to get to the cottage first. They were both perfect gentlemen and very entertaining. When I went out with James he would take a bunch of leaves and make what he called a true lover's knot, which he would present to me.

Mrs. Thick would often ask me which of them I liked best, but I always told her that I didn't know, because they were both nice. I thought she was always telling me to go out with them so that Ella and Alice would have peace and quiet to get on with their work – I didn't realise she was matchmaking. Then one day a farm labourer stopped me in the lane while I was on my way home, and let the cat out of the bag. he told me that he had called at the cottage to see me, but Mrs. Thick had told him to clear off, he had nothing to offer. I asked him what she had meant by 'nothing to offer', and he said, "My boss's son is allowed to see you and take you out because my dad works for Master James's father, and he is sent to Mrs. Thick with legs of pork and large gammons to keep her sweet. And young Mr. Sutton takes legs of lamb and pork from his father's shop for her."

I said nothing to Mrs. Thick of what I had learned, but when James next came calling, I asked him if it was true. He admitted he was paying Mrs. Thick, at her request, so that he could meet me, but he said his feeling had now gone much deeper, and he would have something to ask me very soon. However I told him that I had no intention of ever going out with him again; I had come to Dorset for a holiday and had no intention of being bartered or bargained for.

"I feel insulted," I told him angrily, "and if this is what you Dorset boys call friendship, I want nothing to do with it. I wondered why Mrs. Thick was so generous with her meat in my sandwiches, and now I know why." When Jack Sutton called, I told him the same thing. Both boys seemed discomforted, and I wondered if they thought I had been aware of what had been going on.

Ben and Maud came up to Dorset for a holiday; there was no room for them to stay at the cottage, so they stayed in Maud's stepsister's pretty home, and came each day to visit Maud's mother. One day Ben called me outside, saying he wanted to have a chat with me, so I went into the garden with him, and he said, "Rit, I have been talking to James, the son from the big farm, and he told me he had assaulted you; and he apologised to me, telling me he was very sorry. Now, Rity, I want you to tell me the truth, did he assault you?"

"You got it all wrong, Ben," I said. "He must have said he had insulted me, not assaulted me."

"Are you sure, Rit? Because if he did assault you, I am going back there to knock the devil out of him."

"I'm telling you the truth, Ben," I said. "James is a very nice man, and not at all the type of person who would assault a lady."

"Thank God for that," said Ben. "Because he told me he had fallen in love with you, and wanted to get engaged."

143

I didn't want to tell Ben about the meat bribes, because it might have caused trouble between him and his mother-in-law, so I told him that only my pride had been hurt, and that was all; but I was sorry that this little deception had come between us.

In the evenings now I would sit with Ella and Alice, and repair some of the knots in my lace; by this extra effort I raised my wages from ten shillings to eleven and sixpence a week, and I loved bringing home my pay. We worked for a few hours on Saturday morning, then after dinner the girls and I would walk through the lanes looking for a fête, however small; we loved these festivities.

One evening I came out of the factory with my sack of lace; the girls had already gone off on their bikes because their bags that day had been too heavy to let them take mine as well. Outside, on the road, stood a horse and farm dray. The driver, an employee from one of the farms, spoke to me in a strong Dorset accent, "Would 'ee like a lift, missy? I be goin' past Thick's cottage."

"Yes, please," I said, climbing up into the cart beside the driver. There was only one seat, so I sat on the cart, and had a very enjoyable ride back to the cottage, where the man dropped me at the door. I jumped down from the cart, saying to him, "Thank you very much, that was a most enjoyable treat."

Next day, when I left work, he was there again, but this time there was a young naval officer sitting in the dray beside him. I hesitated, and was about to refuse the lift when the young officer jumped down and helped me into the dray. He told me that he had been abroad for several years, but his ship had just docked and he was on a long period of leave. From that day on he used to meet me and walk me home every evening. Sometimes he would come into the house and spend the evening there, because he knew the Thicks. In the night he would go into 'The Meads', and bring some bottles of cider back to the cottage, then we would sit down to our meal of bread and cheese and cider. By now I had fallen in love with my naval officer, Tom Cox, and he with me, and I knew without doubt that this time it was the real thing.

One Saturday Tom came up to the cottage and invited me to dinner at his mother's house. He told me that he had invited

144

Ben and Maud, and that his kid brother would be there also. He always referred to his mother as 'my old lady', and now he said to me, "My old lady and my sister have gone away for the weekend." His mother's home was a modern, red-bricked house with a slate roof, and there was a beautiful garden at the back of the house. Ben, Maud and I were admiring the house when Tom's young brother said, "Our Tom bought this house for Mum, and he owns three more like it down the road." Tom playfully cuffed his kid brother round the ear, saying, "You old show-off!" Then we all sat at the table waiting for Tom to bring in the dinner – he placed before each of his guests a large plate of beautifully brown chips and fried eggs. We were all hungry and the sight of these delicious-looking chips and eggs improved our appetites still further. Ben said, "Excuse my bad manners, these look so good that I can't wait, I'm going to start my dinner." He set to with a will on his plate of eggs and chips – then jumped up as if he had been stung by a bee, and ran into the kitchen. After he had spat out the mouthful he had eaten, he said to Tom, "Crikey, Tom, what did you cook these chips in?" "Why?" asked Tom. "Just tell me," said Ben. "What did you cook them in?"

"Well," he said, "I couldn't find where my old lady had put the cooking oil, but I found this," and he produced a bottle of what looked like water – but, when the cork was removed, turned out to be paraffin oil.

"You clown," said Ben, "this is paraffin oil!" Tom just laughed and said, "Well, oil is oil, isn't it?"

The eggs and chips went into the bin, and Tom raided his mother's pantry to satisfy our appetites.

I was getting letters occasionally from Fred Jeffries, and had replied to them as I would to a casual friend; when I answered his next letter, I told him about Tom Cox, explaining that he was a young naval officer with whom I had fallen in love. My three months holiday had now come to an end, but I had no wish to return home as there was no work there for me. However Ben and Maud had gone back and now my mother had started to write and ask me when I was coming home; so I had to start saving my one and sixpences a week. I told Tom that I would have to be going home shortly because once the winter came, I would not be able to walk the lanes to and from work, the weather would be too bad.

Tom took me to visit his aunt, who lived within walking distance; it was autumn now, and the weather was getting colder. We went into the aunt's beautiful Georgian house, which stood in its own grounds, and the family made me very welcome; we were shown into a big room, with a floor of highly polished wood and white fur rugs placed around it – though what I liked most was the fire-place. The fire was on the floor, inside an arch, and on either side of the hearth was an iron 'dog'; the whole fireplace was encircled by a heavy brass curb, and brass fire tongs etc. stood inside the curb. Tom's cousin asked me if I would like to see the fruit in the orchard, and she gathered a large basket of fruit from the trees for me to take home with me. Beautiful large apples lay like a carpet on the floor, and I said to her, "There's no need to pick the apples off the trees, I can have these on the floor." "Oh," she said, "they are no good, they are just the wind-blown apples, the pigs will eat those up."

One sunny autumn day Tom and I walked through a beautiful green meadow, and stood under a huge walnut tree, heavy with nuts; Tom picked a walnut from the tree, crushed it in his hands, and said, "Next year when the walnuts are on the tree, we will pick them, you and I, and I will teach you how to pickle them. My ship is in, and I have been recalled, but we will be docking back in England for Christmas. I want you to be my wife; will you marry me at Christmas? I will come straight down to your home in Wales, and we can be married there, then I will bring you back to your own home here in Dorset."

It wasn't my first proposal, but it was my first real love. It was arranged that I would go home and wait for Christmas (which was only two months away) while I prepared for my wedding to Tom.

EIGHTEEN

My mother was impatient for me to come home, and sent me my train fare. Then, when I arrived home, a messenger came up with a message from Fred Jeffries's mother. It said, "Ritty, will you please come down as soon as you arrive home, as Fred is dangerously ill and hasn't long to live. Please come, Ritty, he is calling for you." I showed the note to my mother, who said, "Yes, he's been very ill for some time, and there is no hope for him, poor boy."

Fred's mother was very pleased to see me, and told me I would see a great change in him. "Don't be surprised if he doesn't know you," she said. "He doesn't recognise anyone." She took me up to his bedroom, and when I went in, Fred was laying facing the wall. He seemed to be in a coma, and there was a heavy vallance all around the bed, as well as at the head, to keep out the draught. Mrs. Jeffries walked around to the head of the bed and, resting her arms on the bed, called quietly down to Fred, "Open your eyes, Fred, look who's here." But despite all her calling, Fred didn't seem to hear her, and his eyes remained closed. She tried again, "Come on, Fred, open your eyes, Ritty's here. Come on, Fred, see Ritty."

Slowly he opened his eyes, and seemed to come to life. "Is it really you, Ritty?" he said, fearing, no doubt, that he was seeing an illusion.

"Yes, Fred, it really is me, Ritty."

Then he said either "Have you come back?" or "Have you come back to me?" I couldn't be sure which.

"Yes, Fred, it *is* me, I *have* come back," I answered him. His mother was smiling and nodding at me in approval.

"Have you come back to me?" Fred kept asking, and all I could say was "Yes, I've come back:" I couldn't say "Yes, I've come back to you." To get him to talk, I asked him what had happened, what had made him like this, by now he was facing me, and he took my hand and held it tightly, then said, quite sharply, "It's your fault, Ritty, it's your fault."

"Why my fault, Fred? What have I done?" I asked, surprised.

"If you hadn't gone to Dorset and left me, and then written to tell me you had fallen in love with that Tom Cox, this wouldn't have happened. I went all to pieces."

My feeling of pity for him turned to disgust, that he should blame me for his own weakness; but what could I say to a man who was dying? So I said to him, "You must forget all that, Fred, put it behind you and get yourself well again." His mother smiled at what I was saying to him, but at the same time she was nodding her head to say that he couldn't get better. Fred was leaning towards me, and now he took hold of my other hand, saying, "Promise me, Rit, if I get better, you'll marry me."

I couldn't make a promise that I wouldn't be able to keep and I didn't want to marry Fred, but when I looked at his mother, she was nodding her head for me to say 'yes' to him. I didn't love Fred, and I knew I never could, yet I couldn't let him die believing he was unloved. I didn't know what to do. I had a feeling of revulsion, and I thought to myself, 'If he dies, I'll never forgive myself for not making him happy.'

Then I asked God for His guidance. 'Oh Lord, what can I do? If I don't give him my promise and he dies, I'll always feel guilty of his death, but, oh God, if he gets better, I don't want to marry him, but I will have to keep my promise.' I looked at Fred and said simply, "Yes, Fred, if you get better."

Fred said, "Now that we are engaged, I will get better, and we'll get married as soon as possible." His mother was all smiles, but she could see that it had all been a great shock to me, and she took me out of the bedroom. Now I felt like a prisoner who had just received a death sentence. All I wanted was to get away from that house and go to my own room and lock myself in, to try to unravel the trapped feeling inside me.

Fred made a remarkable recovery, and we started to make plans for our marriage. I would have told Tom my troubles if he had not been abroad, I knew not where, but now there was no-one I could tell. I spoke to Maud, though, and told her the story, asking for her advice; she said, "Well, you'll have to marry him, Rit, won't you?"

"Whom do you mean, Maud?" I asked.

"Well," she said, "Fred Jeffries, of course."

"How am I going to tell Tom?" I asked. "I'm going to have to

148

tell him and stop him coming at Christmas, but how?"

Maud said, "If you married Tom Cox, you'd have a wonderful husband, I know him well; but you'll have to marry Fred now. I'll write to Tom for you and explain everything to him."

Then my friend, also called Maud, came home for the weekend from her place in Cardiff, and I told her I was going to be married. I explained that Fred did not want to start in debt, so we were going to save up so that we could pay for our furniture before we got married; (as he was a preacher, Fred would not be getting big money.) Then I told Maud that it might be six months before we married, and I couldn't live off my parents for that long.

Maud worked as a mother's help to Mrs. Ceridwen John, the daughter of Sir John and Lady Daniel, and she said that Sir John, who was a Cardiff shipping magnate, had lost a lot of money in shipping lately, so they had had to dispense of their valet and lady's maid. However they had found that they could not manage on their own, and as Sir John was very delicate, they needed someone with nursing experience who could also act as valet to Sir John and lady's maid to her ladyship; Maud thought I would be just the girl to suit them.

"Shall I speak to them for you, Ritty?" she asked.

"Yes please, Maud," I said. "I'd be very grateful!"

Meanwhile Colonel North's second wife, the headmistress of Aber Girls' School, of whom I was very fond, and whom I called Auntie Winnie, took advantage of my fondness for her. She was a hygiene fanatic, and when she knew that I was at home, she would always send a message down to my house saying that she needed me urgently. As this was a regular event, I knew that the message meant that either her maid or her washerwoman had walked out on her, and I would go up prepared for a day's hard work; from the moment I got into the house, after walking two and a half miles to get there, she would be merciless in her demands on me. This time Uncle William had been taken into hospital and she wanted the house spring-cleaned before he came home – though the house was spotlessly clean, and didn't look at all as though it needed cleaning.

Auntie Winnie would say to me as I was leaving, tired out after working so hard, "You are a good girl, Ritty, you clean much cleaner than a maid, and you work much harder than the maid, and I don't have to pay you for doing it!" She did not pay me for my hard work; if she *had* offered, I would have taken the money but she never did so.

Uncle William was an old man, twenty years older than his wife, and he did not recover from his illness. Auntie Winnie told me that he had requested that they would cut his throat before he was buried, to make sure he really was dead. (He had told my mother of this wish some years before; the reason for it being that when he was a young man he had been pronounced dead after an illness, but had come back to life in his coffin, and he was afraid that the same thing might happen again, after he had been buried.)

After Uncle William's funeral, a letter came for me from Sir John, requesting me to attend an interview. I went along, and Lady Daniel asked me if I would start right away; I agreed, and that night slept in the best guest room, as my room wasn't ready,

By now I had accepted that I was to become Fred's wife and that I had lost Tom Cox. Fred was very nice, and I knew he was everything that was required to make a good husband. Also I had been brought up in the Christian faith and as Fred's wife I would be living, as I wished, according to my religious upbringing. Every week Fred sent me a large box of chocolates by post, and inside the box I would find two half-crowns, with a note telling me to enjoy myself; he would also write and describe what he was doing to the house in readiness for our marriage. I didn't eat the chocolates or spend the money, instead I would pack up the parcel and readdress it to my mother's house for Violet and Nancy to enjoy. I told Fred time and time again not to send me chocolates and money, because I didn't want them, and he would be better off saving towards our married life together. This went on for some weeks, until I received a letter from him saying that the sweets and money were for me to enjoy, not for my family; that was the last time I received chocolates from him. (Apparently he had gone up to visit my mother, as was his usual custom, and he had seen his box of chocolates lying on the table!)

Sir John and Lady Daniel were a nice couple, and I was very happy there. The work was light, and they were such a lovely couple that it was a joy to work for them. Lady Daniel had a beautiful voice, and sang at all the Cymmrodorion parties, while Sir John was the President of the Cymmrodorion Society; he was charming to work for, but suffered from very poor health.

Every evening I would take their dalmatian for a walk round Cardiff, and one night I was out on my usual stroll, but without the dog which was at Mrs. Ceridwen John's house. I was window shopping, going nowhere in particular, and I must have walked quite a long way. Suddenly I found myself staring into the window of an antique shop, fascinated by some pretty jewellery there; but as it was evening, the shop was shut. Then, from behind me, I heard a voice say, "I told you not to, didn't I?" and this was repeated several times. I thought the man must be speaking to someone with him, and I took no notice, but just went on looking in the window. Next the voice seemed to come from over my shoulder, speaking the same words: "I told you not to, I told you not to, didn't I?" I turned around, and looked into the face of a very big black man. It *was* me he had been speaking to, for there was no-one else around; but I thought he had mistaken me for someone he knew, and I walked away, quickly crossing to the other side of the road.

I had no idea where I was, and I just kept on walking. The man also crossed the road and walked on the left-hand side of me, saying nothing except for those same words over and over again. I was on a road that had no shops; it was dark – night time now – and the road was only dimly lit, with its lamps a long distance apart. I ignored the man, and though I felt frightened, I did not let him see this, but just kept on walking, until, after some time, I saw a policeman standing under a lamp-post on the other side of the road. Quickly I crossed the road towards him, and said, "I am a stranger to Cardiff, officer. Can you please tell me where I am. I was window shopping, and I've lost my way."

"I thought you didn't live in this area," said the policeman. "You are in Bute Street."

"I'm sorry, I've never heard of Bute Street," I told him. "I want to go to Cathedral Road, can you help me?"

"You are in the docks," he explained. "I must get you away from here quickly. Come with me, and I'll put you on a trolley bus."

We walked together to the trolley bus depot, and he hailed one of the buses and told the driver to put me down near Cathedral Road. When I got back, I told Lady Daniel where I had been, and about the black man and the policeman.

"It was very fortunate for you that you met that policeman," she said. "It is so nice to know that there *are* such kind men who

151

will take the trouble to assist young ladies when they are lost."

I had been with the Daniels for about six months when disaster struck and they lost all their money. They decided to emigrate to Canada and take their son and his wife with them, but then another tragedy befell these lovely people, when their oldest grand-daughter, twelve-year-old Hilary, passed away suddenly. (She was their daughter Ceridwen's child.) The house in Cathedral Road had to be sold, along with everything else, and I found it a very sad leave-taking, saying goodbye to them all and going back to Ogmore Vale.

Clutching my suitcase, I stepped off the train in Blackmill, and started my long walk to Ogmore Vale. As I was passing the Isolation Hospital, I saw a group of gipsies just ahead of me, walking down the lane to join the main road, and one of the women, with a big basket on her arm, stopped and waited for me to catch up with her.

"What have you got to give to a gipsy, miss?" she said. Although the road was long and lonely. I had no fear of the gipsies, because the true Romanies are very nice people. (I used to spend hours sitting with them when I was young and they camped in Cwm Nant y Ci woods, and when I was sixteen I had been made blood sister to Isobel Lee, daughter of a gipsy queen.) I said to the gipsy, in answer to her question, "Very little, I'm afraid." Then she took my hand and admired the ring I was wearing; it wasn't an expensive ring, but it was a keepsake.

"Will you give the gipsy that ring, miss?" she asked. I laughed and tapped her on the hand and said to her, "No indeed, I won't give you that ring, it's a keepsake and I can't part with it."

"Well," she said, "you've got a threepenny bit in your pocket, miss, will you give that to me?"

I laughed again, and said, "Yes, I've got a threepenny bit, and you can have it. Now, will this keep the peace? And if you are walking up to Ogmore Vale, I'll walk up with you." She took my hand again, and said, "You are getting married soon, miss, aren't you?"

I sighed, and said, "Oh yes, I suppose so." I was thinking that now I was home, Fred might want to bring the date forward.

"Oh no, miss," said the gipsy, "not to that man."

"Oh Yes," I told her, "I am engaged to be married."

"*But*," she emphasized, "you won't marry that man. Think of the gipsy, miss, when you *are* married, to a tall, dark, handsome

152

man with the initial 'W'."

We walked along together, and when we reached my home she shouted after me again, "Don't forget now, miss, when you are married to that tall, dark, handsome man with the initial 'W'." When I told my mother about this, she just smiled, as if to say, 'that gipsy nonsense!' "Fred is coming by later on," she said, "to take you up to the house; he has a surprise for you."

Before I had gone to Cardiff, Fred had asked me once what was my idea of a warm, cosy evening, and I had said, "A nice bright fire, with brass fire irons, an American rocking chair, a box of chocolates and a good book." Now, when we went into the house that evening, there to greet me was a nice, bright fire with brass fire irons, an American rocking chair in front of the fire, and a book and a box of chocolates at the side of it. Then he took me into the parlour, and there was my photo, enlarged and framed, standing on the piano. It made me feel guilty, because I did not want to marry him although he was everything I had ever wanted in a husband. I couldn't forget Tom Cox. But I vowed to myself, in spite of my heartache, that I would never show Fred that I didn't love him, and I would do my best to make him a good wife, and be a good mother to the children he wanted. (I also loved children, and had secretly wished that I would have at least four.)

On the way home that night, Fred seemed to have something on his mind, but he didn't seem to know how to begin to tell me what it was. We walked a long way in silence, then he said, "Your mother has been talking to me about you, Rit. It seems Dr. Anderson saw the advertisement of our wedding in the paper, and went to see your mother. He asked if she had spoken to you, but she said, no, she hadn't had the heart to, so the doctor told her that if she wouldn't tell *you*, then she must tell *me*. The truth is, Rit, there must be no children. If you have a child, it could kill you. But don't worry about it, Rit, we'll adopt children. We can start with little Nancy, you love her, so she will be our first." Nancy was six years old.

I asked Fred if he was disappointed, secretly hoping that he would call the wedding off, but he said, "I *was* disappointed at first, but I've got used to the idea now, and I'd rather adopt children than take any chances with your life. Now, since our home is ready, shall we make our wedding day Easter?" It was the beginning of Lent, and Easter was only six weeks away, but I agreed to the date. When I got home, I told my mother that we would be getting married then; she was very pleased that I was marrying Fred, of whom she was very fond, but I felt that she was a little worried.

NINETEEN

Next morning Mother said to me, "I'm feeling very down this morning, Rit. I have been thinking about your father. I think I'll go over to Caerau for the day. Will you come with me?"

"I'll come with you, of course," I said. "but why do you want to go to Caerau? We don't know anyone over there."

"I do," Mother said. "I want to go to the Station Hotel to see Billy and Deborah Hopkins. They don't know I've buried your father, they'll be sorry to hear it."

If my mother set her mind on going somewhere, she wouldn't think of going by bus or train, and so, though I wasn't all that keen on walking so far, we started off on foot over the mountains to Caerau. As we walked along, my mother told me that Billy Hopkins had been employed by my grandparents in their hotels and my father had taught him all he knew. After that, to lighten our journey, my mother told me stories of things that had happened years before.

We arrived at the Station Hotel after stop tap, but Mother knocked at the door, and Mrs. Hopkins recognised her at once, though she hadn't seen Mother for many years. She was very pleased to see us and made us welcome, taking us into the living room where there was a strange smell from something cooking on the open fire. She told us she was boiling a haggis, and then she quickly put food on the table – though it was past their dinner time. Then Mrs. Hopkins took the haggis off the fire, unwrapped it, and put it on a plate, where it looked like a large roll of some grey matter, not the least bit appetising.

"Would you like to try some haggis, Rachael?" she asked Mother.

"No thank you," said my mother. "I don't like the look of it."

Then Mrs. Hopkins said to me, "I can't call you Rachael, I'll have to call you Ray. Would *you* like some haggis?" I was so hungry that I didn't hesitate, but said, "Yes, please." I could see there were cakes and bread and butter, but I wanted something

155

more savoury. Mrs. Hopkins cut the haggis in half, and put half on my plate. "There you are, Ray, eat that up. And if you like it, eat it all. I don't know why I make it, Billy won't eat it, and I don't think I will either."

There was a tang on the haggis, and if I hadn't been so hungry, I wouldn't have eaten it, but as it was, I ate the whole lot. My mother asked me how it tasted, and I told her, "I don't know, Mam, it went down without touching the sides!"

Mrs. Hopkins told us that she had three barmaids; two weren't much good and she wanted to get rid of them, but though she had advertised for two new girls, she had had no replies yet. Essie Furnace, who was an excellent barmaid and had been with them for five years was getting married in ten days' time. Essie was from the Rhondda, and she didn't have her mother alive, so she had asked if she could be married from the hotel. Mrs. Hopkins said, "I don't know what I'm going to do. – What are you doing now, Ray?"

"I've only just come home from Cardiff," I said, "and I'm getting married at Easter."

"Oh," she said, "then you've got six weeks before Easter, haven't you? How about coming here and giving me a hand for the wedding? Because the two girls I've got here can't wash a dish clean, let alone lay a table for a wedding. I've invited the vicar and his wife, so I want things done nicely, and you could do that I'm sure, Ray."

"Well," I said, "I don't know, my fiancé is a minister, and I don't think he'd approve of me coming into a pub."

"I wouldn't dream of asking you to go into the bar, or to do anything at all except just spend a holiday here. All I'd want you to do would be to lay the table and wait on the bridal party," said Mrs. Hopkins.

"I know what my fiancé will say," I said. "He thinks public houses are evil places, and it will be the first time I have set foot inside one in all my life. But if it will please you to have me here, I will ask him"

Mrs. Hopkins laughed and said, "Your grandparents were hoteliers, and they were lovely people to work for. And your father was an educated gentleman who never took a drink, even though he was born and reared in a hotel."

So then I said, "If Fred agrees to my coming here, I will go home now and come back this Saturday, so that I can help you make the preparations through the week."

When we got home, I asked Fred about Mrs. Hopkins's suggestion, and he said, "Most emphatically no, I can't have old drunken men looking at my wife." But I had a way of twisting poor old Fred around my little finger, and the next Saturday found him very reluctantly carrying my case up to the Station Hotel. He let me go into the hotel alone, but he did not go home, he just walked up and down the pavement outside all day, making sure that I did not go into the bar. He even found somewhere to stay the night rather than go home, and he told me later that he knew I didn't like drunken men, so he wanted to be there in case I didn't want to stay.

Once the wedding was over, I wanted to go home on the Monday, but was persuaded to stay a little longer. Mrs. Hopkins and the barmaids worked in the public bar and looked after the jug and bottle, while Mr. Hopkins looked after the billiard room and the private bar, three floors up. No beer was sold in the private bar, only liqueurs, but only a few men went there, perhaps two or three at a time, if that. Billy Hopkins introduced me to his friends in the private bar, and showed me how to draw shorts from the fixtures on the wall. It was very pleasant there, with no bad language or drunkenness, and I didn't need much coaxing to stay on. If I did say anything about going home, Mr. Hopkins would say, "But look at the trade you are bringing here. Don't go this week, go next week."

One of the young men who started coming to the bar in the evenings was Ivor Webb, who brought his brother-in-law, Emlyn Lake, with him. Billy Hopkins had let everyone know that I was engaged to be married, but Emlyn Lake started to match-make for his brother Ivor because, as he said, Ivor didn't like to ask me out himself since I was engaged although he had fallen in love with me. I told him he was wasting his time, because I was getting married in Easter, and had no intention of going out with anyone – though in fact I had told Fred that I would like to postpone our wedding until Whitsun, because Mrs. Hopkins didn't want me to leave until she had found someone to replace Essie.

Then, one bitterly cold day, when the snow lay deep on the ground, I decided to take a walk to see what Caerau looked like in the snow. I was standing on the doorstep of the hotel when Emlyn Lake approached me and asked if I would like to go for a

157

run in the car. I said, "No, thank you, Mr. Lake, I'm just going to take a walk."

"I've got my father-in-law's car just over there," he said. "Let me take you for a run, it's too cold to walk."

He was very persistent, so, to get rid of him I said, "No, I've decided to take a bus and go to see my mother in Ogmore Vale." But he still wouldn't take no for an answer, and said, "The buses are very infrequent, and you'll have to go into Bridgend to get a bus to Ogmore Vale. I doubt if you would even get one today, and if you did, it would be midnight before you got home. I'm going to Nantymoel on business for Mr. Webb, and I can drop you off right at your mother's door, and pick you up again on the way back and bring you safely back to the hotel."

The temptation was too great – to think of driving in the comfort of a car and not to have to stand out in the cold, waiting for buses.

"How many of you are going to Nantymoel?" I asked.

"Only myself and Mr. Webb's chauffeur, Mr. Dai Pratt," he said.

"Very well, I'll come with you," I agreed, and I got into the car, where I had the back seat all to myself, and we started off. Just then, as we slowed under the railway bridge on the square, the car door opened, a man jumped into the back seat beside me, then we picked up speed again. The man was Ivor Webb (who, incidentally was just as tall, dark and handsome as the gipsy had said.) However I decided that I wasn't going to speak to either of them, Emlyn or Ivor, because I felt I had been deceived; so I sat back and flatly refused to be drawn into any conversation. Eventually we arrived at Ogmore Vale, but instead of them dropping me off as I expected them to do, they drove up the mountain track to my mother's door.

When she heard the unusual sound of a motor car stopping outside her door, my mother came out to see what was happening; no traffic ever came up that track. I got out of the car and walked past my mother into the house – and the three men followed.

"Where are you lot going?" asked my mother.

Ivor Webb said, "We've come to see you, to tell you that I am going to marry your daughter."

"I'm afraid Fred Jeffries will have something to say about that," Mother told him.

"They told me they were going to Nantymoel on business," I explained, "and they are going to pick me up on the way back."

"That was only an excuse to get you into the car," said Emlyn Lake, "because you always refused to speak to Ivor."

We just had time for a cup of tea, and then we had to go, because my mother had said Fred always came up at the same time every night, and she didn't want him to walk in and see us all sitting there. They were such a jovial crowd that I could not maintain my stony silence on the way back. Ivor told me that it was love at first sight with him; although he was twenty-four, he had never been interested in girls before, and had never taken a girl out. Now he kept pestering me to jilt Fred and marry him, and I felt that in all fairness I should leave the Station Hotel and go back home.

When I had asked Fred to agree to postpone the wedding until a replacement could be found, my reason had not been strictly true, but I hadn't wished to discuss women's ailments with him. In fact, Mrs. Hopkins had had a very serious haemorrhage, and as there was no telephone in the hotel, Mr. Hopkins had asked me to sit with his wife while he fetched the doctor. When I saw Mrs. Hopkins, I was able to use my nursing experience, knowing exactly what had to be done; the doctor told Mr. Hopkins later that my prompt action had saved her life. Although she was better now, and they had found a replacement barmaid, they kept making excuses to stop me leaving, saying that perhaps Mrs. Hopkins might have a recurrence of the haemorrhage and Mr. Hopkins would not know what to do without my help.

However, after a while Emlyn Lake asked me if I would do his wife Alice and himself a favour, because she was laid up with 'white leg' after childbirth. Emlyn was a civil electrical engineer, and as his wife and child had no-one to look after them while he was in work, he asked me if I would look after them for a while. They lived in a big house in Brynmawr Place in Maesteg. I wanted to go home, but I couldn't refuse to look after a woman who was ill in bed, or her new baby, so reluctantly I agreed to go with him, on the understanding that it was only until Alice was well enough to come downstairs.

Meanwhile, though I had remained faithful to Fred, I had also become very attracted to Ivor Webb, and even felt able to confide in him. After I had been at Brynmawr Place for a couple

159

of weeks, and Alice was on her feet again, I told the Lakes that I was going home, and at that Ivor proposed to me, asking me to give Fred up and marry him instead. I still felt it was my duty to marry Fred – he had made a home for us, and gone to a great deal of trouble, and I wasn't even sure that I would have the heart to turn him down. For all these reasons I knew he *should* be the right man for me – but I knew, too, that I couldn't go through with a marriage to him. I realised that Ivor was the only man I could marry, and so, after many attempts at it, I actually wrote a letter to Fred, telling him everything. Fred did not reply to me, but sent a very offensive letter to Ivor (which showed me the other side of Fred, one which he had kept hidden.) He told Ivor that he would never believe that I loved Ivor more than I loved him – not until he saw me coming back from my wedding.

At that point I had a telegram asking me to come home at once, because Violet had had an accident. So I took my bags, left Alice's house, and caught a bus for home, where I found Violet in bed in the parlour with seventeen stitches in her leg. It seemed that she had been caught between a van and a lorry, on her bike; the bike was a write-off. There were no broken bones, and Violet was none the worse for the accident except that she was fretting because the bike had been a present from me; but when I told her the bike didn't matter as long as she was all right, she soon perked up.

Next thing, Auntie Winnie sent down a message that she wanted to see me. This time, though, it was not to work, but to be interrogated! She was younger than my mother, but the way she treated me made me feel as if she was my grandmother. "I hear you have jilted your fiancé," she said, "and are going to marry a boy from Caerau. What is he like, Ritty? Is he a good man? When can I see him? Fred Jeffries is a good man, but when am I going to see what this other man is like, and whether *he's* good enough for you? I promised you your wedding dress because you've been a good girl to me, you've worked hard and I've never paid you for your work. I want only the best for you – but are you fit to wear white?"

"What do you mean, Auntie Winnie, am I fit to wear white?" I asked.

"Well, you've been engaged to Fred Jeffries for nearly two years," she said, "But now you are getting married to a boy we don't know. Is there something the matter with you?"

Then the penny dropped, and I knew what she meant. "Auntie Winnie," I said to her, "I thought you knew me better than to think such a thing of me. Didn't I tell you once that I would never marry a man who dishonoured me? Yes, Auntie Winnie, I can wear white."

"Then we'll go to the Co-operative now, and get the material for your wedding gown," she said. In the Drapery Department she demanded to see the same material that had been sold to the colliery manager's wife for his daughter's wedding dress. "Nothing but the best is good enough for my niece," she said. (Auntie Winnie had been a guest at the daughter's wedding, and knew exactly what she wanted to buy.)

"Now, for your wedding breakfast I insist on you using my best Royal Albert China, as long as you take care of it, and see that it is safely returned after the wedding."

So my wedding dress was a present from Auntie Winnie, while my veil was a present from a well-to-do friend of my mother's, and came straight from a Paris fashion house, complete with a lace Dutch bonnet with orange blosssom, and a sprig of artificial white heather to pin to my gown. The veil was really far too costly for such a small wedding, but it looked very beautiful over my lovely gown. Little Nancy was to be my flower girl, in pale violet satin, and on the wedding day she was so excited that we could hardly control her. My bridesmaids were Violet and Gertie and Winnie Webb, while my stepfather, David Charles (who was also my grandmother's brother's son) was to give me away, and I was very proud as I walked down to the waiting taxi on his arm.

When little Nancy saw me in my bridal outfit, she became hysterical and reverted to her baby name for me; she was terrified, and screaming, "Not my Gigga Boden, not my Gigga Boden!" Nobody knew what she meant, and she could not be pacified, so I had to go to my wedding without her.

My brother Garfield and my brother James Price, little Nancy's brother, were the groomsmen, and after we had gone, Flossie, Nancy's eldest sister, who was twenty-six years old and had come to the wedding as a guest, explained to them why Nancy was so terrified. She had overheard her elders talking about her mother's sister, Emily Gwendoline Harris, who had died on her twenty-first birthday, and was buried in her wedding dress and veil, on what should have been her wedding day. Then they had remarked that 'Ritty looked like Emily Gwen' and, being too young to understand, Nancy had thought that I too was going to be buried in my bridal dress, and had become hysterical.

When we came back from our wedding, some men were holding a rope across the road, and we had to pay a toll before they would let us pass. While we were held up behind the rope, Ivor had to throw money to the children who were crowding around, waiting, and just then little Nancy ran up to the rope and threw herself into my arms. Ivor put a half crown in her hand, and she ran back into the house, to my mother, shouting, "Look, Mam, look what that chap Ivor Webb gave me, a big silver penny, he's not a bad chap after all, Mam!"

When the wedding photographs came out, my two brothers and my sister Violet looked as miserable as if they had been to a funeral; they disapproved of Ivor. When we went into my mother's house, I looked up at my new husband, and the gipsy's words came flooding back to me: 'Think of the gipsy, miss, when you are married to a tall, dark, handsome man, with the bluest eyes you've ever seen, and the initial 'W' – and there it was, 'W' for Webb. It was only a small wedding, and the reception was at my mother's home. There was just the immediate family, with a few neighbours who came in to help with the tables; in those days people did not go in for large receptions, and the wedding breakfast was usually confined to the bride's home.

The night before my wedding, I met my friend Irene Hoskins walking aimlessly down the road, as if she was escaping from something unpleasant, but I was so filled with my own joy that I failed to notice how sad Irene looked; she lived a few miles from my home, and I hadn't seen her since I left school. (She had been the little girl who always took the part of the bride or groom when we played at weddings.) I said to her, "I'm getting married in the morning, Irene, wish me luck, will you?" Irene was married and had one child, but she was alone when I met her that day. She suddenly sprang to life, and taking both of my hands in hers, she said, "Don't do it, Rachael, don't do it, it can be hell." Irene had always been the happiest girl in our group, well brought up, and very much loved, but now she looked very sad, and without another word she went on her way. But I could not get her sad face out of my mind; she was a very proud girl, and I felt that she would not have wanted to tell me what was wrong.

162

TWENTY

We had no honeymoon. Instead, we spent the weekend at my mother's house, and on the Monday morning Ivor said to me, "I want to take you to Ogmore Vale today, before we go back to Caerau. I'm going to buy you a present." As we walked up the road together, I was so proud that I felt as though I was the only girl that had ever got married. I was actually walking to Ogmore Vale for the very first time as Mrs. Webb. As we got into the place we met Mrs. Marsh who was standing at the door of her shop; I had spent many happy weekends with her children at her home, and had often gone to church on a Sunday with the Marsh family. Now she said to me as we drew near, "I saw you coming, and I waited to have a word with you and your new husband." I introduced Ivor to her, and she told him that she had known me since I first came to Ogmore Vale as a schoolgirl. She said a lot of flattering things about me that made me blush, and then told Ivor, "Don't you ever let her lose that smile or you'll have me to answer to." We just laughed and went on our way, but she shouted after us, "Don't forget now, young man, I mean what I say."

That night we came back to our little house in Caerau. It was just two rooms, a far cry from the lovely home that Fred had prepared, but these two rooms, though sparsely furnished with things discarded from Ivor's old home, were much more beautiful to me because they were also furnished with love.

We had been married for just two months, and I was seeing Ivor off to work at five thirty in the morning. (Ivor was a colliery contractor, with a lot of his own employees doing the three shifts, and that week he was taking the morning shift himself; he had to be at the colliery in time to see the night shift coming up, and to have their report on the work done during the night. After that he would go down underground at six o'clock with the day shift men. Then after his own shift was completed, he would meet the afternoon shift and give them their instuctions. Each shift was nine hours long, so Ivor spent a great deal of his time at the colliery.)

On this particular morning, Ivor had gone to work earlier than the other tenant who lived at the back of the house, and as it was only half past five in the morning, I decided to go back to bed. The other tenant left for work by the back entrance; he worked in a different pit, and I assumed that he had left as usual. I started my way up the stairs, but I had only gone up about three steps when I sat down and cried as if my heart would break. I thought that as the men had gone to work and the mother and children of the other tenant were fast asleep in bed, no-one would hear me, but it seemed that the woman had not yet gone back to bed and her husband had not left for work. He saw me sitting there, and said to his wife, "You had better go and see what is the matter with Mrs. Webb, she is sitting on the stairs, crying." So she came out and said to me, "What is the matter, Mrs. Webb, are you ill?"

"No," I said, "I'm not ill, I'm just disappointed. Some people get too many children when they don't want them, and here am I, married two months and no baby yet!"

At that she burst out laughing, and said, "You wait till you've been married as long as I have, you'll be asking me what you can do to stop them then!" She went away, and I heard her and her husband laughing; it was a long time before I lived that down. But I had met and married my husband within six weeks, and I hadn't given anyone the opportunity of telling him that I must not have children; now I was desperate to have a child before someone told him.

One day, some time later, Auntie Winnie paid us a visit, saying she had come to see our new home. We were not expecting her – it was a surprise visit – and I couldn't help noticing that she looked disdainfully at my humble home. I knew she was displeased, and thought that I should have done better for myself, but I told her that we were happy. As we sat on the platform that night, waiting for the train to come in to take her back to Ogmore Vale, Auntie Winnie took my two hands and put them on her lap, and there was sorrow in her voice as she said, "I had such high hopes for you, you are sure you are happy, Ritty?"

"I'm very sure," I answered. The train roared out of the tunnel into the station, and as she got up from her seat, Auntie

164

Winnie said to me, "You are going to have a baby, aren't you?"

"No, Auntie Winnie," I replied. "I wish I was, but I'm not."

But she was still holding my hands, and she said, "Yes, you are, I can tell by your hands." After that I couldn't get Auntie Winnie into the carriage quickly enough, so that I could go home and give Ivor the good news. I ran all the way home and burst in, shouting, "Ivor, Ivor, we are going to have a baby!" Ivor looked startled – he thought I had decided to take someone else's baby – but he was relieved and happy when I told him what Auntie Winnie had said. It seemed that I hadn't been looking too well for some time, but we had put it down to an experience I had had just after we moved to Caerau.

Soon after we had settled into our home, I had taken a walk down to the shops, intent on becoming a member of the Co-operative Society, and as I was passing through the shopping centre, I noticed groups of people standing around, talking excitedly. Then, in the Co-op, I heard a conversation which was evidently the same thing that the people out in the road had been discussing. It seemed that in one of the streets nearby lived an elderly couple who were very much respected; their son and daughter were living away from home, and the son was a local shoemaker. They lived happily together, until one day the old gentleman bought a large, sharp knife from the local iron-monger's store. When his wife saw the knife, she said to him, "Why did you buy that knife, and why do you keep sharpening it all the time?" He told her that it was to cut her throat, and she laughed because she knew they were so happy together; but that morning the old lady had been found with her throat cut, and the old gentleman had gone up in to the mountains to hide.

Then, as I was returning from the Co-op, I could see two policemen coming down the road towards me, dragging something between them; it was the old man, and they were holding him under his arms, with his feet dragging behind him along the road. It was a pitiful sight. They dragged him to the police station, and his daughter, who had been told of her mother's death, happened to be standing outside the station as they were dragging her father in. The police had found the old man hiding up in the mountains, and he was terrified. There was speculation about the old man being hanged, but he did not live to stand trial, dying a few days later.

Some months later we had to call the doctor in. I didn't tell

165

him I was pregnant, and he couldn't understand what was wrong with me, but he called in every day for several days and then told my husband that I was being poisoned. He questioned Ivor as to who was preparing my meals, and what I was eating, and we told him that I prepared all my own meal, and ate the same food as my husband. Then Ivor told him that whenever I needed to go into the back of the house, he would have to go ahead of me to open the doors, after which I could hold my breath and run through them. The house and the people were spotless, and no-one could find a reason for the heavy smell that was present (though only at night) in the back kitchen, which I had to go through to get water. At last they discovered that it was beetles that caused the problem – beetles that came out only at night, and only in the back kitchen (which was near the coal house; the pits were infested with beetles and cockroaches which got into the colliers' clothes.) The doctor told Ivor, "Your wife is allergic to smells, and if you don't get her away from here soon, she will die."

We were sorry to leave the house, because the people we lived with were so nice and kind: we couldn't tell them we were leaving because of the smell, so we said the doctor had advised us to move higher up towards the mountain. We moved into the top house in Bryn Terrace, which was called 'Windy Ridge', and we were very happy there for a while, until my father-in-law sent for Ivor one day and told him to bring his wife and come home to live. We would have our own rooms. Mr. Webb was a well-to-do man who owned a lot of property; he had retired at the age of fifty, and was now sixty years old. His two youngest daughters were keeping house for him. He had a car and a chauffeur, and he wanted to spend some time touring London – he was a Londoner himself by origin – but he didn't want to leave his two girls alone in the house. This was because people brought their rent money to the house, and he was afraid that someone might attempt to break in, and hurt one of the girls. I didn't want to go, being happy where I was, but Ivor's father would not take 'no' for an answer. Mr. and Mrs. Topping of Bryn Terrace were lovely people to live with, and they were expecting their first child as we were expecting ours; but reluctantly we moved our belongings down to Protheroe Street.

I had engaged a midwife, but had told her that she was on no account to ask a doctor to come and see me. However one day she sent for me to come to her house to discuss my pregnancy, and when she opened the door to my knock, I heard Dr. Mebbon's voice coming from the living room. I immediately ran home, because I was afraid that they would terminate the pregnancy if they examined me and found out the truth; I preferred to risk losing my life.

There was great unrest in the valley at that time, and all the talk was of the strike, which seemed imminent. In the weeks before the birth of my baby, I had several attacks of paralysis of the nerves of the spinal cord, but on the last day of April I was seeing Ivor off to work on the night shift. It was eleven o'clock, and he was uneasy going to work that night – indeed he did not want to go, but because he was a contractor he had to go to instruct his men, so I told him to be off. I watched him go along Victoria Street, and then he turned and looked back; he could see I was still clinging to the gate (another attack of paralysis had prevented me from moving, and he came back and said, "I'm staying here tonight."

"You can't," I said. "You can't leave your men without instructions. I'll be all right until you come home." He left, but very reluctantly.

I knew nothing about the birth of a child. My mother had sent my sister Violet, who was now seventeen, to stay with me, so that she could send for help when it was needed, but Violet was in bed, and I was too ill to go up and call her, so I didn't go to bed that night. When Ivor came home at six o'clock, he found me unconscious on the floor. He ran, just as he was, to fetch the midwife who lived just a few minutes away, but she came to the window and shouted down to him, "I'm in bed, I've got the 'flu'."

"You'll have to come down," cried Ivor. "My wife's unconscious."

"You go down, I'll come down later," she said. Eventually she did come down, but by then I had recovered a little, and was feeling better.

"Oh, you've got a long way to go yet," she said. "Call me if it gets worse, I'm going back to bed. I'm not fit to be up yet, I've got the 'flu!" and off she went. Two doors up from us lived a trainee midwife, and now she came down to stay with me; but soon after that I became worse and she rushed downstairs and said to Ivor, "For God's sake tell the nurse to come quick, it's urgent! Tell her I said so."

The nurse jumped out of bed, and quickly ran down to our house. When she saw me, she said, "Oh, my God, it's too late, there's nothing I can do," and she hastily scribbled a note and asked who could run fastest. Violet said she could, and the nurse told her to run as fast as she could and tell Dr. Mebbon to come at once. The doctor ran all the way from his surgery, and walked into my bedroom and asked, "Is this the little lady?" He turned to the nurse then, and said, "My God, nurse, what is the meaning of this? I can do nothing to help." Thereupon he too scribbled a note, asking the other three local doctors to come at once, and once again Violet ran as quickly as she could. Soon Dr. Gillis, Dr. Crawford and Dr. Grey arrived.

Ivor had been sent over to his sister-in-law's house; Mary watched through the window and told him, "There must be something wrong, there are four doctors gone into the house." At that Ivor ran across to our house, but was not allowed in; he was told to wait because there was nothing he could do. Meanwhile the four doctors fought to save my life, but said it was hopeless. They put a sheet over my head and prepared to leave the room, but the nurse stood with her back to the door, and prevented them from leaving. Dr. Mebbon was crying, and said to her. "Get out of the way, nurse, you know what this means, it's manslaughter."

"For God's sake, do something," she said.

"I can't bring back the dead," the doctor told her.

"Well, save the baby, then," she said. There seemed to be nothing they could do for me, but they did try to save the baby by operating; then Dr. Crawford noticed a feeble movement of my heart and worked on it for an hour or more, while the nurse washed the perspiration off his face and those of the other doctors as they fought to save my life. On that afternoon, May 1st, 1926, the baby was born.

They told Ivor that the baby had been so badly damaged that he was unlikely to live more than a few weeks, and for the moment he was too weak to cry. I had been unconscious during the whole operation, and they thought I needed to hear a baby's cry to bring me back to consciousness. Luckily my sister-in-law Dolly Manning hurried up to the house, with her baby, when she heard the news, and the people caring for me knew that they only had to take Dolly's baby from its mother and it would start screaming immediately. So, in desperation, they did this, and the sound of the baby's screams roused me from unconsciousness.

The day my baby was born was the day when all the pits closed down, the first day of the General Strike, which was to last for eight months. All the women in our street were standing at their doors, listening to the latest news coming from our house, and directly opposite us, at their door, stood Mr. and Mrs. Sam Davies. Mr. Davies was the choir master in St. Cynfelin's Church, and on this particular day he was walking up the street while Mrs. Davies stood on the door with their two children, crying bitterly. When he got to his house, Mr. Davies asked his wife why she was crying, and she turned on him in fury and said, "Don't ask me what's the matter! Four doctors are over in that house across the road fighting for the life of that little girl, all because of men like you!"

Mr. Webb, my father-in-law, was a very quiet man. He had been left a widower, with ten children, at the age of thirty-seven. His wife had died soon after the birth of their tenth child, and he vowed then that no woman would ever put her foot over his doorstep – a vow that he kept for twenty years until the day he asked Ivor to bring me there to live. On that morning when my baby was being born, he couldn't stay in the house but went out, and waited outside until someone told him it was all over. When he heard, in the village, that his daughter-in-law was dead, he hurried home to comfort his son, but then, when he heard the good news that I had been revived, he did something he had never done before, not even for his children or his other daughters-in-law: he made a bowl of gruel for me, just as he used to make for his own wife. He carried it to Ivor and told him, "Here, son, I've made this gruel for your wife. Take it up to her, it will do her good. I've made it with rum and pieces of buttered toast in it, just as your mother used to like."

Ivor was so overcome with emotion that he told his father, "You can see the baby, Father – but he can't hold anything less than a five pound note in his hand." However no visitors were allowed to see me yet, so Mr. Webb put a five pound note into Ivor's hand, and told him to give it to the baby.

It was ten days after my baby's birth, when Ivor, who had cooked a nice dinner, asked the doctor (who was just leaving) if he could give me some of the food, because up until then I had only been spoonfed. The doctor put his hand on Ivor's shoulder and said, "If your wife can eat dinner a week today, you'll be a very lucky man. But thank God she's alive. She should never have had that child, and she must certainly never have another one – this will have to be your only child. Ten days ago a miracle was performed – because though your wife is outwardly normal, inwardly she is no more developed than a child of six." And with those words and a final warning, he left the house.

Some weeks later, on a warm Sunday afternoon, Ivor and I were taking our baby for a little walk up the hill towards Cymmer when we saw Mr. and Mrs. Sam Davies and their two daughters, Dolly and Mary, coming towards us. Mrs. Davies said to her husband, "Oh look, Sam, there's little Mrs. Webb and her baby." But at that Mr. Davies said, "Don't ask *me* to look or I'll have the fault for that again!"

TWENTY-ONE

The strike had been on for several weeks now, and our valley, like the other Welsh valleys, was very short of money. The men had no wages coming in, and though the miners were given parish relief notes, the amount varying according to the size of their families, these notes were a loan which had to be repaid when the strike ended. The relief notes were for food only, and had to be handed in to the grocer. The sum allowed for food for a man, woman and child was then ten shillings a week (50p). Ivor said that he didn't want charity, he was going to look for work, so he brought a dilapidated old push-bike for a few shillings and said, "I am going to ride to Somerset to look for work." Our rent in Protheroe Street was seven shillings and sixpence (37½p) a week, and Ivor paid his father the rent for several weeks in advance in order to keep our rooms for us. He also told him that all the vegetables in our allotment at the top of the street were his in lieu of rent while the strike lasted. (It was a large allotment, which had been set out with peas, beans, potatoes etc; they were now coming up and ripening, ready for use.) Meanwhile I had arranged to take the baby and go and live with my mother until Ivor could send for me.

He set off for Hensridge in Somerset, the home of my brother Ben and his wife Maud, who had invited us to go there to live. Ben had told Ivor to cycle up to Cardiff, then take the ferry across to Weston-super-mare where Ben would meet him; from there they could cycle to Hensridge. But though Ivor was a good horseman, he was certainly not a good cyclist, and before he reached Cardiff, both the tyres had burst. He wheeled his bike into a garage, and found that he had to have two new inner tubes and two tyres, which took all his money; then when, after the delay, he reached the landing, the ferry had gone – which was just as well, because he had no money left to pay the fare. So he had to cycle all along the roads to Weston, where he had arranged to meet Ben, only to find that, after waiting for some

171

time, Ben had assumed that Ivor had changed his mind about coming, and had gone home. It was very late that night when Ivor arrived at Hensridge; he did not know the way to Ben's home, so he had had to stop several times to ask the way. (And I was told later that Ivor had been so saddle sore that he had been unable to sit down, even at mealtimes, for several days – and he threw the bike away!)

Ivor managed to find casual work on the farms and in the quarry, and his wages came to one pound ten shillings a week (£1.50). Two weeks later he sent for me to join him, and the baby and I travelled to Somerset, to Ben and Maud's house. It was arranged that I should pay half the rent each week while we were there. Ben and Maud lived in a semi-detached cottage, with a large garden, surrounded by lovely lanes and scenery. They had three daughters: Beryl Emma, who was a pretty child with dark, curly hair, very much like her father, and three and a half years old; Bronwen Pearl, two years old, with long blonde curls; and the baby, Margery, who was nine months old, a beautiful child with dark brown curls. The two eldest children had been born in my mother's house in Ogmore Vale, and the baby had been born in Somerset.

Maud brought me a second-hand pram, and we would take lovely walks down the lanes; soon I could see that the country air was working wonders with our Jack, who was such a delicate child. Then one day Ben called my attention to the fact that Jack was ruptured, and he asked the district nurse to call and see him. The nurse told us that the baby would have to be taken into Bristol hospital immediately, to have an operation as he was suffering from a double hernia. The doctors in Wales had not told me that my baby was likely to die within a few weeks, and as Ivor was against the idea of taking him into hospital, I told the nurse that I would prefer to wait until we got back to Wales, when I could see what my own doctors thought about it.

I was very worried about my baby, but I did not want him to go into Bristol Hospital, because it was such a long way off. I didn't know what to do. Then I wondered what my father's advice would have been, if he had been alive, and I seemed to hear his voice telling me, 'Ritty, do what I always taught you to do, take it to the Lord in prayer'; so I knew what I had to do. I went to see the vicar of Hensridge and asked him if he would christen my baby on the following Sunday because it was urgent.

I explained that I was a Baptist, but I wished my baby to be christened in Church, and he agreed, saying that I must get two godmothers and one godfather, and the ceremony would be held after Sunday School. On that following Sunday our baby was christened as promised, with Mr. and Mrs. Trim as godparents, and my sister-in-law Maud as the second god-mother. After the ceremony the vicar took me to one side for a moment, and asked, "I am curious to know, Mrs. Webb, why you chose to have your child christened here when you are a Baptist."

"You will have noticed that my child is very delicate," I told him. "Before I was married I was told that I must never have a child, or I would lose my life. But I desperately wanted a child, and I have a great belief in the power of prayer, so I prayed that God would grant my wish. When I discovered that I was going to have this child, I knew it was God's answer, and if God was giving me the child, He would give me my life to rear it. Only now the district nurse has told me that my baby needs an urgent operation for a double hernia. I don't want him to go into hospital in Bristol – I have more faith in my own doctors in Wales, but I can't go back there until the strike is over. So I wanted to give my baby to God in Holy Baptism, then I can safely leave him in God's care."

"You have a very strong faith in Christ, haven't you, Mrs. Webb?" said the vicar.

"Yes," I agreed, "I have a strong faith that all is well that is done by God," and I went home, knowing my baby would find new strength.

The wonderful air of Somerset was working wonders for my health as well as the baby's, and I felt much improved. Maud and I spent hours walking round the lanes with our babies; we were great friends, and that stay in Somerset was very happy. We were allowed to go into a nearby orchard and pick as many apples as we liked, while there was an abundance of black berries and Ben's garden was well filled with fresh vegetables, so we benefitted not only from the good air, but also from the fresh food.

One day I took a walk into the village to buy some wool, so that I could knit a warm suit for the baby (Winter was drawing in by now.) As I was walking back with my baby snug in his cradle-style Welsh shawl, we passed some men, who were re-thatching a cottage roof, and they called out 'Good afternoon' to me. They evidently mistook me for a gipsy because of the way I carried my baby, so they added 'bad weather for your trade today, missus!' I just laughed and bid them 'good day'. When I told Maud about it later, she said they thought I was a 'didikoi' because I carried my baby like the gipsies.

Another day, when Christmas was near, we received a message from the colliery, asking Ivor to come back as the strike was all but over, so reluctantly we said goodbye to Somerset and to my brother and his family, and returned to Wales. When we got to our home in Caerau, we found that my youngest sister-in-law had got married and taken up residence in our rooms. We were welcomed back by my father-in-law, but Winnie resented our return because now she had to get out of those rooms (for which we had continued to pay rent all the time we were in Somerset), and set up home in her father-in-law's sitting room.

The next day I went up to see Nurse Aubrey, and tell her what the district nurse in Somerset had said. Jack looked every inch a beautiful, bouncing baby in the blue and white suit I had knitted for him; he was eight months old. Nurse Aubrey was amazed to see him looking so well, and said, "Yes, my dear, we knew about the rupture, but your baby was so delicate that we didn't expect him to live more than two or three weeks, and we didn't like to tell you about it. Will you bring your baby to the clinic on Tuesday, because I would like the doctor to see him?"

So on Tuesday I took my baby in his little blue and white suit to the clinic. There were two doctors there, and one of them took Jack from Nurse Aubrey and held him up for everyone to see him, while they told all the people who were there, "Look at him! Here is the wonder baby – his mother died before he was born, and we brought them both back to life."

Then the doctor said to me, "When you didn't bring the baby to the clinic, we thought it was because he had died. I don't know what you have done for this child, but he must have had wonderful care, and if you continue to give him the same care in the future, then he will never need an operation." At that I told them of his christening and said, "He's had no special care, and I prefer to think this is the work of the Lord, and the result of the power of prayer which is free for everyone."

Life was not the same now in Protheroe Street. Everything was all right while Ivor was around, but the minute his back was turned, Winnie was badgering me to go back to Windy Ridge to live, and telling me "This is *my* home." Life became intolerable; Winnie committed spiteful little acts to make my life unpleasant, and I couldn't tell Ivor or my father-in-law. My husband would have defended me against these things, of course, but that would have caused an upset in the family; still, the pressure was beginning to break me and my nerves were getting bad.

We provided all the coal for the whole house, but we only had a small fire grate in our room, while my sister-in-law had a large fireplace which also heated the water. It took an awful lot of coal to keep that fire going, so as well as paying the rent, we also paid for their heating. Whichever shift Ivor was working on, before leaving he would always give me instructions to make sure that the water was kept hot and that there was plenty of it, so that he could have his bath when he came home from work. Miners came home in their pit dirt in those day, and most of them had to wash in a tin bath in front of the fire; there were no pithead baths. We were fortunate enough to have a bathroom in our house, and Ivor's first words when he came in from work were always, "Is the water hot?" I would say, "Yes, it's lovely and hot for you, I've been out stoking." Then Ivor would go into the bathroom – only to find that someone had drained all the hot water out of the tank and it was filling up with cold water. I would have to build up my own little fire, and put a bucket of water on it to boil, so that Ivor could have a wash before eating his dinner. Then I would have to put sheets of paper down on the floor in front of the fire, ready for Ivor to wash in the tin bath.

Ivor knew what the trouble was, and said, "I know what's happening, they are trying to push us out so that Winnie can have our rooms, but they won't get rid of us. We'll stick it out." Then they tried different tactics, using my baby. (All this, of course, was done behind Ivor's back, while he was at work.) There was a little three-year-old boy living in the house, who was allowed to do whatever he wanted to do, but my baby was not even allowed to go out to the passageway – they said he would mark the wallpaper. We had French windows in our one and only living room, and these led out into the back yard, while from the back yard a long flight of steps went down into the garden. To give little Jack a bit of fresh air, I would let him out into the back yard to toddle around, but first I would place his

175

high chair across the top of the steps to prevent him from getting too close and falling down into the garden. By the side of the back door was a tap, and under this was a wooden tub which had to be kept wet to preserve the wood. For my baby's safety, while he played out there, I would empty this tub into the drain and turn it upside down; then I would go into the house to do my chores, thinking my child was safe – but as soon as I was indoors someone would come out, remove the chair, and refill the tub with water.

Every time this happened, I would have to fish Jack out of the tub by his legs, and this completely shattered me and damaged my health. I didn't discuss their treatment of me with Ivor, for fear of creating animosity, but I did tell him that I had to fish our baby out of the water, and I told him that we would have to go from there. However Ivor would not hear of this; all he would say was, "Keep the baby in from the back then." Soon my life became so intolerable and my state of health so low, that I thought I must be pregnant again to account for it, but when I told Ivor he said it was impossible, and I couldn't be. I made him promise me, though, that if I *was* pregnant and I died in childbirth, he would take our baby away from that house and out to his eldest sister, in America. Her husband was the commissioner of police in Maryland, and I knew that Arthur and Ginny would take great care of our baby. Ivor promised, but still insisted that I could not be pregnant.

Although I knew that I could not discuss this mental strain with Ivor and his father, I knew I could take my troubles to my Heavenly Father in prayer, and that is what I did. It was a wonderful relief to unburden myself, and to know that I would be helped. I had not been pregnant when I thought I was, but soon I really was so.

One day I put my baby in the shawl and left that house of unhappiness, not knowing where I was going or what I was going to do. I just walked, and talked with God, asking Him to direct me in the right direction, wherever that might be, until I found myself knocking on a door half a mile away, in Humphries Terrace.

A woman of about forty came to the door, and behind her stood her mother, a woman in her sixties. I told them that I was seeking apartments, and asked them if they had rooms to let. "I am Mrs. Webb," I told them, "I've come from Protheroe Street and I want to move in with people who will be kind to my baby, because I am expecting another child."

The woman asked me in and gave me a cup of tea, then asked me if I was Mr. Alf Webb's daughter-in-law. "Yes," I said, "I married his son Ivor."

"This is Mr. Webb's house," they told me. "We are his tenants, did he send you to us?"

"No," I said, "No-one has sent me here. I live with the Webbs in Protheroe Street, and I was directed here. But now that you know who I am, perhaps you won't want me here?"

"We have two rooms," they told me, "and you will be very welcome here."

The older lady took my baby in her arms while Mrs. Morgan, her daughter, showed me the rooms. They were a far cry from the lovely rooms I had in Protheroe Street, but when I looked at my baby in Mrs. Howells's arms, I knew that what the rooms lacked in comfort would be compensated for by love and peace for my baby and myself. Mrs. Howells said, "Don't worry about your baby, I'll take care of you when it comes."

After Ivor had bathed and had his dinner, I broke the news that we were moving from Protheroe Street. Ivor was up in arms at once. "I am not leaving Protheroe Street to go and live down there," he said.

"If I stay in this house," I said, "I'll only be fit for a mental home, and then what will become of my babies? I know that my baby and I will be happy with those kind people, and I will get my health back there. If you don't want to come with us, Ivor, you can stay here, but the baby and I are going as soon as possible. The choice is yours: this house and your sisters, or me and your child."

I left it at that, but when the van came to pick up my furniture, Ivor was ready to come with me. He helped the men to load the van, and there was no question as to where he wanted to be. When we put our furniture in the new rooms, I quoted my father's saying – "In a cottage there is joy, when there's love at home" – to Ivor, and we truly found love in that house. Mrs. Howells adored my baby from the moment we walked in, and Jack adored her and soon learned to call her 'grandma'; she never ate a meal without him on her lap. There were four other children in the house, two girls and two boys; the girls were in their teens, while the younger of Mrs. Morgan's boys was about

177

six years old. That street, too, was nice to live in, and though there was no bathroom in the house and Ivor had to bath in front of our living room fire, we were as happy there as we had been in Windy Ridge with Ethel and Will Topping. (They had now sold up and gone to Australia to live.)

TWENTY-TWO

We were now looking forward to the birth of our second child. At least, I was looking forward; Ivor was very worried, remembering the last time. The midwife had been down to see Mrs. Howells, to arrange for the care I would be needing, and Dr. Mebbon had also spoken to both Mrs. Howells and Mrs. Morgan; although I was not included in that interview, Mrs. Howells was told about my first childbirth and the difficulties that might be expected with the second. The doctor told Mrs. Howells that he would be watching me carefully, and he asked her to do the same, and in particular to call him immediately she noticed any sign of my going into labour.

"Don't wait for her to be ill," he insisted. "Call me at once. Don't call the nurse, call me. I will see to everything."

After this Mrs. Howells became very worried, and would not let me out of her sight. I scarcely knew I had little Jackie, she took such care of him, and she insisted on my bed being brought down into their parlour, both so that she could take better care of me, and for fear of little Jack, who was now a year and five months old, might fall down the stairs.

On a Saturday at the beginning of October I had a 'false alarm'. Now, according to the old wives' tales, a 'false alarm' meant that the mother would go round the clock before the real event, or else she would go the full circle of another week. Ivor was working the afternoon shift that week, and I would cook a full dinner for him when he came home at eleven o'clock at night, but earlier on Mrs. Howells had a cooked dinner with me in my room, because her daughter only cooked dinner on a Sunday. Every night, after we had had our meal together, Mrs. Howells would sit by the fire, with Jack in her arms, and wait with me for Ivor to come home. Her eyes seemed to bore into me, and sometimes my hair would stand on end with the force of her staring at me. She wouldn't let me put the baby to bed, but would say, "No, let me hold him until you are ready to go."

179

Quite unknown to me, Mrs. Howells had gone to see 'Marie Jolly', a fortune teller who lived in Tonna Road. (Her real name was Mrs. Davies). She was considered to be an excellent fortune teller, and she had told Mrs. Howells that on the coming Saturday the house would be filled with doctors and police, and there would be crowds of people around the place. That Saturday would be the day of the 'full circle' for me, when my baby should be born, and this was why Mrs. Howells would not let me out of her sight, because she assumed that according to the fortune teller, I would be dead on Saturday. This fear for my safety was the cause of a bad dream she had. According to her dream book, blood on hands meant death to the dreamer, and in her dream her hands were covered with blood. Then again, I was very fond of reading, and some weeks previously I had bought a book called 'Ashes to Ashes'; now Mrs. Howells had taken it away from me, saying "You mustn't read this until after you've had your baby. I'll read it first as I've nothing to read, and when you are comfortable, with your new baby in your arms, then I'll give you the book."

On Friday night we had corned beef hash, green peas and creamed potatoes for our dinner, (I always gave Mrs. Howells the same sized dinner as my husband, as she was a hearty eater), and we both thoroughly enjoyed it. Later we were sitting, waiting for Ivor to come in – Mrs. Howells had refused to go to bed until Ivor came in, and at eleven o'clock we heard his footsteps. Mrs. Howells got up, and said, "I'll go now, Mr. Webb is here."

She met my husband at the door, and said to him, "I'm going to bed now, Mr. Webb. Watch Mrs. Webb, won't you?"

"Yes, I will," Ivor told her.

"At the first sign, call me," urged Mrs. Howells. "Don't wait for her to go bad."

We had a paraffin oil lamp in our room; there was electricity in the house, but Mrs. Howells liked to read in bed, and she was only allowed to read by candle light. She was given one candle to last the week, and by that night she had just an inch left, which she lit. She had walked up just two stairs when she called to Ivor, "You will call me, Mr. Webb, won't you, you won't let her go bad."

"Yes, I'll call you," Ivor assured her, but she called out two or three times more, as if she was afraid to go to bed and leave me.

She reached her bedroom door, and called again, "I'm going into my bedroom now, Mr. Webb, I'll leave the door open. You will take great care, won't you?"

"Don't worry, Mrs. Howells," Ivor said. "I'll take great care, and I'll call you at the first sign. Good night, Mrs. Howells." (We didn't know, of course, of her great fear, or her visit to the fortune teller.)

That was my husband's last shift of the week, but most miners worked on the Saturday, and Mr. Morgan would be going to work in the morning. (Miners worked nine hour shifts, six days a week, and it was not an unusual sight to see half a dozen men walking down the street, covered in pit dust and carrying a stretcher, bringing home a dead or injured miner.) When we had cleared up after Ivor's bath, we retired to our bed in the parlour, which was all prepared for the arrival of our new baby. I was feeling in pretty good form.

Just after six o'clock the following morning, when Mr. Morgan had gone to work and his wife was taking a cup of tea up to her mother, we suddenly heard her voice calling, "Mr. Webb, come quick, come quick!" Ivor was half asleep, and while he was feeling around for his dressing gown, the voice came again, "Come quick, Mr. Webb, come quick, I think my mother is dead."

Ivor ran quickly upstairs to Mrs. Howells's bedroom. The little bedroom table was drawn up to the bed, with her candle close so that she could see to read, and Mrs. Howells was in a crouched position, where she had settled herself for reading, with the book close to the candle. She must have died immediately she started to read, because the book had fallen across the candle and put it out. There was a brown smoke stain on the page she had been reading. Her little nine-year-old grandson was sleeping at her side and when his mother came into the room, he told her that Granny was cold. The house was filled with police and doctors just as Marie Jolly had foretold. My little boy and I were taken into a house lower down the street and my bed was taken back upstairs so that they could put Mrs. Howells's body in the parlour. She had been dead for such a long time, in a sitting position, that they had to break her arms and legs in order to lay her out.

It was thought that the shock of this death had killed my baby, because although it was due at the end of September or the

181

beginning of October, there was no sign of anything happening; also I had felt no movement for the last month. Mr. and Mrs. Morgan had to attend an inquest in Cardiff because of the sudden death of her mother, and as Iris, their eldest girl, was in bed with tonsillitis, they asked me if I would keep an eye on her until they returned, and show the doctor in when he called. When Dr. Mebbon arrived to see Iris, I took him into her bedroom; he looked at her, and then at me, and said to me, "Get out of this room at once. What are you doing in here, Mrs. Webb?" I told him about the Morgans having to go to Cardiff.

"I'm taking her into hospital at once," he said. "It's the worst form of diphtheria." She was removed immediately. When Mrs. Morgan came back, she said her mother had died from malnutrition.

I missed Mrs. Howells very much; I had become very attached to her, and my little boy kept asking for 'grandma'. She had been a very good friend to me since I had moved down to Humphries Terrace. My father-in-law, as I have said, was a very shy and quiet man, but from the things that Mrs. Howells had told me, he seemed to be very concerned about the birth of my baby, which was due any day now. Although he was a man of property and owned the house in which I was now living, he engaged a rent collector to collect his rents and look after the property. Mrs. Howells and her daughter had never met their landlord, but several times while she was out with baby Jack, Mrs. Howells had noticed a man looking over our garden wall, and one day she stopped and spoke to him, discovering that he was Mr. Alf Webb. He was very interested in the baby, which was why she asked him who he was, and she told me that he was very concerned about us, although he was a man who hid his emotions. He was trying to discover from Mrs. Howells why we had chosen to go down to live in Humphries Terrace.

I had been very unhappy while I lived in Protheroe Street, but I had never disclosed my feelings either to my father-in-law or his daughters. We had not quarrelled, and there were no ill feelings between us, so he had not known at all why I should have wanted to leave there and go elsewhere to live, and as I hadn't even told Mrs. Howells why I had left Protheroe Street, she could not satisfy Mr. Webb's curiosity. However she gave him a very good account of Ivor and myself, and told him that we were very happy living there, while she was happy to have us, and loved my baby and was very anxious about my forthcoming confinement. Now poor Mrs. Howells was gone, and I felt her loss.

I still felt no movement from my baby, and it wasn't until the sixth of November that Ivor called on Mr. Morgan in the middle of the night, and asked him to fetch the doctor. The doctor's surgery was three quarters of a mile away, and the snow was deep on the ground, and when Mr. Morgan returned with Dr. Mebbon, we could see that he had gone through all that snow in his stockinged feet.

Such was the haste with which he had run for the doctor, that he hadn't even stopped to put a shirt or jacket or shoes on. The doctor sent my husband to fetch Nurse Aubrey, while the other doctors stayed on standby, and my little girl was born later that day. It was a forceps delivery, and I was given an anaesthetic, but there was only the one doctor and one nurse in attendance this time; the birth was easier than they had anticipated.

A few days later, Iris came home from the fever hospital, and her mother brought her into the bedroom to see the baby – though I couldn't allow her to nurse the baby, because I knew from my own nursing experience that it would be unwise to allow a patient newly discharged from a fever hospital to nurse a baby just a few days old. Soon after my little girl was born, Ivor brought Jack up to see his little sister. Jack looked at the baby, slapped her face, and said to her, "Go home, you made my mammy cry!" But when we explained to him that this was his little sister and she was going to live with us, he became devoted to her, and called her 'his Pearly'. One day I was showing him a picture of Goldilocks and the Three Bears, and Jack looked at the picture and said, "Dat am my Pearly, dat Pearly my goldilock"; that is what he always called her until she started school, she was always his Goldilocks. Jack had very dark hair and his father's colouring, but my features, whereas Pearl was like me entirely. She had a mop of golden curls and bluey-green eyes.

Very early one morning when the baby was just a few days old, my throat became vey sore, and once again Mr. Morgan had to run to fetch the doctor in the middle of the night. After he had gone, Ivor realized that I was choking and something had to be done quickly. We had no telephone, and the doctors attended their patients on foot, so we knew it would be a long time before the doctor arrived. Ivor ran downstairs and rekindled the fire with the dried wood prepared for the morning, then put an onion between the burning sticks to soften. In those days colliers wore thick woollen stockings for work, and while the onion was softening, Ivor got one of his working stockings; then he put the softened onion inside it, ran back up the stairs and clamped it quickly to my throat. I was fighting for my breath when Ivor put the burning hot onion on my throat, and I didn't feel the heat of it, but it did the trick, because whatever it was that had caused the blockage burst, just as the doctor came into the room.

The doctor stood gasping for breath after his long run, then he took my husband's hand and shook it, saying to him, "Thank God you had the sense to do that, you saved her life. She would have choked before I got there."

The next day, when the doctor called at the house, I told him that the baby was having difficulty in breathing, and wasn't taking her feeds, and that I feared there was something wrong with her throat. He looked at the baby and then he told me to turn my head away. "She is going to scream," he said, "but don't be alarmed. I will hurt her, but only for a very short while."

I saw him put his two fingers into her throat, then she screamed, and I turned my head away. After that the baby was all right. The doctor said he would have taken us both into hospital, but the diphtheria ward was so full that they were sleeping two to a bed.

The day my daughter was born, Ivor sent a telegram to my mother telling her of the birth, and she and my stepfather came over, and took Jack back with them for a few days. But the following day they came back, and my mother said, "I had to bring him back, Rit, God love him, he was breaking his little heart. If he had been crying, we could have comforted him, but he didn't cry, he didn't make a sound. We took him to bed, but he wanted to go 'bye bye' with his mammy. So we didn't go to bed, and Dai spent the night riding him around on his back. It broke our hearts to see him so sad. He went into the passage and pulled on my coat, which was hanging on the stand, and said, 'Take me to my mammy – please!' And so, God love him, I had to bring him this morning, I can't see him suffer. He'll be better with you, Rit."

"I'm glad you brought him back," Ivor told my mother. "I

don't think Rit could have lived much longer without him."

We had a young girl from Tonna Road who came in each day to help with the children; her name was Harriet Davies, and she loved them.

(She was the daughter of Marie Jolly who had told Mrs. Howells her fortune.) When Pearl was three months old, she had chicken pox, and to our surprise, I also had it, although it is a child's complaint. We took a weekly paper called 'John Bull' that carried an insurance policy with it, covering adult readers. They would pay out five pounds to any adult reader who contracted chicken pox, as it was a child's complaint – and they knew it would be very unusual if they had to pay such a policy to an adult! So we sent a medical paper to 'John Bull' and duly received our five pounds. There were placards outside every newagent telling the world that 'John Bull' had paid out five pounds to Mrs. Webb of Caerau because she had suffered from chicken pox. (Five pounds was more than some men's weekly pay packets in those days.)

Our daughter Pearl was nine months old, when I was passing through the kitchen, one day, on my way out to the garden and I heard the tenant telling Mr. Gould, the rent collector, "I'm sorry I can't pay the rent today, the 'partments haven't paid me again." I turned and went back into my room and got my rent book, then, when Mr. Gould was passing my door, I handed him my rent book. He looked at it, and said, "But you don't owe anything, your rent book is clear. – I see your name is Webb. What Webb are you?"

"I am Alf Webb's son," Ivor answered.

Gould turned to my husband, and said, "Good heavens, what are you doing down here, Ivor, in a place like this?"

"We live here," said Ivor.

"Why doesn't your father give you a house?" Gould asked.

"My father's houses are all occupied," said Ivor. "He hasn't got an empty house to give us."

"Well, then," said Mr. Gould, "you shall have this house. I'll put the rent-book in your name, instead of Mrs. Howells's. I haven't had any rent since she died."

"Oh no, Mr. Gould, don't do that," we both said. "We won't accept it. These people were kind enough to take us in when we needed a place, and we won't repay their kindness by robbing them of their home."

"But they owe a hundred pounds in rent," said Mr. Gould.

"I'm sorry," I said, "but that's not my concern. I pay my half of the rent regularly, as I did when I lived in Protheroe Street, and I'd like you to tell my father-in-law that my rent book is clear. Perhaps if you were to put the book in Mrs. Morgan's name, you might be more successful."

Mr. Gould left then, but a few days later he returned, and said to Ivor, "Pack up, you are going from here. Here are the keys to your new house in Cymmer Road." So a few days later we moved up to a house of our own in Cymmer, and instead of two rooms, I now owned eight, four up and four down. We didn't have enough furniture to fill all the rooms, but we made a few rooms very comfortable, and I used to carry my little ones around the house, showing them the empty rooms. "Look, this is all ours," I would say to them. The only thing that marred my happiness was the fact that I was nervous when Ivor wasn't there. He couldn't work the night shift at the colliery, because I was afraid to be alone.

Someone gave me a kitten, a persian cat, and as it was growing, I taught it to do tricks. It took to its training so well that at meals I would put the baby in her high chair and with one cushion, Jack would have two cushions to lift him up to the table, and puss would sit on three cushions, with his front paws on the edge of the table. Before meals I taught the children, and the cat, to put their hands together, and then, heads bowed and eyes closed, to say grace. The cat was so quick to learn that as soon as he heard me say 'Time for grace', he would put his head down on his two paws and leave it there until we said 'Amen'. Puss knew that 'Amen' meant he could tuck into his food, which was placed at the side of the table, and the children would do the same. After food I would say 'heads down', and puss would do the same as before; then again, at the sound of 'Amen' he would jump down off the chair.

One morning there was a knock on the door. It was Gertie's little boy Desmond, and he said, "Hello Daunty Day (Auntie Ray), I've come to play with Jackie." He stayed with me all day, and then came every day for a whole week; now that Jack had someone to play with, it gave me more time for my chores, and they played so happily that week that it was marvellous for me. On the Sunday, though, Gertie called at our house and asked me, "Ray, does Desmond call here?"

186

"Yes, Gertie," I said. "Thanks for sending him up, they've had a wonderful week together thanks to Desmond, he's been a little gem."

"I'll give him little gem," said Gertie. "The little so and so, he was supposed to have been in school."

"I didn't know he had started school, Gertie," I said. "How did you know that he was here, then, if you didn't send him?"

"I had a letter from the headmistress," Gertie told me, "to tell me he hadn't been to school for a whole week. I asked him where he had been, and he said to me, 'To school, of course, Dertie' (he couldn't pronounce Gertie), and to stop me asking him any more about school, the cunning little devil said, 'Dertie, Daunty Day got a shop in her house.' 'Where is the shop then?' I asked him. 'In her pantry,' he said, 'she's got a big shop in her pantry'."

"I suppose he has seen the extra tins of food I am getting in for Christmas," I told Gertie. "They are on the top shelf of my pantry. Still, any time you'd like to send him up to me when he is not in school, Jack would be thrilled to have him."

I was nervous about being left alone in the house with the children mainly because I had always lived in 'rooms', where there were always a lot of children about and activities going on. Cymmer Road was a very select part of Caerau, and the people there kept themselves very much to themselves; thought the houses were bigger than the rest of the houses lower down the road, they did not sublet their rooms. Every night at seven o'clock Ivor would go down to the sweet shop and buy me a bar of chocolate, and this was meant to bribe me to let him go down to the Station Hotel, where he could have a drink with his workmates and talk over the plans for the next day's work. He didn't stay out long, it was his rule that we should all be in bed by nine o'clock when he was working on the day shift, because he had to be in the colliery before six o'clock in the morning.

One night Ivor had settled himself for sleep, but my own restlessness kept him awake, and he said to me, "What is the matter with you, Ray, can't you go to sleep, I won't be fit for work in the morning if I don't get my sleep."

"I can't sleep, Ivor," I said. "There's something that won't let me go to sleep, the voice of my old friend Renee Hoskins. She's calling me all the time, and by the sound of her voice, she's very distressed, she keeps calling me, Rachael, Rachael. Don't you remember me telling you about her, Ivor? She was the tall girl who always played the bride in our 'wedding games' at school because she was tall and very pretty. I told you how one night I met her and told her I was getting married in the morning; and if my eyes hadn't been filled with stardust, I would have seen the sadness in *her* eyes. She took my hands and begged me not to marry because it could be hell. Then she went on her way. Later Mother told me that Irene now had a baby girl as well as her little boy, but she was not happy in her marriage."

"Try to forget her and go to sleep," said Ivor. "Put her out of your mind. It's probably just your imagination because you were thinking about her."

But I couldn't get her out of my mind, and the next morning I wrote to my mother, asking her to find out for me if there was anything wrong with Irene. For several nights after that I was haunted by her voice calling me. I couldn't stop hearing it, try as I would. Then a letter came from my mother, saying that Irene has passed away. Rumour had it that she had fallen down the stairs and broken her neck. My mother said that the little boy, now six years old, was being well cared for by Irene's parents, while the little girl had been taken away by her father. It had not been a happy marriage.

That night I was again very disturbed by Irene's voice. Ivor had read my mother's letter, and I told him that I believed Irene was unhappy about her litte girl and was trying to tell me something. Ivor believed in spiritualism, and he surprised me when he said, "Tell Irene if she wants us to have her little girl, then we will have her and bring her up as one of ours. We've got two children, another one wouldn't make any difference. We would give her a good home for your friend's sake."

But after that night Renee was at peace, and I did not hear her voice again.

TWENTY-THREE

By now it was nearing Christmas in our new house in Cymmer Road, Caerau. We had previously been sub-tenants in a house owned by my father-in-law, where we had kept geese, but Council regulations forbade us to keep live poultry in the back of the house in Cymmer Road, so Ivor killed the geese and the one gander, and gave a goose each to my mother in Ogmore Vale and my father-in-law in Protheroe Street, for Christmas.

Our next problem was how to cook the gander for ourselves, since it weighed twenty-five pounds (after cleaning), and the oven was too small to take it. On Christmas Eve Ivor brought his brother-in-law home to supper, and afterwards, when the children's stockings had been filled and their toys had been put out, ready for the morning, he said to me, "You go to bed, Ray, Ted and I are going to stay up all night to cook the gander." Then they began to clear the brass and the fire irons away from the fireplace in the back kitchen, after which they took a big nail, a meathook and some string and improvised a spit, from which they hung the gander by its legs. On the floor, underneath the gander's neck, they put a large grease-pan, and then they settled themselves down with their bottles of beer, one on each side of the fireplace, taking it in turns to rotate the gander over the roaring fire.

Next morning, after putting a match to the sitting room fire so that the babies would be warm while they played with their new toys, I went into the kitchen, expecting to find a greasy mess. But to my surprise everything was spick and span: not only had the men cooked the gander beautifully, but they had cleaned up all the mess as well. Yet my biggest surprise was still to come; for as they had talked in the night, the men had decided to emigrate to Australia!

When I heard that, I told Ivor that though I had always had a wish to live in Australia, now that I had a husband and two beautiful children and a little home of my own, I wanted to stay in Cymmer Road, not be uprooted again. However Ted, who was a Londoner and had no work in Wales, was anxious to go to what he called 'a land of opportunity', and when he left my house that day, he took with him the address of my sister Emily in Western Australia; he said he would write straight away.

Ivor had said he would be quite happy to stay in Caerau, but Ted had been persistent. Now Ivor looked at me. "Don't worry, Ray, nothing will come of it," he said. "Dolly won't want to go, she'll put a stop to it." And so we decided that that would be the end of it, and we'd hear no more about the scheme. But a few weeks later, to our surprise, we were called to a medical examination, as required by the emigration authorities because my sister Emily had nominated not Ted and Dolly, as they had hoped, but Ivor, our two children and myself; although we did not know it at the time, she had flatly refused to be responsible for two families.

Soon it was Easter, and on the Thursday before Good Friday a stranger called at our house. He said he was a representative of the Australian shipping company, and asked where my husband was. I told him Ivor was at work in the colliery, whereupon he said my husband would have to be sent for immediately so that he could go with him to London, ready to sail for Australia on the Saturday. So I sent a message to the colliery asking Ivor to come home at once, and while we waited for him, I told the man that it would be impossible for us to travel back with him, because my baby had pneumonia. However it seemed that it was only Ivor who would be going as yet, and the man asked me why our family wanted to go to Australia. I explained that my child had been ill and the doctor had advised us to take both of the little ones to a warmer climate. Naturally we wished to travel as a family, and I was anxious to know why only my husband was wanted.

"Well" said the man, "It's like this, the S.S. Orsova will be sailing for Australia on Saturday and one of the passengers has died. The passage is too precious to waste, and the authorities have chosen your husband to fill the place because he intends to go up into the wilds, not to the big towns like everyone else. Australia's great need is for pioneers like your husband."

"But I can't manage on my own, with two babies to bring up," I protested.

"Put it this way," suggested the man. "Your husband is doing

190

a dangerous job in the colliery and if you stop him from coming away with me, he could go to work tomorrow and be killed. Then you would be without him forever. Perhaps this is fate giving you a chance to save his life?"

I had always been afraid of the colliery, and the man was so persuasive that I could not argue any longer. "If my husband is willing to go on alone, I won't stand in his way," I said.

When Ivor did arrive home and heard the news, he protested that he could not leave his wife and family, but the man pointed out, "You can't take a woman and two babies to the place where you are going without making proper preparations for them there. And your wife will soon follow you." At that I asked him how he thought I was going to travel fourteen thousand miles alone but for two small babies, one of whom couldn't walk at all, while the other was just toddling, but he assured us that there would be plenty of people to help me and the children throughout the voyage.

After that we had just a few hours to dispose of all our furniture and give the tenancy of the house back to my father-in-law, in time for us to leave Caerau early on the Friday morning. Luckily we did not have much furniture to get rid of, but though it was all new and fully paid up, we had to sell it so quickly that we were forced to take whatever we could get for it. Soon only our bed was left, and my sister Dolly was going to take that when I went to stay with my mother until it was time for me to go too.

Early next morning Ivor borrowed his father's car and chauffeur to drive us and our small possessions to Ogmore Vale. We had Ivor's two suitcases, labelled for Australia, and our babies' cots. On Saturday morning I left the children with my mother and went with Ivor to see him off on the ten o'clock train from Blackmill to Bridgend. While we were waiting at Bridgend Station Dolly and Ted arrived, having also come to see Ivor off, but we were all too upset and emotional to make conversation, and all I could do was to repeat over and over again, "Don't worry, we will be alright." When the moment of parting came, Ivor's face was as white as a sheet, and neither of us could speak. Then Dolly and Ted went back to Caerau, and I returned to my mother's house with a very heavy heart.

Ivor had not been able to get the money – some £300 – due to him from the colliery, but he had arranged for someone to collect it and give it to me the following weekend when I went over to Caerau. Meanwhile, when we had got to Ogmore Vale we had divided the money that we received from the sale of the furniture equally between us. I put twenty pounds of my half share on one side towards my passage to Australia, and a further ten pounds or so for landing money and spending money for the journey, after which there was enough left to give my mother a little for our keep.

The following weekend I went back to Caerau to collect the three hundred pounds due to Ivor from the colliery, but, to my dismay, when I went to see Mr. Petty, the man Ivor had asked to collect the money on his behalf, he gave me four pounds, and ten shillings (the exact amount that Ivor gave me each week for the housekeeping), and said that that was all that was due to me. I couldn't believe this, and felt sure that there must be some mistake, but in my distress I went straight up to my two friends Rene and Oscar in Corn Hill.

Rene and Oscar were anxious to buy our perambulator, which was practically new (I had never used it, not being strong enough to push it up and down the steep hill). As it happened, I had bought the pram on hire purchase from Mr. Lockyer of Maesteg; the total cost was seven pounds ten shillings, of which I had so far paid four pounds, and the idea now was that Rene and Oscar should keep the pram and take over payment of the debt, if Mr. Lockyer was willing. I told them about the £300, and then we went down to see Mr. Lockyer, who was an elderly gentleman with a very abrupt manner. I explained what had happened and gave him my repayment book, whereupon he said, rather sharply, "Well, and what do you want me to do about it?"

Evidently he had not quite grasped what I was trying to tell him, but I told him that I wanted the account transferred to Mrs. Rene Jones because my husband had gone to Australia and I had left Caerau to live with my mother until I was able to go to join him. "What is your mother's address?" Mr. Lockyer asked. I told him, feeling very nervous by now, and he looked at my repayment book.

"You've paid more than half of it," he said. "Why don't you take the pram with you?"

"I can't take it with me, Mr. Lockyer," I explained, "Because I can't afford to pay the three pounds ten shillings still owing on it."

"Then what do you expect me to do about it!" he shouted. "It's nothing to do with me, your husband has left these waters and his debt goes with him."

"But it wasn't his debt," I tried to explain again. "My husband didn't know it wasn't paid for, it's my debt, and I'm the one that cannot pay."

This time he seemed to understand, and, turning to Rene, he said, "Very well then, Mrs. Jones, if she wants to lose all that money, take it." And so Rene went home happy with her pram, while I went home bitterly disappointed at not receiving the £300 as expected. But at least the episode of the pram had a happy sequel. A few days later a note was sent down to my mother's house from the lesser hall in Ogmore Vale, asking me to call in as soon as possible. Although I went, I felt very worried, not knowing what on earth they wanted of me, but sure it must be something very unpleasant. I gave my name to the clerk, and then I was taken into a large room so filled with the most beautiful clothes that it looked just like a draper's shop.

"Mrs. Webb," said the woman in charge, "you are to choose anything you require, to the value of ten pounds, with the compliments of Mr. Lockyer of Maesteg." And so I left there weighed down with parcels containing the best quality clothes for both myself and the children.

But despite this piece of good fortune, I still had no money to provide for my babies. My mother told me not to worry – somehow we would manage: but I knew my stepfather's wage was small, and in desperation I spent my last few precious shillings on a second-hand sewing machine. There was no dressmaker in Lewistown, and soon I had plenty of orders coming in – so many, indeed, that my mother and stepfather cared for the children while I spent from early in the morning to late at night at my machine.

In August came the news that we were to travel in the S.S. Ballranald to join Ivor in Australia. In the meantime I had been receiving weekly letters from him, but as his writing was so small, and I was only partially sighted, it sometimes took me as much as a week to understand them; they were far too personal for me to be able to ask anyone to read them to me. They would begin with "Don't be in a hurry to come out here, love," and end with "For God's sake come out quick, it's terrible out here without you," and I hardly knew what to make of them! I knew that if Ivor was not happy in Australia, his father would pay for him to come home, but since he did not say exactly that, in the end I decided he was just lonely for me and the children.

After receiving confirmation that I was to sail on the S.S. Ballranald, I wrote to my sister Violet in London, asking her to meet me at Paddington at six o'clock in the evening on the day before I was due to sail, as I wanted to say goodbye to her. Then, on the morning of my departure, I wished my friends and neighbours goodbye and my mother and I set off, carrying the children and some hand luggage, on the mile and a half walk to Blackmill. (The main luggage had been sent off in advance.) At Blackmill we caught a train to Bridgend, and there, waiting for us on the platform, were Ted and Dolly Manning. Dolly asked my mother how I was taking it, and Mother told her that I had been wonderful about it and not the least bit upset; she did not know of all the tears of sorrow I had shed in the darkness of the night after parting from Ivor. And yet now my heart was breaking because I was leaving my mother and all those others I loved, and I said under my breath, "Please God, send the train quickly." The words of an old song kept running through my mind – 'Now the time has come for parting, and the tears are starting.'

At last the train arrived, and I kissed Ted and Dolly goodbye, fighting back the tears as I did so. Then Mother came into the compartment to help settle my little ones, and as she turned to leave, I could not stay dry-eyed any longer. My little three-year-old asked me why I was crying, and I said 'Because I won't see Granny any more', 'Don't cry,' he said, 'You *will* see her again.'

There was a young girl in the compartment with us, sitting near the window, and she asked me where I was going, saying that she herself was on the way back to London after a holiday at home. I explained that I was going to Australia, and would be sailing on the S.S. Ballranald in the morning, but in the meantime my sister was meeting us at Paddington and I would spend the night with her at Isleworth. When we reached Paddington, the girl helped me to get my babies and my luggage off the train, and then offered to wait with me until my sister arrived; but at half-past ten that night we were still waiting. It was very cold on the platform, and we only had lightweight clothing because it had been a warm day; but I believe much of my own cold and numbness was due to fright, because I had realised by now that my sister was not coming.

Just then a woman in station uniform walked up to us and asked me why I was waiting there.

"My sister was supposed to meet me here at six o'clock to take me and the children to her place for the night," I explained.

"If your sister had intended meeting you, my dear," said the woman, "she would have been here hours ago. It is ten-thirty now, and you have been sitting here since six o'clock with your two babies in your arms; you must be very cold indeed after that, and my advice is that you should try to find your sister. Where does she live?"

"In Isleworth, in Middlesex," I answered. The woman could see that I was a stranger and so she asked the young girl who had been so kind already if she would look after me now. The girl readily agreed, and set off, carrying my luggage and her own suitcase, while I followed behind with a baby on each shoulder. She knew her way around London, and led me down the steps to the underground railway. It was my first experience of this, and I found the rapid opening and closing of the doors very frightening; I was tired, too, and confused by all the crowds, so that all I could do was to follow in the girl's wake and hope not to lose her. Then there were escalators to ascend and descend, and these terrified me even more, because I did not know how to get either on or off them, and prayed silently "Please God, let me get off safely, don't leave me!" Then, after what seemed like hours, we finally emerged in the crowds and the traffic of the road.

After a while we left the crowded street and walked until we came to a small country station, with just a tiny platform and one set of tracks going to the suburbs, By now my arms and legs were so numb that when the girl led me to a seat I could hardly sit down. She helped me as much as she could, and after seeing that I was as comfortable as possible in the circumstances, she went to the booking office and got me a ticket. She put it safely into my hand, and then explained that she would have to leave me now, but I would get a train in half an hour.

It was very dark and lonely on the platform, with not another soul in sight and not even a sound of passing traffic, so that we seemed to be out in the heart of the country. Even my brain now was numb with cold and fear, and I prayed again, "Oh God, don't leave me, help me, stay with me." And then at last the

195

train came in – but, to my horror, I found I was quite unable to move. I knew the train would only wait for a few minutes, but there was nothing I could do: and then, just as I was giving up, a voice called out, "Don't worry, we'll help you, Madam," and two young men appeared. One went to either side of me, and lifted me up, off the seat, and into a compartment on the train, explaining that they had seen my predicament and jumped off the train to help.

One of the young men asked me where I was going, and I told him the whole story – that I was sailing for Australia in the morning, and had intended to spend the night with my sister, but she had failed to turn up at Paddington. He listened patiently, and then aked if I was willing to trust myself to him for the moment; we were nearing my destination, but there was still a bus ride ahead before I reached my sister's house. I looked at him, and considered that he might be a criminal or even a murderer; but I had to have help, and so I had to trust someone. 'I prayed a little while ago,' I thought, 'and God has heard my prayer and sent this young man to help me.' "Yes, I will trust you," I told him.

He helped me off the train and asked if he could carry one of my babies. Jack refused to leave my arms, and so I entrusted Pearl, who was still asleep, to the young man. We walked down a cinder path to the road, but when we got to the bus stop, the last bus had gone, and we faced a mile-long walk, because the train had been late getting in. The young man was very concerned, and asked if I could manage the walk; I said that I could do it if he could!

It was pitch dark and the road was badly lit. It was not a main road in any case, and there was no sound of traffic and no pavements, only a wire fence on each side of the road. There were no houses either, and as we seemed to be out in the country, I assumed the wire fence was to keep stray animals off the road. I wondered, too, why there was no traffic on the road, because even though it was now almost one o'clock in the morning, I had expected to find busier roads near London. By now it had started to drizzle and I was worried that the children would get wet, as they had no coats on. The young man walked ahead of me, so that we could not talk as we went, and I had difficulty in keeping up with him, but whenever he felt he had got too far ahead, he slowed down and waited for me.

"Not much further now," said the man at length. "What is the name of the street?"

"Southall Street," I answered.

"Well, then, here we are," he said.

The street was so badly lit and the drizzle so steady that I could hardly see the houses. The young man opened my sister's front gate, walked up to the front door, banged on it loudly, and waited. Suddenly a window opened and two people glared down at us.

"What do you want?" shouted one of them angrily. "Don't you realise it's nearly two o'clock in the morning?"

"Come down and open the door," my friend shouted back. "I have a woman here, and two babies. She is looking for Mrs. Grant."

"I'm not Mrs. Grant," called out the woman at the window. "She moved from here this morning."

"Tell me where I can reach her, then," said the young man, angry with them now. "I must get these babies out of the rain, they are getting soaking wet."

"You will have to go back to the shopping centre," said the woman. "They are living in a flat over Pratt's Stores where Mr. Grant works."

"Can you go a little further?" the young man asked me. I nodded wearily, and we set off again to walk the mile back to the shopping centre.

When, at long last, we found ourselves outside Pratt's Stores the young man banged on the door with his fists, but there was no response.

"They are probably too far back from the front of the shop to hear us," he told me. Then we heard the footsteps of two people running towards us, and as they reached us a woman's voice said, "I'm sorry, are you Ritty?" It was the woman who had yelled at us from the window. "Why didn't you write and tell Violet you were coming?" she said.

"I did write," I told her. "Violet should have had my letter two days ago."

"It's all right, young man," she said, turning to my helper, "we'll take them home with us now, the Grants will never hear you knocking, they are right back at the far end of the stores."

At that the young man asked me if I knew these people, and I admitted that I had never met them before, but I believed they were an aunt and uncle of my brother-in-law. He was not happy with the situation, and wanted to know more about these people before letting me join them, but I explained that I was quite happy to go with them because they had called me 'Ritty', a pet name known only to my sister.

Then the couple thanked the young man for taking such good care of me, and asked how much they owed him. Much to their surprise he told them, "You owe me nothing. I do this often, and it has been a pleasure to help." I guessed then that he must belong to some kind of protection organisation, and I thanked him for his kindness and told him that I did not know what would have happened to us if he had not come along when he did. He smiled at this, and left us. Then I went back with the man and woman down the same track that I had already tramped along twice that night.

By now it was three o'clock in the morning, but soon the children were safely tucked up in a nice warm bed, and as for me, I was so exhausted that I fell asleep as soon as my head touched the pillow.

Next morning, as I was enjoying a cup of tea, my sister Violet came running in. It seemed that my overnight host had called in to tell her that we were staying at his house, and advised her to come over right away if she wanted to see us. When she heard the story of our ordeal, Violet was very upset, but we kissed and hugged each other, and she told me, "I'm sorry, Rit, I'm so sorry, I didn't know."

All too soon then we had to leave, to catch a bus to take us to the boat train to the Royal Albert Docks. We got to the siding just before the boat train pulled in, and Violet, her tears streaming down her face, went over to a young man who was standing alone on the platform, and asked him, "Are you going to Australia?"

"Yes, indeed I am," he answered, in a strong Irish brogue, and with that Violet asked him if he would keep an eye on me, because I was going to Australia all alone. Then she turned back to me, just as the train was coming in, and we had only enough time to say our goodbyes. (All we could find to say to one another was "Don't cry, you'll have a red nose."!)

The Irishman helped me to get my babies, my hand luggage and myself into the compartment, and away we went, right into the docks, where the S.S. Ballranald towered above us like a huge floating palace. There one of the officers standing on the ship's deck noticed my burdens and came down to help me aboard and take me to my cabin. In the cabin there was a life-jacket on each bunk, and I was told that a steward would soon be along to teach me how to put the life-jackets on, but rather than wait we went up on deck and found a vacant space by the rail where we could watch the ship leaving the shore. A Salvation Army band was there to see us off, and the ship's crew threw streamers down to the men on the dock; as the huge liner slowly moved out to sea and the long journey began, the streamers waved in the breeze while the band played 'God be with you till we meet again.' Many of the passengers were in tears, and as the liner drew away from the shore and the streamers broke apart, we took it as a sad omen that we were leaving old England far behind.

TWENTY-FOUR

Our journey was quite an eventful affair. On the Sunday after sailing, we attended a religious service and I asked the Padre if it would be possible to have my little girl christened before we reached Australia. He said that this would be unusual, but not impossible, and he would christen her when we reached the north coast of Africa. Meanwhile the weather proved very rough in the dreaded Bay of Biscay, and all the decks except the promenade deck were put out of bounds to the passengers for their own safety. As for the promenade deck, it was sealed off with tarpaulin to prevent the high seas washing over the deck, and we were advised to stay clear even of that. The sea was rising so high that I feared it would engulf the whole ship, and the vessel dived deep into the waves and came up again awash with sea water, like a huge rocking horse. It was a terrifying experience, but mercifully the sea calmed as we passed the Rock of Gibraltar.

My daughter Pearl was christened, as the Padre had promised, on the north coast of Africa. The service was attended by two hundred children, and my cabin mates, Hilda Kellet, a Lancashire lass on her way to Queensland, and Marie Grimball-Denstine, a nursing sister from Guy's Hospital who was also on her way to Australia, were Pearl's two godmothers, while Wilfred Martin, a young missionary on his way to Queensland to spread the Gospel story, was her godfather. After the service the Padre gave Pearl a prayer book.

Our next port of call was Malta, and Pearl's godparents invited me to go ashore with them. There had been a drought in Malta, so that the place was very dirty and the smell was terrible, but the streets were fascinating, like a huge staircase with shops on either side. Before we left the ship we had been told not to pay the price asked by the traders, but to beat them down as low as possible, so when I went into a toyshop to buy each of the children a teddy bear and was told that the price was £2.10.00

(£2.50) each, I managed to knock that figure down by half to £1.5.00 (£1.25) each. As it happened, Pearl's godparents insisted on paying for them, and after leaving the toyshop we walked a little further on and bought some fruit – though we were careful to take it back to the ship and wash it thoroughly before we ate it. It was very interesting to watch the milkman bring his goat right up to the front doors of his customers' houses and actually milk the goat straight into their jugs.

A few days after leaving Malta, my little son Jack became seriously ill with Mediterranean fever. He was taken to the sick-bay, but since there were no nurses on board, I told the doctor that I would prefer to look after Jack myself. I had had five years' experience in nursing fevers, so I knew what had to be done, and I spent hours sponging my boy with cold water to keep his temperature down. My meals were brought to the cabin, and the only time I left Jack was to go down to dinner; then a sick-bay attendant would stay with him until I returned. It was three weeks before my son was well again.

For quite some time I had noticed a shark following the ship, and this made me very uneasy because there is a superstition at sea that a shark will follow a ship because it knows that there is going to be a death on board. Naturally I was afraid my son might be the victim, but my faith in God made me fight for my boy; when eventually the fever left him and he was on his feet again, the shark was still following us. Once my son was well enough to leave the cabin, I took him up on deck, and there one of the passengers told me that a man who had been returning to Australia with ten young emigrants had died suddenly of a heart attack. The passengers were invited to attend the burial service, and when the body had been prepared and placed on a plank, ready to be buried at sea, those who wished to witness the event stood silently and respectfully behind the officers and crew. The ten boys who had been travelling with the man stood sadly beside the captain as he conducted the service. The Padre led us in prayer, and then we sang one or two hymns; when the body slid from underneath a Union Jack into the deep sea, the ship's engines were silenced for one minute, the climax to a very moving service. As we walked sadly back to our cabins, one of the passengers remarked, "Now we've had a christening *and* a burial at sea," and as we looked down into the sea we saw that the shark had stopped following us. We did not see him again during

201

the voyage.

On our first day at sea we had had a boat drill, and been shown our stations, so that in the event of a disaster we would know exactly where and how to get into the life-boats without confusion or panic. We were told then that though this was only a drill we must not take it lightly because the next time the alarm sounded, it could well be the real thing – but we had no idea how soon we would be put to the test.

Our next port of call was Port Suez, where our ship anchored a mile from shore, and small boats came out to ferry passengers to the mainland. It was a pleasure to go ashore and stretch our legs for a while. Later on, when we were all back on the ship, a pilot came aboard to guide us through the Suez Canal, a manoeuvre which took some thirty-six hours to complete. Next came Port Said; at each port the liner was surrounded by small boats, each one carrying men and women loaded with goods of all descriptions which they would try to sell to the passengers crowding the liner's decks. If we wished to buy anything from them, we merely pointed to the article of our choice; at that the boatman threw up a rope which we caught and secured to the ship's rail. He then put the goods into a basket attached to the other end of the rope, we pulled the basket up to the deck, took out our purchases, put in the money, and lowered the basket to the boatman.

There was a tremendous babble of voices, what with the boatmen shouting their wares and small boys shouting for pennies: "Throw a penny, Mister, and I'll dive for you! Throw threepence and I'll dive under one end of the ship and come out at the other!" The passengers duly threw pennies into the water and the small boys dived under the surface and came up holding the pennies between their teeth; someone told me later that this was how they made a living.

Just before we reached the Red Sea the captain's voice came over the loud speakers. "Attention all passengers, we are about to cross over the Line. Please hold tightly to the rails, as the ship will leap over the Line, and if you are *not* holding tightly, you might have an accident! Father Neptune will come aboard aft of the promenade deck at precisely ten o'clock, and all passengers are invited to meet him."

That night we all went along to see Father Neptune, a white-bearded old man dripping with sea-water, and with fish hanging from his clothes, as he ascended to the deck by rope ladder. After the arrival came the customary ritual of some of the members of the crew being 'shaved' by Father Neptune. The victim was tied to a kitchen chair while the yard-long 'razor', first sharpened on a strop, was placed in position, then the victim's head was plastered with shaving foam, his mouth was filled with very large tranquilizers (cotton balls!) to calm him down, and the shaving began. It was a mock ritual, of course, but the crew played their parts well, and a good time was had by all.

After the shaving ritual was over, we had to sing a French song. The words were written on a large board and held up for everyone to see: they went something like 'It ain't tray bong on the Continong, San Fairy Anne, you are a loony', and the result was hilarious. We returned to our cabins later, smiling happily. (Unfortunately I had to miss most of the entertainment because my babies were too young to be left alone; I had to keep them with me at all times, which proved very exhausting, so we spent most of our time in the cabin.)

It was now about ten days since we had last seen land, and the heat was unbearable. Several times a day we were issued with sweat towels to put around our necks, but our bodies were sweating so freely that we dared not touch each other, and the resulting odour was overpowering. We were given a ship's biscuit (which resembled a very large, very hard dog biscuit), and told to chew on that, and we were also given an orange to suck. The ship that had preceeded us by one day radioed back to us that they were keeping their passengers alive by getting them to lie down on the bare deck and playing hosepipes over them; they suggested that we should do the same. The suggestion was welcomed by the passengers, who also asked our captain if they could bring their beds up on deck as the cabins were stiflingly hot. (The cabin walls were made of iron, and because of the intense heat they were almost red-hot – certainly too hot to touch with bare hands.) The captain agreed, but just as the last beds were being carried up on deck, when some passengers had already settled down for the night, the captain's voice boomed out over the loud-speakers: "Beds back in the cabins at once."

Later that night the alarm bell sounded and we had to leap out of our beds and into our life-jackets. I was so agitated that I became all fingers and thumbs, and had great difficulty in doing up the jackets; the din of the warning bells and the noise of the crew running about in all directions did not help, and though I managed to fasten the children's life-jackets, I was shaking too much to fasten my own. The ship was lurching badly, and it was with great difficulty that I got up the companionway steps; voices were coming over the loudspeaker urging us not to panic, but to go to our boat stations at once. I saw the lifeboats being swung out of their cradles and lowered to the boat deck, and the crew were just opening the gates to let us get in, when the captain's voice came over a loudspeaker, announcing, "The danger has now passed. Will passengers please return to their cabins." We were not told what the danger had been, but at least our terrifying experience had ended happily, and the passengers, though very frightened, had remembered their boat drill and remained calm.

We sailed on to Colombo, where parents were advised not to take their children ashore. As in other ports, we anchored a mile out, and the little boats came out to meet us; some of the boatmen were Indians, wearing colourful turbans on their heads. They were very noisy and a number of them came on board and asked the passengers to let them tell their fortunes. I had just taken my two babies down to the ship's nursery to join the other children (where I could happily leave them with the person in charge while they played with some of the many toys provided for their use), and was coming back on deck when one of the Indians insisted on telling my fortune. I managed to escape from him and went to see what was happening on the lowerdeck, where I watched as the foreign seamen brought cargo aboard. I was told they were 'mulattoes', and they were certainly a peculiar-looking bunch, naked to the waist, with long pigtails and long skirts. They went bare-footed, and the big toe on each foot stood out and away from their other toes, just like a letter t; this was caused because the big toe was used to wrap around the rope which pulled the cargo in, but it was a strange sight. I found it hard, too, to tell whether the seamen were men or women.

Later I went to join the rest of the passengers, only to find the Indian who had pestered me earlier standing, looking at me. "Tell your fortune for a pound, lady," he said. I told him that I couldn't afford it, but he kept bringing his price down until at last I told him that I had no money at all, and turned to walk away. Suddenly he said, "I must tell you something, you got little boy, so high, he got hair like me" (which was black) "beautiful hands, very clever, brain very clever, make name for himself some day. Also little girl, so high." He could not describe fair hair, but said, "like a fairy". Then he stretched out the fingers of both hands and said, "Very clever, play music. Another boy, clever, different, make beautiful music with mouth."

"I've only got two children," I said.

"Another boy to come," he said, and with that he salaamed and left me. It was quite incredible. He had described my two children down to the very last detail and there was no way he could have seen them, since they were already playing in the ship's nursery when he came aboard.

Soon we were entering Australian waters, and we were issued with declaration forms. Among other things we were asked if we were carrying any brass items, or sewing machines, or various other household goods and were told we would have to pay duty on them. I had all the listed items in my iron-bound trunk, but as I had already paid out most of my money for excess baggage charges before I left England, I had no money left to cover the duty. This was a great worry, but one of the passengers advised me to draw a big cross over the page and write on the form 'Settlers' household goods only' and leave it at that.

When we arrived at Freemantle, I stood at the rail eagerly scanning the faces on the quay, searching for my husband; but to my bitter disappointment he was not there. However I did spot my sister Emily, whom I had not seen for eleven years. She was scanning the rail, but she didn't recognise me, since I had only been a girl of fifteen when she saw me last, and now I was a housewife and mother of two children. I called out to her, and she looked up and said, "I'm cold." It was a scorching hot day, but I threw down my trench coat and shouted "Catch!"

The ship was low in the water, so I had only a short gangway to go down to reach the quay, where I greeted Emily and her two children. I had expected to hear her speaking with an Australian accent, but to my surprise she sounded more Welsh than I did, and told me, "I wouldn't change my Welsh accent for all the tea in China."

"Where is Ivor?" I asked her. "Why didn't he come to meet us?"

205

"A farmer gave him some work," said Emily, "so I asked him if I could come in his place."

I asked her if it was far to Northampton, because I was longing to see my husband.

"Oh no, not really," she said. "It's just about six hundred miles, and if you think I'm going straight back there, you've got another think coming. I haven't had a holiday since I came to this god-forsaken hole, and I am not going back until the money runs out. I've booked us into a hotel."

"Emily," I said, "I can't stay in a hotel, I've only got my ten pounds landing money."

Meanwhile the Customs men were waiting patiently for my keys, so that they could open my trunk. I was scared that they would find things on which they could charge me tax, so I pretended to act a bit daft. I pushed my keys into their hands and asked them eagerly if I could open all my boxes for them. They began with my cabin trunk, and then, just as they were about to search it, I said sharply, "That's right, expose all my dirty linen!" At that the men looked at each other, then slammed the lid shut, marked it, together with all my other boxes, and handed me back my keys. I gave in my declaration form before leaving the quay, and it was plain that everything was all right, for they gave me my ten pounds landing money and a small Testament.

Next we caught a bus to Perth, and Emily took me to the 'hotel' she had booked for us. No wonder she had been silent when I told her I had no money for a hotel, for the place we were booked into was a Salvation Army hostel, where it cost a shilling for bed and breakfast! I was very hurt and disappointed because I didn't want to stop there anyway, I wanted to get home to Ivor, but it was to be another fortnight before we left Perth.

In fact Perth was a very interesting city. Emily took us to see the black swans on the Swan river, and then we crossed the water into a park where all the animals ran free, which made me rather nervous. (I was afraid for the children, because there was nothing to stop the wild animals coming out on to the footpath.) Next we came into a leisure park, where people could sit at tables under colourful umbrellas and be served with drinks. It was nearing the end of winter in Australia, and the flowers were magnificent. We stayed in the park for some time because we were too nervous to walk past the animals again, and there were no other people walking in that direction just then. We were told that the animals were quite harmless and used to people, and that as long as we stayed on the path we would be all right, but we hired a sulky (a two-wheeled carriage with a hood on top, the only type of vehicle on the roads there), and for a few pence it took us back to the hostel.

On the Saturday night we went to the square in Perth where the Salvation Army held its meetings. The Salvationists formed a large circle in the square, and as it was six o'clock and quite dark, and all the pubs had just closed for the night, the crowds of men leaving the pubs stopped and listened to them. They sang a hymn, inviting everyone to join them, and then some of the songsters went around among the crowd with the collection plate, asking for money. One of the lady Salvationists shouted to the crowd, "Come along, throw your money into the circle. I don't want coins, I want notes!" Then she pointed first to one man, then to another, and said, "Come on, I want a pound off you," until in the end the whole floor was littered with pound notes. I said to Emily, "Perth must be a very rich place if men can throw their pound notes away so freely," but she told me, "Now Australia is feeling the depression after the war. The Salvation Army wait until the men come out of the pubs, because when the beer's in, the wit's out, and they don't know what they are doing with their money."

After all we didn't stay the whole fortnight in Perth, because there was nothing to do after a while, and it became boring; so on the tenth day we caught our train to Geraldton. My luggage had already gone on ahead, but just as we went to board the Southern Cross train, Emily explained that Ivor had given her the money to travel on that train with us, but she had travelled on a cheaper route to save the expense. "But you can use your ticket for the Southern Cross on the cheaper route, the Wongan Hills trains," she told me. "Only they won't take my ticket on the Southern Cross, so you will either have to come with me or travel alone. My train only has a small wooden engine, and it will take us all round the wilds, but that is the way I've got to go."

It seemed that Emily's line was one used mainly by coloured people to get from one outpost to another, but I thought to myself, 'One line is just as good as another if it gets us to our destination.' I was taken aback, though, when I got to the train and saw that there were just bare slatted seats with no cushions, while the train itself was like a long bus, just one carriage with seats going in all directions. It had one tiny toilet and one small hand basin to serve the whole train.

We sat on those slatted wooden seats for three days and three nights, quite unable to stretch our legs. I had thought that the journey to Geraldton was only a short trip, and I had expected to get food on the train, so all we had to feed six of us for the whole journey was a few biscuits, a few slices of cake, and some fruit. We travelled all around the wastelands of Australia, with nothing to see, not even any scenery. Emily said that nothing could be done with these hundreds of miles of barren waste because there was no water, and in all the six hundred miles we didn't see a living being or even an animal. When we needed a drink we had to put our heads through the window and take a drinking glass from a rack attached to the side of the train, then pour a drink from a plastic bag which hung near the rack; we had to be careful with the water because that was all we would have for the whole journey.

There was no-one else on the train except for one half-caste man in our compartment and another a little lower down the train. The journey was very painful for our bones, and though the mornings were bad enough, the nights were especially painful for the children and myself. The nights were freezing and the days were sweltering, we had no blankets of any kind, and I had to lie on the hard wooden seat with my babies in my arms to try and keep warm. We left Perth on the Friday and arrived at Geraldton on the Monday, changing trains there and catching a freight train to Northampton, a journey of another fifty miles. This train, too, had just the one carriage, rather like our old steam trains at home in England.

At long last we reached our destination, which had just a small wooden platform and a tiny office, and there, on the platform, stood Ivor, the only person at the station. I was standing at the window, holding Pearl in my arms, and when Ivor opened the carriage door, she sprang from me into his arms, shouting, "Daddy, Hiyah, o!" I was very frightened because she had sprung out of my arms so suddenly that if she had slipped she could easily have fallen down between the rails. Luckily Ivor was able to catch her as she jumped, but we were both very shaken. Ivor picked up the two children in his arms and walked towards Emily's house, which was just a ten minute walk from the station. This house was a two-roomed stone building, put up by the R.S.F. It was built on short wooden piles, and had a small verandah at the front, as well as a living room, and a bedroom along which ran another verandah which they had closed in, transforming it into an extra bedroom and living room, so that they now had four rooms.

I asked Ivor why he had not come to Fremantle to meet us, and he explained that he had found a few weeks' work with a farmer. "I wanted to come and meet you," he said. "But Emily said if I gave her the money she would go in my place, and I wouldn't have to lose the work." Then he told me to go indoors with Emily and have a good night's rest, and he would see me in the morning. Naturally I asked him why he wasn't coming in with us, and he said that Bert had lent him the horse so that he could come and meet us, and he had to go back right away, because he still had a few more weeks' work there and he could not afford to lose it. I understood, but it was a poor homecoming when, after all those years apart, Ivor and I had to be separated on my first day back with him.

TWENTY-FIVE

My luggage had arrived ahead of us, but I was so tired after my journey that I left it alone and went straight to bed. The small room into which Emily showed me held only two single beds; there was no room for anything more. Eleven-year-old Beryl and eight-year-old Edna slept in one bed, and seven-year-old Peter and four-year-old Roy slept in the other, so there was a little shuffling around to make room for me and my two children, and having crowds of midges making a meal of us and mosquitoes dive-bombing us, buzzing and biting, I had no sleep. Instead I had to keep brushing the insects off the children, to protect their faces, and I was glad to see the coming of the morning.

In the morning the children carried the overlays off the beds and laid them on the earth at the back of the house. I asked Emily why the beds were being taken out, thinking that perhaps they were going to sunbathe. "Come," she said, "I'll show you why." We went down four wooden steps to the yard, and there I saw that the beds were covered with millions of ants who were eating the bugs and bugs' eggs that had got into the beds. Emily said they had to do this every morning, and that because of the hot climate every house had the same problem, there was nothing else to be done.

"Oh, Emily," I said, "I hope there aren't any in my cottage."

"What sort of cottage do you think you've got?" she asked.

"Oh," I replied, "I have been picturing a whitewashed cottage with roses round the door."

"Oh my gosh!" she said, but she would enlighten me no further, try as I would.

Later Ivor came in, and I asked him, "Are we going to our own home today?"

"Don't be in a hurry to go there, Ray," he told me. "Stay here with Emily for a few days."

Each day Ivor rode in on horseback, and each time he came, I asked him if we were going home; but he kept putting it off. He would stay only a short while, and then he would say he had to go back; each day he promised to take me to the cottage in the morning – but always tomorrow. Emily begged me to stay with her.

"You'll never be able to live up there," she told me. "You'll be terrified. It's been empty for years, and there are many people in Northampton who are desperate for houses, but wouldn't live in it for all the tea in China."

"Emily," I said, "after all I've been through these last few months, I'd live anywhere as long as I could be with Ivor. I haven't come all these thousands of miles and endured all those hardships just to be separated from my husband again; if it's good enough for him, it's good enough for me!"

When Ivor and Emily saw that I would not be moved, Emily said to Ivor, "You'd better borrow Rae's sulky." (That was a child's chair, with two wheels and a long wooden handle.) "What do I do with it?" I asked, and Emily explained, "Put the children to sit in it, and when the road is smooth you can push it, but when the road is rough and sandy, you will have to get in front and pull it behind you." When we set off, Emily shouted after me, "You'll be back, you have neighbours here and houses all around you. When you see what's facing you there, you'll be glad to come back."

The sun was hot, and we were wearing colourful clothes. Just then I had stardust in my eyes, and I thought if this was how an Australian lived, then I would have to be an Australian too; I felt so proud as we started out on the long trek to our new home, my tall bronzed husband at my side, wearing shirt and vest, with a stetson on his head. Half a mile of rough track from Emily's house brought us to the main road, but once we were on that, nothing passed us, not even an animal. It was not a surfaced road, and the sand piling up made heavy going of our walking.

The walk was unending. After a while I took Pearl out of Ivor's arms, to give him a rest, but the further we walked, the lower my heart sank, and I could see Ivor getting very depressed. There was nothing to break the long, lonely mono-tony, no life at all, just bush on either side of the road, and we did not even speak, except when I asked how much further we had to go. After a mile and half of walking, we came to a rough track going downhill into the bush, and turned off onto this. It was

211

difficult to pull the sulky; we had to walk in single file, and with each step my heart sank still lower, and I began to understand what Emily meant. I asked Ivor why there were so many ruts in the road, and he said, "This is the road that used to be used for bringing up the copper from the copper mine below. The miners used small two wheeled carts which were drawn along this track by cows, and the ruts in the road were caused by the wheels digging into the track."

At the bottom of the hill was a gully – fortunately dry – and that was the end of the road. Now we had to make our way through the wild bush, on a track that Ivor had made himself. I looked around for houses, but saw nothing but dead bush. I could not go on, I was so exhausted, but Ivor said we were nearly there. We took a left turn up another hill, and soon I could see the outline of a building through the scrub. Ivor walked on ahead, leading the way, until we came to a gate of sorts, and he said, "You'll have to wait until I can make a path for you to walk through." The weeds stood four foot high, sticky, with little bobbles at the end of them, which tore my stockings and legs if they brushed up against me. When we came to the building there were two steps to get up onto a platform, and corrugated sheeting covering the platform and the verandah: it was not a house, but a shack.

I followed closely behind Ivor through what was supposed to be a front door into a long empty shed. Ivor had made a partition down the middle out of the hessian, and painted or whitewashed it, and this partition divided the space into a living room and bedroom. When Ivor first found the place there had been no walls at all, because they had been blown away, but he had gathered together some timber and iron and nailed it all back together again – thought it was as rusty as an old horseshoe; where there were gaps he had opened some four-gallon kerosene tins and nailed them to the walls to cover up the holes. The only furniture in the entire place was a rough, home-made table. This was the whitewashed cottage with the roses around the door that I had dreamed about.

In one corner of the shed was a wood burner, with a makeshift chimney going through a hole in the roof to let the smoke out. On the other side of the room were a window and a little back door. I crossed the room to the little window, put my head on my arms, and cried as I have never cried before – we had come all

212

those miles only to end up in a horrible shack like this. My dreams were shattered and my whole world had collapsed. I said to Ivor, "Tell me this is just a terrible dream, and I'll wake up soon; this can't be real." Ivor said nothing, but I could see the misery in his face. Then he said, "I told you not to be in a hurry to come out, this is a terribly lonely place." I didn't have the heart to remind him that he had also said, "Come out as soon as you can, it's dreadful here without you." Instead I dried my tears and said, "We've got each other, and we've got our children, we'll make it into a home," and a look of immense relief came into his face, replacing the misery that had been there before.

He said, "Come, I'll take you back to Emily's," but I said, "No, it is too far to go back, I'm staying here."

"Then I'm not going back to Bert Ash tonight," he told me. "I'll stay here, but you can't stay, there's no bed."

"We'll sleep on the floor as you've been doing," I said, and there we spent the night, the four of us lying on the floor, with just one blanket covering us.

Sunrise came at five thirty in the morning, and we had to get up then and do what we had to before the heat became too intense. Although it was on a hard floor, we had had the best night's sleep since leaving Perth. Ivor told me, "I have to go back to Bert Ash's farm today, Ray." We had no supper, and there was no food in the house for breakfast, so I said, "You can't leave me and the children here in this lonely place with no food. I'd be terrified if you didn't come home tonight."

"It's all right, Rit," he said. "I'm taking you all with me."

"Do you mean I am going to be a servant working on a farm?" I asked. "I couldn't do that and look after two babies as well."

"No," said Ivor, "you are not going to work, you are going to have a holiday. Mrs. Ash insists on it."

"I don't want to go," I said. "I'd rather stay here and you come back at night." I didn't think a farmer's wife would want to be burdened with the family of one of their employees.

"She's a very nice woman," Ivor explained, "and Bert was the only one who offered me work out here, I couldn't turn it down. I was so desperate for work that when he asked me if I could drive a tractor, I swore I was a good tractor driver, though I'd never even seen one. You see how desperate I was, with you and the children coming out, and me with no money to come and

213

meet you or to buy food. I couldn't even offer you a home, so I did what you had always told me to do, trusted in God and waited on his help. And the tractor and I took to each other like old friends. Bert is very pleased with my work; he only needs help for a month, so I must stick it out."

I was very unhappy about going to the Ash farm, and I was sure that I was going to have to work for our keep – I was not afraid of work, but I was tired and I needed a rest after our long journey. Just then we heard Bert Ash's horse and farm cart coming up the track. He had called at my sister's house to see if we were there, and when she told him we hadn't been back, he picked up our boxes, and was bringing them to us. I opened my cabin trunk and took out some clothes for the children and myself, then we went with him to his farm, which was small and isolated.

Mrs. Ash proved to be very nice, and gave us a warm welcome. "You don't realise how much it means to me to have another woman in my house," she said. "I don't see a woman from one year's end to another." Mrs. Ash had been twice married, and had a six-year-old son by her first marriage, but she was not too happy as a wife; Australian men regarded women as necessary for their creature comforts, but not much more. She had inherited the farm from her late first husband.

The next morning I asked her if I could help in any way around the house, but she said, No, she had invited us there for a holiday. Then I suggested that if she was not prepared to let me work, maybe I could do some sewing for her, as I was a good dressmaker. At that she told me that she had a sewing machine, but didn't know how to use it; however, she had some material to make her son David pyjamas, but had no idea how to make them, so she would be very grateful for any help I could give. The she added, "I don't want you to work, I want you to get to know about the country, and learn how to cope with this terrific heat."

"Don't worry about me," I said. "It's enough for me to see how well the little ones have taken to each other, and to see them so contented."

"David has never had a child to play with before," Mrs. Ash told me. "He's as overjoyed to have your little ones with him as I am to have you."

She put the treadle-type sewing machine on the back verandah, away from the sun, and I taught her how to use the treadle. She watched as I cut out and sewed the pyjamas for David, and was very pleased with the result. I told her to bring me anything she needed to be done, and Bert went into town to buy some more material. Then I spent the next two weeks happily sewing. It made me feel that I had not been imposing on them.

All too soon the fortnight ended, and we had to go back to that awful shack. The problem now was to find food for the children, since we had two babies and not a drop of milk for them, while the only baker was several miles away, and in any case, owing to the heat of the climate, the bread would have been hard by the time we got home. Ivor went into town to get a few stores, but as he had to walk both ways, it was almost a day's journey. We still had no furniture or beds, just the old makeshift table, but an old lady had died and Ivor had been promised that after the share-out he could buy the bed. I said to him, "Do we have to have a second-hand bed? There may be bugs in it."

"There are no furnishers this side of Perth," Ivor pointed out. "I have ordered a new overlay for you, and we will have to manage with that for a while."

Ivor showed me how to make damper bread out of the plain flour he had brought home, using the flour and a pinch of bicarbonate of soda and a little salt. It was just wetted into a dough, rolled into a ball, and then cooked in the oven, and ended up filling, but not very digestible, especially for the children. It was the best we could do for the moment, but I would have to look for someone to teach me to make balm.

The next morning we found a lovely white cot on our verandah. We didn't know who had put it there, because the local people had been hostile towards us, blaming the 'pommies' for taking work away from them, but I believe it was Bert Ash who had left it for us, because he had seen our predicament when he called that day. Later that morning a man came to our house with a hen and a couple of chicks, and Ivor introduced him to me as Mr. Hendley, our next-door neighbour – next door being a mile and half away, further up in the bush. When he handed the hen and chicks to Ivor, he said, "This is a start for you. I am repaying your husband for his kindness to my wife." He went on to explain that he and his wife were elderly people, but he was the local water diviner and grave digger, and he continued, "I want to ask you, Mrs. Webb, to do me a favour if you will. Your husband tells me you were a good milker." I looked at my husband in surprise, because I hadn't been near a cow since I was very young. I had learned to milk on Abergarw Farm in Brynmemin, as a Land Army girl, but I left there when I was sixteen to take up nursing.

I could not let Ivor down, so I asked Mr. Hendley what he wanted me to do. He told me. "I've got a Jersey cow up at my farm. This is her third calf, and she has never allowed anyone but myself to milk her. Now I have a job going out to the Bowes estate to divine water, so that they can sink a well, and although we have reared Blackie from a calf, my wife won't go near her. What sort of stripper are you? Because the last man I had was a bad stripper and ruined a cow."

"I enjoy milking," I answered, "and I am a good stripper and a wet milker.

"Good," he said. "She likes a wet milker. Can you come up this afternoon and see her? You will have to come early and follow in my tracks."

"I'll be pleased to come if you give me some milk for my children," I told him.

"She's a good Jersey, and a heavy milker," he said. "Bring your milk bucket if you have one, and if you give my wife a billy can of milk each morning and afternoon, you can have all the rest for yourself. But when you come up, don't bring the children. Blackie goes raving mad when she hears children, and she would be unmanageable. She hates women and children. My daughter Lulu lives in town; she has three children and they daren't go near Blackie's paddock. Also, while I have been waiting for you to come out, I have been making a trail through the bush from my house to yours. Whatever you do, don't go off the trail, and shuffle your feet and make a noise with your bucket as you are walking."

"Why must I do all this?" I asked, and Mr. Hendley explained that it was to frighten snakes away if there should happen to be one on my path. "Never get behind a snake," he said, "always be in front of it, as they will rear back and spring on you."

So in due course, with a new shining bucket that Ivor had made from a four-gallon kerosene tin, I started my mile and a half trek through the bush to meet Blackie and bring home milk for my children. When I reached Mr. Hendley's bungalow, he took me to the paddock; from there we could look down on Blackie because we were on hilly ground and the cow was in the lower paddock. Mr. Hendley rattled his pail and called out to Blackie, but when she looked up, she saw me and then started pawing the ground, throwing up clodges of grass. Then she stampeded towards us, snorting with rage at seeing a woman in her paddock. I didn't wait for her to reach me, but ducked quickly out through the fence, while Mr. Hendley patted her and calmed her down, then put his stool and pail beside her and started to milk her. Then he told me to come in and have a try. I changed places with him, and succeeded in squirting some milk into my hand to warm them: then I started to milk her, but she knew the difference in the hand and started lashing at me with her tail and holding her milk back. Her tail lashing was painful, but I tried to coax her into giving her milk, until eventually she kicked out and knocked the bucket over. It was hopeless.

I changed places with Mr. Hendley and he milked her, then he asked me to show him what sort of stripper I was, and we changed places again. I stripped her successfully, and he was very pleased, so I came away with a nice bucketful of milk. Ivor had caught a rabbit, and we had damper bread and rabbit that night, with plenty of milk for the children. I had to go back the following morning and face Blackie again, but with the same result. Twice a day I walked the three miles for milk, but was unsuccessful with Blackie each time. The cow terrified me, and I was afraid that I would have to tell Mr. Hendley that he must get someone else. I knew he was anxious to go to his new job, but there was no other way I could have milk for the children, so the next morning I set out with a heavy heart. Each time that I had gone up to the farm, my mind had been concerned about snakes, and I couldn't think of anything else, so on the fourth morning, instead of banging my tin, I turned my thought to God, and all the way up to the paddock I kept asking Him to protect me from that cow. "Give me courage, dear God," I prayed, "to stand up to that cow, please help me to master her, I need her milk so badly."

When I reached Mr. Hendley's house, I got into the paddock and waited for Mr. Hendley to call the cow. Maybe I couldn't master my fears, but I knew now that I was not alone in my fight. Blackie looked up at me and started her capers, snorting and

217

charging at me, and I kept repeating, "God, please don't let her gore me." I shut my eyes and stood firmly where I was, praying all the time, "God, don't let her hurt me, don't let her kill me," while Blackie stood a few yards from me, pawing the ground, her hot breath fanning my face. I couldn't move, I was rooted to the ground – but nothing happened, and I opened my eyes, wondering who was the most astonished, Mr. Hendley, myself or the cow. Then from inside me a voice spoke to Mr. Hendley – my voice, but not my words. "Leave me, Mr. Hendley, go into the house and leave me alone with Blackie."

"Shall I start her?" he asked, but I said, "No, leave me please." As soon as he had gone out of sight I started to sing softly to the cow, and Blackie turned her head to look at me. I patted her neck as I had seen Mr. Hendley do, and she got into the right position for milking; then, still singing, I placed the stool beside her, and put my pail under her, sat down, and put my head against her flank. I squeezed a drop of milk into my hands, rubbed them together and started to milk. The sound of the milk squirting into the pail was like music.

Blackie gave just one slash of her tail and no more; her head came right around towards me, and she started licking me. All the time I milked her she licked me, as if I were her calf, and this was the first bucket of milk to come from Blackie in four days. I put the bucket safe and called Mr. Hendley. When he saw the milk he shouted to his wife, "She's done it, Matey, she's done it!" Then he said to me, "What miracle have you performed?"

"No miracle, Mr. Hendley," I said. "You can go to work now, I'll have no more trouble with Blackie, we're friends. That, Mr. Hendley, is the power of prayer."

Now that they were sure of plenty of milk Ivor had to make me a large pan out of kerosene tins. Kerosene was the only means of lighting our home, and it could only be purchased in four gallon containers. When the tins were empty, Ivor would cut away the lid, bend and flatten down the edges, and make a hole on either side of the can, then thread through the holes to make a handle, then, when it was finsihed, we had a nice shiny container for carrying our water and milk. One day, instead of cutting the lid out of the tin, he cut out the side, and after washing it thoroughly, I poured the milk into it, covered it with a piece of muslin and left it for the cream to settle on top. I made

218

jam from pumpkins, flavoured with a little strawberry essence, and then we had jam and cream and plenty of fresh milk for the children. And with the tin cutters, Ivor was able to make all kinds of useful containers from the kerosene tins.

TWENTY SIX

We were still sleeping on the floor, as our furniture consisted of only a table and two hard kitchen chairs, but we had blankets and sheets that I had brought out from home to make us more comfortable. One day I heard a horse and cart approach the house, and Ivor said, "There's our bed coming at last," He went out to help the man carry in the bed, and I said, "Bring it round the back, I want to see it. Lay it down in the back yard, I can smell bugs on it, and it's not to go into the house until it has been cleaned."

"There can't be bugs in it," Ivor replied. "It has an iron frame," and he introduced me to the driver, whose name was Harry.

"There's no way of getting out of this part of the world but by me and my horse and cart," Harry said. "There *is* a freight train, but that only passes through once a week. If you wish to go camping on the coast, you hire my horse and cart. Alive or dead, Harry is the only one to take you out of here, this cart is your bus, your train and your hearse."

"Well, Harry," I said, "Will you take my husband back into town with you? I need lots of caustic soda, we are going to be sleeping on the floor for a little longer."

When Ivor returned with the caustic soda he took the mesh away from the wooden frame. We laid it flat on the ground, weighed it down with heavy stones and left it there for the ants to eat up the bugs and their eggs. Then we filled a bucket with boiling water and poured the caustic soda into it, and poured that over all the cracks and openings of the frame, and over the whole bed. After that we left it out in the open for a few days, for the soda and the ants to do their work.

A few days later we were able to wash and polish the whole framework, and carry the bed into the house, cleaned and fresh. We eagerly awaited the arrival of our overlay, which arrived a few days later; with the two snowy white cots which had miraculously appeared on my doorstep earlier, our bedroom was complete. I had brought with me a mirror from Wales, and our little house soon began to look like a real home. Finding the cots on our doorstep had shown us that the people who had earlier been hostile towards us were now showing us that we had been accepted, and were being very friendly without appearing to be giving us charity.

Ivor found two old deck chairs whose frames were good, though their canvas was missing; he also used the iron frame of an old sulky seat which he had found earlier, and made a two seater settee. We washed and painted the frames of the deck chairs and the sulky, then, with corn sacks given us by the storekeeper, we repaired the deck chairs. After that we filled some sacks with wild cotton which we had picked out in the bush, and completed our settee. I had taken yards of floral cretonne out to Australia with me, and with my little sewing machine I made four large cushions with frills all round for the deck chairs and settee, covers for the backs of the deck chairs and a large cover for the settee, so that now we had an easy chair each side of the fireplace, as well as a cretonne-covered settee, with matching curtains on the little window. A red chenille curtain covered the bedroom doorway, and there was a matching red chenille tablecloth, both of which I had taken out from England.

Our little shack was beginning to take on the appearance of a pleasant home, and we christened it Caerau Cottage, which became our postal address. One morning, to our surprise, a little bread van pulled up to our door. The baker had travelled miles to bring us a small loaf, and he introduced himself as the only baker in Northampton.

"I don't usually deliver bread," he said, "but as you've come out from England and are not used to our rough ways, if you wish, I will deliver a loaf of bread each day."

I couldn't help suspecting that he had come out of curiosity, just to see us, for the baker was a rich man and did not need to travel all those miles for the price of a loaf.

(Before I arrived in Northampton, Ivor had heard that men were betting against each other in the public house that "That Pommie's bleeding wife must be an old shrew, as he had run up into the bush to get away from her – for no-one came to live in that godforsaken hole unless they were running away from

221

something." But Bert Ash had told them they were barking up the wrong tree and they had lost their bet.)

I was very glad to have a piece of fresh bread, but the trouble was that I couldn't keep it fresh in that very hot climate; though it was such nice bread when it was new, in no time at all it had become hard and stale. Strangely enough my husband never seemed to be there when the baker came with the bread, but we never had much of a conversation except to discusss the bread. The baker never came further than the verandah, and I never asked him into the house, but one day when my two little ones came out onto the verandah to take the bread from him (they liked to pay him in turn for the loaf), he turned to me and said, "Mrs. Webb, you are a very rich woman."

"You must be joking," I said. "With my husband tramping miles each day, looking for work he can't find, no money coming into the house, and all of us living in a tumbledown shack like this, I must be the poorest person in Northampton."

"You are wrong, Mrs. Webb," he told me. "You are a very rich woman indeed, for you've got these two beautiful children. I've got a beautiful house, the only two-storey house in Northampton, and I am considered to be a wealthy man, but I'd give every penny if I could say one of these children was mine." With that he turned sadly and left without another word. When Ivor came home I told him what the baker had said, and added, "He was right, you know, I *am* very rich."

The baker never came again, and Ivor told me that he and his wife had been married for years, but had no children, and were now on the point of divorce. (Ivor was a jealous man, and I believe he had stopped the baker calling.)

On the day Ivor left Caerau, his father had told him he was a fool to go out to Australia, and they had parted with just a cool handshake; Mr. Webb told Ivor that when he saw the size of the ship he'd run back home. Then, on the day before I left to join Ivor, I took the two little ones to say goodbye to their grandpa; my father-in-law had never seen our little girl before, and had only seen our little boy Jack when he was a baby. Father-in-law was a very proud man, and did not like to show his feelings, but he told his daughters that he had never believed that Ivor would really go, and now he felt that he had lost us for ever. Ted Manning had been keeping in touch with Ivor by letter every week; the first letter I received when I got there was from Ted, and though it had been written a day or two after I said goodbye to Grandpa, it had taken seven weeks to arrive. It told us that Ivor's father had taken to his bed and was very ill.

Ted kept us informed of Ivor's father's progress, but each letter was very disturbing. Then, after several weeks of anxiety, Ted was pleased to be able to tell us that my father-in-law was improving. The day that Ivor collected this letter from the Post Office my sister Emily and her four children came to visit me, her first visit to us. I was so pleased to have my sister as a guest, since I had seen no-one but the baker and Mr. Hendley since coming to the bush, and it was a very happy visit. Emily's four children were very friendly and lovable, and they enjoyed themselves climbing the gum trees and bringing down 'bubble gum' to my two children. (There were little bubbles of gum oozing from the tree, and the children loved chewing them.) It was a scorching day, and the children, who were playing in the shade of the trees and wearing large sunhats, were really enjoying themselves.

It was too hot inside the shack, so Emily and I sat outside in the shade, at the back of the house, behaving like two silly schoolgirls. We were recalling the happy days of our childhood, and were so hysterical with laughter that the tears rolled down our faces. I left Emily for a moment, to go into the house. There was one step from the yard into the house, and as I came back out, I was just going to put my foot on the step when a terrible cold wind surrounded me and I was frozen to the spot. An awful strangeness came over me and I clutched the doorpost for support. I knew I was in the presence of death.

Emily was a few yards away from me, and her laughter vanished. She looked fearfully at me and said, "My God, Rit, whatever is wrong?" I said, "Mam's gone." Then a man's cold, dead hand caressed the side of my face, and I called out, "No, Father's gone." Emily said, "Don't be a fool, Ritty, we haven't got a father." I came to myself and found I was crying; I told Emily, "Ivor's father has just passed away." The coldness had gone and I was back in the heat of Australia, but there was a sense of gloom now. "How am I going to tell Ivor his father is dead?" I said.

Emily felt the gloom, so she called her children together and said, "Come on, kids, we're going home." The children did not wish to leave so soon, but when they asked their mother why

223

they had to go, she told them that I had just had bad news from home. They looked at me and wondered why I was crying.

On the mantelpiece, over the wood stove, stood the brass candlesticks that I had brought out from home, and also a solid brass collier's pit lamp, engraved with the name 'Alfred Webb'. The lamp had been presented to my father-in-law as a prize for being the best colliery contractor in Wales, and he had given it to me to keep for my son, Alfred John, when he became a man, in memory of his grandpa. I knew my father-in-law had just come to wish me goodbye, and I wanted to honour his memory, so I placed a piece of black cloth over his lamp – the only way I could show my mourning for him.

Ivor had built a bough shade (a place of shelter from the heat), and when I heard him coming through the bush I went to this shade because I could not face him with my eyes red from crying. He came to the bough shade and asked me why I was standing out there. I had my back to him and didn't answer, so he came over and turned me round to face him; then he said, "My God, what's the matter?"

"Ivor, Father has passed away," I said. He looked incredulously at me and said, "We've just had a letter to say he's better."

"Yes, Ivor," I said, "but that was written seven weeks ago." Then I told him exactly what had happened. "It was Father's hand, so like yours, Ivor, and I heard Alice's voice cry out, 'Oh my God, Father's gone!'" Ivor was convinced. He turned on his heels, and went out into the bush to hide his sorrow; he was very upset.

We wrote down the exact time and date of my premonition, and our next letter from home confirmed that Father had indeed died at that precise moment; exactly five days later I had another strange feeling, and found myself an unseen mourner in Protheroe Street at my father-in-law's funeral; I saw them bringing his body through the door, and heard them sing a hymn. I noted down the name of the hymn and in due course this was confirmed by Ted Manning. Alice, whose voice I had heard, was in the house at the time, though she lived miles away.

TWENTY SEVEN

By now we were nearing our first Christmas in Australia. Ivor had enquired around town whether there was a place of worship, and if so, which was the nearest to our home. He was told that there was a little Anglican church at the lower end of town, but this only had services when the travelling priest came round. There was also a Presbyterian chapel, but it was a long way out and the way there was too complicated for Ivor to understand or explain. I was determined to find this chapel and see if I could discover a short cut to it, because I was anxious that my little boy should attend Sunday School.

Then I had a message from Emily, over the grapevine, that the travelling priest was in Northampton; she asked me if I would go with her to the service on Sunday because Emily and her two daughters were going to be confirmed on Monday. My brother-in-law was a Catholic, and the two girls had been attending a convent school in the township, but Emily was caretaker of the little Protestant school, a job which was being sought after by many women who were Anglicans. So Emily had taken her children from the Catholic school, and on the Monday they would be confirmed into the Anglican church.

Soon after sun-up on Sunday morning I hurried up to Mr. Hendley's; there I went into the paddock and milked Blackie, then, after leaving Mrs. Hendley's milk in the usual place, I hurried home. I got home at six o'clock, to find visitors waiting for me, a Mr. and Mrs. Raymond and their children, who introduced themselves as Dick and Mary, with ten-year-old Dicky and eight-year-old Molly, originally from Barry in South Wales. Dick was a farm labourer, and they lived eight miles away in a place called Badra. They had started out early because their old banger would become too hot to travel in later in the day. With them they had brought a large butt of flour (approximately 25 pounds) and a large shoulder of mutton, the first fresh butcher's meat we had seen since coming to the bush; our diet had consisted mainly of rabbit. The Raymonds planned on staying for the day and going back after sundown when it would be cooler to travel. (The day-time temperature just then was a hundred and twenty-four degrees in the shade.) After cooking dinner for eight of us, I was reduced to a grease spot!

As the house was so very hot, we ate our dinner out in the bough shade. Then Mary made a sponge cake for tea; as she was rather a large lady, I would have expected the cake to be heavy, but it turned out to be the lightest and tastiest sponge I had ever tasted. She taught me how to make bread scones by adding cream of tartar and bicarbonate of soda to plain flour, and these too were delicious, so much nicer than the damper bread. I told her that I would like to make real bread, but was unable to get yeast; she said, "You will have to make your own. We'll come again to see you in a fortnight, and I'll bring you a dirty bottle." I wondered why on earth she was going to bring me a dirty bottle, but there was no answer yet.

I had to leave our guests for a while, to do the afternoon milking, and when I explained about this I also told them that I had promised to go to church with Emily; Dick asked me how I was going to get there, pointing out that it would be dark when the sun went down at five o'clock. I had not really thought about it getting dark, but I had given my promise and I intended to keep it, regardless of the long trek there and back through the bush.

"Oh no, you can't travel alone through the bush at night," Dick told me. "I'll take you in the car, then I'll wait around for you and bring you home again."

At six o'clock each night my two little ones always asked for their 'co-coke' to go to 'Beddie Byes', but that evening I did not want them to know that I would be leaving them for a while as I knew it would upset them. So I got them off to bed before I went. They had been up since five o'clock, so it did not take them long to get to sleep. I did not want to disturb them, so I did not light the candles, but got dressed in the dark, having earlier in the day seen that my clothes were all ready laid out on the bed. I was wearing, for the first time, a new salmon pink two piece and a matching georgette hat which I had taken out to Australia with me, and I had a beautiful pair of shoes to match my suit. I walked proudly into the living room, asking everyone how I looked, and they all agreed that I looked very nice – Dick said I would 'knock them for six'! Then he took me down to Emily's in his car.

Emily was not quite ready; she was preparing to put on a beautiful white dress that I had made for her back home in Wales. It was a long walk to the church, at the entrance to which there was a wrought iron archway with an arc lamp hanging in the centre. There were several small lights on each side of the drive going up to the little church, then four wooden steps went up to a railed platform, and we had to walk up one at a time. Emily led the way, with her two little girls walking behind her, while I was at the rear. The people were already assembled in their seats, and as we walked in, every head turned to stare at 'Mrs. Douglas's sister' who had arrived from England, for although they had heard of my arrival, this was the first time they had laid eyes on me. I felt like a peacock, strutting in my fine feathers, but we walked proudly down to the front row and took our seats.

There was no choir, and though the man taking the service was supposed to be a bishop, he wore no surplice or cassock, and the service was conducted just as a chapel service would be, with no kneeling, just bowing of heads in prayer. We stood to sing the hymns, and there was a short address; I don't think there was an organ, so we sang unaccompanied.

As we stood to sing the last hymn my eyes went down to my feet, and I had a sudden feeling of horror. Then I had a terrible urge to burst into laughter, though remembering where I was, I suppressed this. I was thinking how I had strutted down the aisle in all my finery, with one elegant shoe on one foot and a milking shoe, white with dried milk, on the other! Emily nudged me to stop laughing, and I pointed to my feet, whereupon she too started shaking with suppressed laughter. We stayed in our seats until every one had gone out to where the Bishop stood waiting to shake hands with them, then we went too. When the Bishop shook hands with me, Emily having already introduced me to him, he asked me if he would have the pleasure of confirming me on the following day. I stammered "No, no, no," and ran down the steps, where the people stood waiting to meet me, flew past the crowd – and there, standing in the archway with the arc light full on him, stood Ivor in his working trousers and vest.

The sight of my husband standing there in those old clothes outside a church on a Sunday evening nearly caused me to die of

227

shock. "What are you doing here like this?" I asked.

"I've come to take you home," he said.

"Where are the Raymonds?" I asked.

"They've gone home," said Ivor. At that I asked where the children were and Ivor said, "They're all right, they are asleep."

"Oh my God!" I cried; I was filled with a terrible fear. There were Pearl, only two years old, and Jack, just three, alone in that shack out in the heart of the wild Australian bush, with all the windows and doors left wide open to let in the air. Ivor had had a lift down in the Raymonds' car, and he had been so concerned about my safety coming home through the bush that he had forgotten about the children. I caught hold of his hand and said, "Run!" and we ran as never before, fear lending speed to our feet. I think if we had trodden on a snake, such was our haste that it would not have had time to bite us. We covered those three miles in record time, and collapsed into the house, exhausted. The children were still fast asleep, and all was well. We looked at each other and burst out laughing; then I showed Ivor my feet and we laughed until the tears ran down our faces.

Next day I took the children walk about to see their Aunty Emily, so that I could apologise to her for running away without even saying goodnight. After we had discussed her confirmation, she asked me what we were doing for Christmas. In fact, because the weather was so hot and we did not have any newspapers or a calendar I had not realised that it was December, but Emily told me "Christmas is on Saturday." I had bought no toys and made no preparations at all, but Emily gave me an old doll that someone had once given her; it was called a 'waggy head dolly', and she had always been afraid of it. She told me to come into the township on the Friday, because they were going to hold a bazaar in the Town Hall, and all the farmers' wives would be bringing in their home-made produce to sell. "Come," said Emily, "you will enjoy it," so I promised her I would and we went home because I still had my milking to do for Mr. Hendley.

I didn't show the doll to Pearl, but after the children went to bed that night I washed it, and before Christmas Eve I had repainted the head brown, the eyes blue, and painted two lovely rosy cheeks on it; then I dressed it beautifully so that it looked like a new shiny doll, and hid it away till Christmas. Meanwhile Ivor made a horse's head out of a piece of wood and painted it, and attached it to a broom handle and put some reins on it and a crossbar at the bottom; When he had finshed, it looked like a new hobby horse. My mother had sent a little parcel from home containing some small toys she had bought from Woolworths – in the parcel were a large packet of balloons, a set of carpenter's tools for Jack, and a baby toy for Pearl.

On Friday I left the children with Ivor and went to the bazaar with the few shillings that Ivor had been able to give me. The Town Hall was just one long brick-built room, the inside of which had stalls all around, so that it looked just like a market, with the farmers' wives competing with each other in selling their home-made goods. Emily asked me if I had any poultry for Christmas, and I said, no, but if I could afford it, I would like a little chicken, and I would also like to buy some fruit for the children's stockings. Emily said the only way I could buy fruit was by the tray or half tray, which contained two oranges, two bananas and two passionfruit; there were no apples, as apples couldn't grow in Australia, and they couldn't import them because the country was too dry. The half tray of fruit cost me one shilling and threepence. Emily asked me how much money I had left to buy a chicken, and when I said I only had a shilling, she told me, "Mrs. Chick, the farmer's wife, has one chicken left. It's very small and I think she'd let you have it for a shilling."

That night we filled the children's stockings, and they were very excited on Christmas morning when they got up and saw them. It was a real contrast with the Christmas before when we had been worrying because we didn't have a pan big enough to cook our gander, where this year all we had was a chicken weighing less than two pounds. We laughed at the comparison, but said, "Never mind, we'll enjoy it just the same." Mr. Hendley called in to wish us a happy Christmas; we had no drink to offer him, but as he was a teetotaller, it didn't matter. He asked me what I was going to do with the chicken, and I told him that after I had picked out all the bits of feathers, I was going to wash it, stuff it and cook it. He said, "My advice to you would be to take it to the farthest end of your paddock, dig a hole and bury it!" And this I did, because it had turned green due to the intense heat. So instead of a traditional dinner, we had a tin of rexpie – something similar to boiled ham.

Mr. Hendley invited us to afternoon tea with his wife and

himself at their place. We went up after dinner, and as it was too hot to go indoors, we sat on the verandah which looked down on to the paddock where Blackie was standing together with Mr. Hendley's horse. Their house stood on a rise, so they were able to look out on fields and paddocks, and in the far distance could be seen other shacks. Mr. Hendley was busy blowing up the balloons that the children had taken up with them; then he handed one to each of them, having tied the necks with string, and they ran up an down the length of the paddock, with the balloons floating above them. But when they reached the end of the verandah, the balloons went pop! They kept coming back for more, but each time they got to that part of the verandah the same thing happened again. Mrs. Hendley called to her husband, "You had better go and investigate, and see what is causing the balloons to burst." He found that on one of the posts of the verandah was a cone-shaped hornets' nest; a hornet was a flying insect which looked like a large grub and had what seemed to be a sharp spear on the end of its nose. They had been darting out each time a balloon passed the nest and pecking at them until they burst.

Mr. and Mrs. Hendley were an aristocratic couple, well spoken, seemingly well educated, and English. Mrs. Hendley was a recluse, and they had come out into the bush some forty years before with a young baby, a little girl called Lulu. Lulu was now married to a Pommie who was a deserter, and they had gone up into the bush to hide. We were told later that we had been very honoured indeed to be invited into the Hendleys' home, because they did not speak to anyone or make social visits to town. They kept themselves to themselves, not bothering with anyone and were considered to be a strange couple. The only time that their neighbours had found out anything about them had been when the little girl was in school; she had said that her parents had lived in the grounds of a mansion and her father had been head gardener to a lord, so it was assumed that he had at some time committed some terrible crime and been deported, together with his wife and child.

I guessed that the reason we had been favoured by the Hendleys was because when Ivor had first gone out to the bush looking for work, he had come across their house by accident, and seen an elderly woman near a log-pile trying to chop some heavy logs. He had taken the axe out of her hand, and had told

230

her to go indoors out of the heat and leave the work to him. She had gone in, and he cut a pile of logs for her, then put the axe in the shade and disappeared. She had recognised from his voice that Ivor was an Englishman, and knew of Mrs. Douglas's brother-in-law, hence the gift of the hen and clutch of chicks when we settled in our home.

TWENTY EIGHT

Ivor decided that we must get a horse because it was a must for a man out in the bush who was engaged on the hopeless quest for work. He had walked for miles without success, and he felt that with a horse he could travel further into the bush. There was a delivery man in town who had a horse to sell, a fairly elderly mare which he was selling cheaply because he needed a younger, faster horse and didn't have room in the paddock for two horses. He would sell it, he said, for eight pounds. I asked Ivor, "If this is an old mare, is it going to be any use to you as a saddle horse?"

"All she needs is a good rest and plenty of feeding," he said, "and she'll be fine for me. I won't be riding her too hard."

I told him that I still had a few pounds left of my landing money, and he could have that. Later that day he came back proudly riding his horse, with a big black labrador running alongside him, and I asked him where he was taking the dog. He said that the man had given it to him for my protection when Ivor was out in the bush. I told Ivor the dog wouldn't stay with us, he was a fully-grown animal and he would surely run back to his former home; but he came into our house and settled down as if he had been there all his life. Ivor had paid two pounds deposit on the horse and the rest was to be paid by instalments.

He set the mare loose in the paddock where there was plenty of food for her. We could only claim 'our' paddock as ours because of a wire fence at the bottom of our land, so Ivor cut back some of the wire to make an opening for the horse to go through to the gully where there was plenty of couch grass. Then he put a fence from the top end of our paddock across the gully to the neighbouring fence, to prevent the horse from straying into the bush, and although the water in the gully ceased to flow in that hot season, there was plenty of drinking water for the horse in the water traps. Lastly Ivor fenced off another three

232

acres of crown land running down to the gully, so that the mare had eight acres of land to run around in, and I had become a 'horse widow'! Ivor spent all his time with the mare, and doted on her, and Daisy, as we called her, soon became a member of the family. In a short time she was in perfect condition, and then my lonely life started, because Ivor would ride out early on the Monday morning, and I would not see him again until the next Saturday.

The R.S.L. (The Returned Soldiers' League) had made it an unwritten law of the bush that all available employment must be given to the returned soldiers. Many of the men in Northampton were sheep shearers; they would travel hundreds of miles to the bigger farms and only came home once a year at Christmas, when they had large sums of money on them because they had had no chance to spend any while shearing. They were men of honour as far as their debts to the storekeepers were concerned, and they would call in at each store before going home to their wives, to see what money was owing, so that their wives would be in credit with the stores and could live on this while their husbands were away. There was no unemployment money or sick relief, nothing at all for the family of a man who could find no work.

I had asked Emily to ask around to see if anyone needed a washerwoman or a needlewoman, because I had to find work to support myself and the children. It was very hard to live in that shack alone when Ivor wasn't coming home at nights, and I was terrified of the loneliness. Darkness came on so suddenly, and on the longest days it would go dark at five o'clock, so before darkness fell I would get in all the logs for the fire, then shut the back door and put a piece of wood against it, hoping that I had jammed it so that it could not be opened from the outside. I pretended to myself that no-one could get past that, though I knew in my heart that the slightest push would open it. I had to have something to hold on to. Then I would shut the front door and put a peg in it. The water and the wood I would bring inside just in case the children were ill in the night, because I was too frightened to go outside in the dark.

I would not see the dog all night because he would be out exploring, but it was better that way, because if there was a moon about, it would be so big and low down that Australian dogs would sit on their haunches and howl, and I would be much

233

more frightened of that. Thousands of bull frogs in the gully made such a din throughout the night that for a long time I had very bad headaches. The children would be soundly asleep, and I would not hear one solitary human sound, only the strange sounds of the bush which were very frightening to listen to; I would sing quietly to myself to blot out the sounds of the bush. During the wet season the rain would be so deafening that I would stare up at the roof expecting it to cave in at any moment. On some nights we would have tropical electric storms, which sounded like gunfire, and the whole shack would seem to shake with the fury of the storm; but the worst nights of all were those that were hot and still, when the little one would be perspiring and the mosquitoes were biting, and I knew I would have to take the children's beds out on to the verandah.

The only light we had was a little oil lamp in the kitchen. I would struggle with my fear before opening the front door, and I would have to master it and step out to see if there was anyone about. I would not really have been able to see anyone if they *had* been there, because it was so black, but I would strain my ears and listen for the slightest sound. Then I would start singing again, softly at first, then louder and louder to give myself courage, and tell myself that no-one could come up there because the snakes would kill them. That was my only comfort. The front door was wide, and the cots had wheels on them so I was able to pull them outside onto the verandah without disturbing the sleeping children.

Ivor had bought a second-hand twenty-two Winchester rifle from a young boy who had been his friend when he lived alone in the shack. When the boy discovered Ivor's lonely plight he had given him his gun, saying, "Ivor, you can't live up here alone without a gun. Borrow this from me." When Ryan bought himself a new gun, he sold the old one to Ivor. Ivor knocked in two six inch nails over the front door frame and rested the gun across them; he always left the gun with me when he went off into the bush, and taught me how to use it, so each night, early on, I would take the gun down, put a shot in it, and replace it on the nails. Then I would put a kitchen chair by the curtained doorway.

I had now become quite adept at pulling my bed down, dragging it out on the verandah, and putting it together again outside. I would not light the hurricane lantern for fear of

234

attracting attention, since sometimes there would be an aborigine roaming the bush. Then, before getting into bed, I would take the rifle with me, and I would go to sleep with one hand on the barrel of the gun which would be standing by the side of the bed. I always slept with a shot in the gun, but with the safety catch on, and I felt much safer, although I was told that it was a foolish thing to do, as I was putting a weapon in the hands of an intruder.

There was a tree shading the kitchen end of the verandah, and one day I knew that something had got up into the tree; all night long it kept calling out repeatedly in a deep-throated voice, as if it was talking to me, "More pork, more pork." I got out of bed, stood between the two cots, and tried to tell this thing to go away, but I could not get the words out. When Ivor came home on Saturday I was a complete wreck. I told him about this thing in the tree every night – but Ivor laughed, and said it was only a 'morepork' and it would not harm me. (A morepork is a large bird with a head like a fish.) Ivor shot up into the tree to frighten it away, and it did not come back; we were told later that it was unlucky to kill a morepork.

Ivor came back that time with half a sack of beautiful Washington navel oranges, and said he had been orange picking. He had found a little casual work and had been promised tomato picking and peach picking in their seasons, and though he had not made a lot of money, he had earned his keep for the week, and the oranges were his perks. Hence he was able to do a little shopping, for the things we would need to see us through the coming week, such as flour, sugar and potatoes, all that the money would run to.

Australia is a man's country, and the bush is no place for a woman or her children. Ivor had fenced all round the house and garden to stop any animals coming into the house, but the back of the house was open to the wilds, and I knew now that this was going to be my life, alone with the children all the week, and seeing my husband only at the weekend. The Raymonds called in to see us every second Sunday, and each time they came they brought with them a shoulder of mutton and a bag of flour; they arrived at sun-up and left just after sundown. On one visit Mary brought me a 'dirty bottle' and I asked her what I was supposed to do with it. When Ivor went shopping on the following Saturday I told him that I wanted him to get me a block of

235

compressed hops, because on her last visit Mary had showed me how to make yeast. The compressed hops looked like a block of wood, and I had to break off an ounce or two, with a whole peeled potato and a tablespoon of sugar. When the potato was cooked I had to strain the liquid off into the 'dirty bottle' (it got that name because it had a sediment of yeast all round it); I then had to cook the liquid and leave it to stand for twenty-four hours, after which I had to boil another potato, a tablespoonful of sugar and a few more ounces of hops, pour out the liquid which had been standing for twenty-four hours, and then pour the second lot of liquid into the bottle. This whole process then had to be repeated for a third time. After the third boiling the liquid had to be left for another twenty-four hours, and then it was ready for breadmaking.

On the following Sunday Dick Raymond came out in his car and took us to Badra for the day. The Raymonds lived in a two-roomed bungalow, with a verandah front and back, only a small place, but solid and good. They had closed in the back verandah to make a kitchen, and this was filled with remarkable furniture; it was none too clean, and there was nothing on the floors, no carpets or mats of any kind. Mary gave me a guided tour of the bungalow. The kitchen contained a dresser cum food cupboard cum saucepan cupboard which Dick had made from rough Nestlé's Milk boxes, made as only Dick could have made it (he couldn't knock a nail in a piece of wood), and unpainted, so that whichever way you looked at it you could see 'Nestlé's Milk' staring at you. Mary kept literally everything in this, and though the cupboard was almost indescribable, it was her proudest possession.

The kitchen was a shambles, and since Mary was very large, it was a miracle that she managed to get her body round it. However she cooked us a beautiful dinner in spite of the shambles, and her 'Spotted Dick' was as light as a feather. She told us she would set the table out in the dining room, because we were too many to eat in the kitchen; the dining room consisted of one scrubbed table, one kitchen chair, one chair with the back broken off it, and one three-legged chair with a block under. Dick carried some boxes in for us to sit on. The bedroom held a double bed and two single beds, home-made by Dick who had used sawn-off branches of trees lashed together with cord, and made spring mattresses of netting wire nailed to the four sides of the bed. The overlays were sacks filled with wild cotton. How the double bed took the weight of Dick and Mary I'll never know, because it rocked like a cradle!

Mary told me that in her letters home she told her people about her house in such a way that she gave them the impression that she had a beautiful home; she had also told them about her farm with six hundred sheep, the family swimming pool, and the children's private education. It gave her people something to boast about back home, and let them think that she and Dick were doing well out in Australia, but the truth was that the farm and the six hundred sheep belonged to Dick's boss, and the luxury home was the bungalow as I have described it. The children's private education was a correspondence course given free by the State for children who lived too far away in the outback to attend a state school. As for the swimming pool, it was the gully that ran down near their house, and the children would paddle in a little pool they had made by damming the gully.

On this Sunday the Raymond children took Jack and Pearl to paddle in their pond, but Jack stepped on a piece of glass and gashed his foot underneath.

The glass had pierced a vein and he was bleeding badly; he lost a lot of blood before we could get him up to the house. Dick got the car out quickly to take Jack to the Doctor, but the doctor's place was ten miles away, and I knew Jack would never make it if he went on bleeding like that. I tried to staunch the flow of blood, but it was still pumping out of him, so I asked someone to give me a penny and a clean white cloth. I wrapped the penny in a piece of linen, pressed it tightly into the ball of the foot and held it there to let the blood congeal.

I held him in my arms until the bleeding stopped. He seemed lifeless and all the blood had drained out of his face, so that we feared he would die through loss of blood. But once again faith and prayer, which had always played a major part in my life, brought him back to us, and the following morning he was none the worse; however a few days later I noticed that he was limping a little. I put some cushions on the table, and laid him down on them, telling him I was going to tickle his feet. Where the wound had been, there was now a lump as big as a marble. I sterilised a needle in a milk saucepan, and let Jack think I was tickling him; while he laughed, I scraped at the ball of the foot and cleared away a piece of quartz which had been lodged in his foot. I had thought that I had cleansed the wound completely, but because he had been losing so much blood, I hadn't been able to see it properly. Now I put some of my homemade ointment on it, and all Jack kept saying was, "Tickle me more, Mammy." He had enjoyed himself through it all!

Since Ivor was not at home during the week, it meant that I had to take the children with me when I went milking. (Ivor did not have a regular job, he just did odd jobs when he could get them, to pay for his keep, and this made it a little easier to manage for food for myself and the children because I did not have to find any for Ivor during the week.) I always left the children on Mrs. Hendley's verandah when I went milking, because Blackie did not like them. Mrs. Hendley was a strange woman, and it was difficult to have an intelligent conversation with her; she once asked me, "Mrs. Webb, what have you run away from?"

"My sister nominated us," I explained. "We didn't know what part of the country we were going to until we landed in Northampton."

"No-one comes up here unless they are running away from something," emphasized Mrs. Hendley, and it was pointless to argue with her.

One day when I went up to milk Blackie, Mr. Hendley was there. "Mrs. Webb," he said, "you must have a very loving home life."

"What makes you say that, Mr. Hendley?" I asked.

"Well, you have two lovely chilren, and very often I come down into the bush, hide so that they can't see me, and watch them at play. Listening to them, I know they are being brought up in a loving home. And when I get home, I have to repeat everything that I've heard to my wife. The best thing that has happened to us in all the years since we've been out here is to have you and the children where we can see you each day. Did you know, Mrs. Webb, that when they are playing in their cubby house they are 'Mate and Matey Hendley?' And when I tell Mrs. Hendley how the children mimic us, she laughs as I've never heard her laugh before. The game I enjoy watching most of all is when 'Mate' picks up his little wooden axe and struts off to chop wood for 'Matey', and little Pearl shouts after him 'Bye bye Mate, see you at tucker time.' Then Jack tries to fell a tree with his little axe, and 'Matey' calls out to him 'Tucker time in the Hendley camp', and Jack answers her 'Coming, Matey!'"

Walking back and forward with the children for such a distance every day was exhausting; it was still one hundred and twenty-four degrees in the shade and all through the summer months the gardens were like cement. It was hard to believe that a blade of grass could ever grow again, and gardening was out of the question. Life became boring and monotonous. I couldn't even see my sister through the nine months of the summer because it was too far to walk in the sweltering heat to think of visiting. People did not leave the shelter of their homes during the heat of the day, and usually they rested then, but I could not rest because it was too hot. Most houses were built of weatherboard, with ventilators, but our shack was iron and unlined, and had no ventilation. I had hung two oval-framed pictures on the wooden framework inside the shack, and even though the doors and windows were all open, the intense heat had warped the one picture hanging on the back wall of the living room, twisting it and breaking the glass. It was as if a giant hand had taken hold of it and wrung it like a woman wringing a cloth.

To relieve the monotony of the day, I took the children walk about, hoping it would be cooler in the bush, and we found a cleared path which had been a track made by the miners years before. We did not know where it led, but I felt sure that it *would* lead us somewhere, even if that meant a long walk; and as long as we kept on the track I knew we would not get lost, and our way back was safe. After a while we came to a clearing where we could see a bungalow not too far ahead of us. I saw a woman coming towards us who called out in a friendly voice, "Hello there, come in out of this terrible heat and have a cup of tea. You are Mrs. Douglas's sister, aren't you?"

She took us up to the bungalow, which was on stilts with steps leading up to it. It was very dark inside, for all the blinds were drawn – to keep out the heat, she said. The building was double fronted, with a passage going from the front to the back and two rooms leading off on each side; it was the biggest bungalow I had seen. The verandah at the back had been closed in, making a long narrow kitchen. I did not see inside any of the rooms, but the passage and the kitchen were wooden; there was no floor covering and the interior was very rough, the furniture being home made.

The woman poured me a cup of tea, but before I could raise the cup to my lips, it had become a swimming pool for the flies, and had to be thrown out. Three times she tried to pour a cup of tea, with the same result, and by then I had lost my thirst; but we were so busy talking that she did not notice I hadn't drunk any of the tea. She said she was moving out on the Saturday because her family had grown up now, and the place had become too small for them, so her husband and sons had built her a pug house just across the road. The garden in front of the house led down to the main road which in turn led to the large estate owned by the Carruthers, and on the opposite side of the main road from the bungalow stood the 'pug' house that the men had built. ('Pug' is like a mud, and when dried it looks just like stone, which is then whitewashed; buildings made of it are very cool inside.)

The woman asked me, "Why don't you come here to live, Mrs. Webb? It would be better for you than that old shack. I'll speak to the owner for you, I know he will let you have it for twelve and sixpence a week rent."

"It would be wonderful," I said. I imagined myself living there. There would be a bedroom each for my two children, and I would open up the verandah again and make my kitchen in one of the other rooms. The idea made me so excited, for though the house was on its own, it was not lonely as mine was, and although the town was miles away, there was a main road I could walk on instead of going through the bush. Then I remembered – twelve and six a week. I had no money, but when I told her this, she said, "My dear, you must take it, you will find the money somehow."

I explained that I had been looking for work, needlework or anything I could get, but so far I had found nothing. She said, "Take it, my dear, it is terrible for you living in that old shack, you must be roasted alive in the summer. No-one else would live there – I wouldn't myself, for all the tea in China. And how can you live there after what happened to the other people?"

"What happened to them, Mrs. Smith?" I asked.

She told me then how when the Rays were drummed out of Northampton several years before, a young couple with a boy of five or six years old went to live there. The boy's father had caused an aborigine to recieve a police sentence by reporting him for some misdeed that he had committed, and the tribe had sworn vengeance on him. One morning the couple woke to find their little boy's cot, which had been standing by the window, was empty. The child was nowhere to be found, and the black trackers, who are highly skilled in their craft, were called in. The little boy had been stolen out of his cot, and they found the place to which he had been taken; he had been roasted alive and eaten.

I told the woman that I would speak to my husband about the bungalow as soon as he came home; I didn't want to go back to the shack after hearing that story. Mrs. Smith said she was sorry to have upset me, she had not realised that I hadn't heard the tale. I had to leave then, as I still had to do my milking for Mr. Hendley and get home before dark, but I was sure that when I told my husband the story, he would agree to us moving out to the bungalow, and he would find the money somehow.

TWENTY-NINE

With Ivor away, my days were filled with fear. There was so much out in the bush that could kill, and it came right up to the shack on every side, filled with poisonous snakes such as adders. And then there were the bobtailed goannas, which strutted around like tame cats but could be deadly dangerous if you got close to one. The Aussies called them 'land lizards', but they were more like land crocodiles; some slept under my house at night, and it was quite the usual thing to see one of these creatures with its body under the house and its head on my doorstep, looking around inquisitively. If either of my children had gone near it, it would have snapped their legs off. My brother-in-law once told me that if a goanna buried its teeth in a man's leg, the only way they could release the man was by lighting a fire under the goanna's tail or by putting a red-hot shovel under its belly.

And if I just walked to the clothesline I would carry a stick to hack my way through the cobwebs that were made by the giant spiders which wove their webs like pieces of rope; if you happened to touch one of these, you would be hit in the face by a spider as big as your hand. The worst thing of all was the red-backed spider; this was very small – some were only as big as the top of your nail – and would hide anywhere, so that you dared not put on a coat that had been hanging up on a door without first beating it, in case one of these spiders had made a nest in it. They were tiny black spiders with a red spot on their back end, so that they were known as 'red arse spiders', and their favourite breeding place was under the seat of the toilet, the toilet being a bucket with a wooden seat over it and a canvas screen round it for privacy. However desperate one might be to use the toilet, one would first have to inspect all round underneath it before sitting down. There were also dingos, wild cats and race-horse goannas; the dingos were like vicious alsatian dogs, and the race-horse goannas were about six feet long, like crocodiles, but standing on their legs.

When we got home from our walk, I set about making a meal for myself and the children. Then a man came to the back door. I could only suppose he had followed us back through the bush, for he was a complete stranger, not even an Aussie. He spoke like an Englishman and was dressed as a commercial traveller would dress in England, though in that heat no Australian man would wear a suit and an English hat; he carried a little bag with him. He evidently didn't know the unwritten law of the bush, or he would have stood outside the ten chain space and cooeed to give me warning he was there. Instead he came right up to the door and put his foot into the kitchen. I asked him what he wanted, and said, "Why didn't you cooee and let me know you were there instead of coming up to my door?"

"I wanted to see you ," he said.

I told him to stay outside and tell me what he had come about, and added that my husband was a big strong man and very jealous, and that I would call him if the man did not go away. He asked me where my husband was, and I said, "Probably up at the wood stack, tidying up the woodpile."

The stranger was a goodlooking, smart young man, aged about thirty, and he was smiling as he said, "Your husband is not here."

"He is," I said, and we argued for a few minutes, then he said, "I know where your husband is, and he won't be back until the weekend."

I backed away from him, but he kept coming towards me, so then I told him that I had a big black dog. He only said, "I've made friends with your dog, so I'm not afraid of him." By now I was standing with my back against the wall, beating him off. He wanted to kiss me, and kept asking me what was the matter. In desperation I called out 'Jack', though I did not know what I was calling, or even if the dog was anywhere around, because he was inclined to roam; but wherever he was that time, he must have heard the fear in my voice, because he came charging into the house like a streak of lightning. He got himself between the man and me, with his two paws on the man's shoulders, and was snarling and showing his teeth. He got the stranger out of the house in quick time – I feared at one point that he was going to tear the man's throat out – and it didn't take the man long to clear out of sight. I owed a lot to that old dog!

The next day I felt a little better; I had been terrified of the

243

night after hearing that dreadful story and then having that man come into my house, but I felt much safer knowing the dog was near me. However, I didn't know if he was still around, because if he was at the back of the house he would have been outside the fence, and he loved to roam around there in the shade. When we came back after milking, I couldn't settle in the house, so I took the little sulky, and putting the children to ride in turns, we went down to see my sister.

I told Emily about my visit to Mrs. Smith, and her offer of the house. I said, "I must have it, Emily, I can't live in that shack any longer," and told her that I was afraid to go to sleep at nights in case something happened, though I must have fallen asleep some time during the night, because I woke up shouting "We're alive, we're alive!" A prayer of thanks went up to Heaven that morning.

I did not tell Emily about the man in case Ivor got to hear of it; he was very jealous, and I was afraid he might say I had encouraged him. However I did tell her that on the way home from Mrs. Smith's I had met an elderly lady. It seemed that she had seen me going to Mrs. Smith's, and had looked out for me on my way back. "How are you, my dear?" she asked. "I have heard so much about you, how are you managing, my dear, with your husband not working and your two little ones to keep?" Her name was Mrs. Davidson, and she sounded like a nosey parker at first, but it was her real concern for me that made her ask this.

"I asked my sister to enquire about work for me," I told her. "I am willing to do a week's washing for half a crown a day, and I am also a good seamstress."

"I asked your sister how you were managing," she said, "and Mrs. Douglas told me not to worry, because you had plenty. Have you got plenty, my dear?"

"Oh Mrs. Davidson," I said, "I've not got plenty, I would consider myself rich if someone gave me a few days' work to do."

"Would you like to come and wash for me on Monday?" she asked.

"I would, with pleasure," I said, "but I must bring the little ones with me."

"Certainly, my dear, you must bring the little ones," she agreed, and she showed me the way to her bungalow, telling me

244

to use that track instead of going through the bush, as it was a short cut. Even so, it was still a mile from my shack to her bungalow, and it could only be travelled by daylight.

Emily made no comment on anything I said; it was as if she wasn't interested. Ivor came home on the Saturday, and I told him about the house. He said it would be lovely, but we could not afford it, so then I told him about my job with Mrs. Davidson, and the probability that she could get more work for me. Then I told him the story Mrs. Smith had told me, and explained that my head ached with the strain of fearing for the children; I had to get away. So Ivor said I could have the house, we'd manage somehow. He would try to pick up more casual work – now that he had the horse, he could travel.

I hurried home on Saturday morning after milking, and went to give Mrs. Smith the good news. But when I emerged from the bush into the clearing, I saw Emily, Jim and the four children carrying their furniture into the bungalow. They had got there before us. I did not show myself, but hurried home, heart-broken; they had left a good home to go and live in the new one. When I told Ivor, he commented, "So much for a loving sister! You shouldn't have been in such a hurry to tell her your business, you'll know better next time."

After the first disappointment of losing the house had worn off, I came to my senses and realised that I could never have afforded to pay that rent. I knew, too, that Emily's need was greater than mine, as she was under pressure to get out of her own house at the time. I looked around my old tumble-down shack and remembered the work and love that had gone into it; the words of an old song came into my mind: "Though it's only a tumble-down shack, but with love burning there, surely no love can compare with my little grey home in the west."

Ivor came home one day, to my surprise, with Daisy in the shafts of a sulky, which in this case was a lightweight two-wheeled trap with one seat going width-wise, and a box to rest your feet on; it would seat the driver and one passenger. I asked him to whom it belonged, and he said it was ours. "I'll be able to take you and the children out shopping now at weekends."

I was worried about the expense because I thought we still had to pay for the horse, but Ivor said the horse had been paid for, and he would pay for the sulky the same way. The people who had sold him the sulky had had two boys, one eleven and one nine years old. They had called in the doctor to the older boy who had a bad throat, and he advised them to take the boy to the coast for a few days; they set off in the sulky with the boy, but he died the next day. His parents asked Ivor to take the sulky because they didn't want to see it again, since they felt that if they hadn't had it they could not have taken the boy to the coast, and he might still have been alive. (He had had diphtheria.)

Just then I had a message from Emily asking me to go and clean the school for her, something which I had often done for her when she was not well. I had to be at the school when the children came out, so I took my own children and the dog, and we walked to the school. We watched the children playing tennis for a while until the school had closed, then, as it was a very hot day, I left the little ones in the shade watching the tennis. It was a very small school, just two rooms and a verandah, and the floors were oiled, so they just needed to be mopped. In one of the rooms hung a large mural which could very well have been a picture of Maesteg open market at home; this day I sat on the floor in front of the picture and was back in dear old Wales. Then Beryl, Emily's eldest daughter, came into the room with my two children. She was very excited.

"Look, Auntie, what I've bought," she said. She was holding several pairs of white cotton gloves in her hand, and she told me that they were being thrown out in Stokes's shop and she had had them all for tuppence. Then Beryl hurried off home, and my little ones played on the verandah while I finished cleaning the school. Before we went home I took the little ones to watch the adults playing tennis, and I must have dozed off in the heat. When I woke, some time later, the tennis players had gone, and so had my two children and the dog. I searched the school and the grounds, but there was no sight or sound of them anywhere. I was frantic, and, looking at the sun, I realised that I only had about half an hour in which to search for them before sundown, after which the whole place would be plunged into complete darkness.

I knew they would not go home without me, and I racked my brain, wondering where they might have gone; then I remembered Beryl and the gloves. By now I was so demented that the heat meant nothing, and I ran to town to see if I could catch up with them. I ran towards Stokes's shop, but there was no living creature to be seen, not even a dog. I asked the girl in the shop if

246

my two little ones had come in looking for gloves, and she said, "Yes, Mrs. Webb, they asked for gloves for Mammie. They came in through the side door and went out through the other one, so I thought you must be outside, waiting for them."

On the left of Stokes's shop was Barlow's, the baker and newsagent. Ivor had taken the children with him one day when he went to have his hair cut, and Mr. Barlow had taken them out back to play on the swing with his children; his little girl was also called Pearl. By now I was terribly distraught, with my hair hanging limply down my back, and I could hardly bring the words out.

"Are my little ones playing with your children?" I asked Mr. Barlow, and I saw his face go as white as chalk as he said, "No, Mrs. Webb, I haven't seen them. What's happened?" I told him about Beryl and the gloves, how I had fallen asleep, and how the girl at Stokes's had told me they had been there, but gone. Mr. Barlow advised me to go home as quickly as I could, and perhaps I might find they had made their way back. He did not offer to help me, and I felt terribly alone. I ran back to the school, but there was no-one there. I knew the children did not know their way home by the road, because we used a short cut through the bush, but I did not think they would have enough sense to stick to the little sheep track that led to our house, and I was afraid that I would never see them again.

What I did not know was that Mr. Barlow was neither callous nor cruel; he had just wanted to get me out of the way quickly while he gave out a distress signal; a cooee which men would pick up and pass from one to the other. Every man had his own horse, which would be within easy reach of his working place, tethered and ready for an emergency, so that within minutes men were galloping in from all directions, and the place, so recently almost a ghost town, was filled with men on horseback waiting for instructions from Mr. Barlow. Each man knew it was near sundown, and if the children went too far into the bush they would never be found alive again. Meanwhile I was up at the school, trying to decide which way to go. I knew I had to get back home quickly, and decided to take the track back through the bush, and prayed as I went, "Wherever they are, turn them back, oh God, turn them back." I kept repeating the words over and over again, as my only hope. My hair caught in the brambles as I ran heedlessly through the bush, and the trackers could have followed me by the clumps of my hair left clinging to the spikes, though I did not even notice the pain because my fear was so great.

As I neared our home, I could hear a horse galloping down the gully at the side of the house, and as I came out of the bush I could see it was Ivor. I called to him, and he said, "We are looking for two children lost in the bush." He did not realise that they were our two children, but I shouted out, "It's our children!" Just then I heard another horse coming down the same track, and when I looked up, I saw a man on a horse with two children in front of him and the dog running along at the side of them. The relief was so great that I collapsed, sobbing, on the ground.

The man handed the children down to Ivor, and they ran towards me, calling out, "Don't go to bye byes, Mammy, wake up, we were losted, but we're not losted any more, and Pearl was very tired, and I was very tired." They were babbling with excitement. "Jack gave Pearly a piggy back, then he give Pearly another piggy, 'cause we were losted, and Jack made us come back see Mammy!"

The man told me he had found them up near the burial ground; they must have taken the road leading there, but it was far out into the bush.

"I took that road by chance," he said. "Mr. Barlow said it was unlikely they would have gone that way, but that was the very road they had taken."

It was only a few minutes to sundown, and if the man hadn't taken a chance and gone that way, it is certain that they would never have been seen alive again, because the area was inhabited by so many snakes that it was called 'Snaky Patch'. It was definitely a place of no return for any wanderers. Had the children not been found before sundown, the search for them would have had to be abandoned because no horse will go into the bush at night – even if the rider was willing, the horse would refuse. These men who had searched for the little ones had been hostile when we first arrived, but they were no longer so; I owed my children's lives to all of them, and we would no longer be Pommies, but dinkum Aussies. (We owed a great deal, too, to that wonderful dog who had turned the children back, knowing the danger they were walking into).

By now people were preparing for the Northampton Show, an

agricultural show which was the town's main event, and all the conversation was centred around what the children were going to wear for the day. Mrs. Davidson had been to Perth for a few days, to visit her son, who was a vicar; he had given her half a dozen silk shirts he no longer wanted, and she passed them on to me. There were too many for Ivor, and so I unpicked one of the shirts and made a silk blouse for little Jack; then I made some little shorts to go with the blouse, and bought a quilted silk pith helmet (or 'fisher hat', as the children called them.) Before leaving England I had been given a white embroidered dress, to be a christening gown for Pearl; at that time it had been too big for her, but now, with pink and blue silk cotton, I embroidered over all the flowers at the bottom of the skirt, bringing out the blue and pink forget-me-nots. I also bought Pearl a blue organdie bonnet, with a brim made up of blue petals which stood right out to shade her face.

One night, after the children were asleep in bed, when I was busy embroidering the dress, I heard a peculiar noise coming from the back of the house, like great claws climbing up the iron of the wall. Then I heard the creature slide down, then climb up again. I did not know what it was, and I was too frightened to go out and look, but I could hear it climbing towards the roof. The corrugated iron roof of the shack did not come right down to the walls, but left a four inch gap all around for ventilation, and now I sat perfectly still, my tongue going down into my throat almost, to stop the sound of my breathing, watching the gap and expecting see hands or claws coming through it, because I had no idea what was outside. I could hear it claw its way the whole length of the roof and then back again; then it settled down just above where I was sitting. It stayed there all night, and so I spent the entire time standing at the door with my gun. Later I was told that it was a racehorse goanna, probably some six foot in length.

On the day of the Northampton show, Emily came over with her children, and we set off for the show with our picnic baskets. The six children were very excited and looked lovely in their fresh new clothes. Emily knew a short cut which would save us a few miles along the dusty road, and eventually it led us into the show field at the lower end of the paddock. It was a very hot day, but the weather was a little cooler that it had been and we picnicked and had quite an enjoyable time, then went in to see

249

the exhibits, the home-made bread and cakes and so on. Emily explained that she usually made something for the show, but she had not bothered that year.

From there we went to see the live-stock, and noticed a young man of about twenty-two, riding a beautiful horse which had evidently won some event because it was wearing a rosette. Nearby there were some fine cows and ferocious-looking bulls, and several rows of newly made sheep pens, with no sheep in them just then. We were watching the bulls, fascinated by their size and strength, when the sight of the young man on the prize-winning horse proved too much for one of the creatures, and it broke loose and charged, throwing both horse and rider into the air. It was terrible to see this, and to hear the horse screaming. The bull made ready to charge again, and everyone shouted for the animal's owner, but he was not there, and before the young man could get out of its way, the bull charged again. The horse quivered and got up on its feet and we saw that its side had been torn out. Now the bull was raging around the enclosure, and men were dashing about everywhere, but seemed to be doing nothing.

I put my little ones and Emily's youngest child over into the sheep pens, and shouted to the others, who by now were so frightened that they didn't know where to go, to join them; they all managed to get into the sheep pens, and we told the children to go further back inside. As Emily and I were climbing over into the pens, the bull saw us, but just as he was about to charge us, we both fell into safety, and the weight of his body carried him past us. Suddenly he wheeled around and came looking for us, but I heard someone shout 'Let the cows out', and this was done, to calm the enraged bull. Sadly, the horse had to be shot, and the young man was dazed and upset. After that we did not want to stay for any more, and made our way home, feeling sickened and shocked after our experience, especially Emily's youngest little girl, who was trembling violently. It was a terrible tragedy for the young man, who had seen his horse so dreadfully hurt after his triumphant win earlier on. Men were still to be heard shouting for the owners as we left.

THIRTY

Ivor had searched for miles around, looking for odd jobs, but all casual labour had finished until the wet season, and the little money that we had managed to save from Ivor's casual work had gone to pay for the horse and the sulky. At least we made sure that the little ones were well fed. Although Ivor suffered from the poor diet, he never complained, but would get up from the table after our meagre meal and tighten his belt; when I asked him why he was doing this, he would say, with a smile, "Oh, it's all right, I'm letting it out, I've eaten too much!" It worried me, because I could see that he had gone back several notches on his belt, but I let him think that I believed him. Anxiety took away my own appetite, and I did not want food.

Although Ivor was at home now, I still took the children with me on washing day – one time, at least, when they would have a good meal. The Davidsons were a lovely old couple, though Mr. Davidson was as deaf as a post and he and his wife had not spoken to each other for years, or so Mrs. Davidson told me. She said that Mr. Davidson never came into the house except for meals, and slept outside on his own verandah. Mr. Davidson, who was Swedish, was her second husband.

Before starting to eat my dinner one day, I took my meat off my plate and placed it on the little bread plate at the side, asking Mrs. Davidson if she would mind if I took my meat home with me for my supper. She handed me a serviette, saying, 'certainly she didn't mind', and I wrapped up the precious piece of meat which I was, of course, taking home for Ivor's supper. After that I noticed that every washday there would be a larger piece of meat put on my plate, and I always took this home for Ivor. During the meal I used to act as a link between the old couple; he would say to me 'tell her . . .' and she would say, 'tell him . . .', yet there was no bad feeling between them and they were quite contented and happy together!

One day Mrs. Davidson asked me, "How are you managing,

my dear, now that your husband is not working? It must be very hard for you."

"It's much easier now, Mrs. Davidson," I said, "since I've had this job with you."

She thought for a while, and then said, "Can you use a treadle sewing machine, my dear?"

"Oh yes," I said. "I prefer a treadle machine, but mine is just a hand machine." Then she asked me if I would come over on Wednesday to do some sewing for her. Now I had two jobs a week, and I would be taking home five shillings, which was a godsend. The dear old lady was deliberately finding work for me because she knew how desperately I needed the money. The Davidsons had a windmill over the well in their paddock, and a pipe pumped the water up into the wash-house, and one day some time later, while we were having dinner, the old man said to me across the table, "She go down windmill, take hammer, and bang bang, send for Mr. Webb, windmill broken." I told Ivor about this, and he said he had been wondering why they had been sending for him all the time to see to the windmill; the old lady had been deliberately breaking it, to make a job for Ivor. It was only a small job, but Ivor was very grateful for the few shillings she gave him when it was completed.

I was still doing the milking morning and afternoon for Mr. Hendley. My first milking was done at six o'clock in the morning, and it meant a walk of one and a half miles there and back, and then a further three mile walk to do my washing. Ivor looked after the children while I went milking, but I still took them with me to the Davidsons where they would always be sure of a good meal. (Now that I was working there twice a week, Ivor would get his meat suppers more often.)

The children were worrying me to take them to see their cousins, and since Ivor was going down to the town one day, leaving the horse and sulky behind, I asked him to harness the horse to the sulky so that I could take the children down in it to see Emily that afternoon. But Ivor told me to wait until he came back, then he would harness the horse, as long as it seemed likely that I could drive her. However, he did not come back in time for me to go, so I decided to harness the horse myself. I did not have a clue as to how to do it, and I had never watched Ivor, so I said to Jack, "You have watched Daddy harness Daisy to the sulky, haven't you? Will you show Mammy how it is done?"

Together we struggled to find out where all the bits and pieces had to go, and once that task had been done, we climbed aboard.

There are no sides to a sulky, so I had to balance to keep from falling out, which was very difficult on rough roads. We jogged along happily and I was amazed at the ease with which we travelled along the old mine track; Daisy was quite at home pulling the sulky – it had belonged to her last master. Suddenly she stopped, and although I kept saying nice things to encourage her, she wouldn't budge. I got down from the sulky and went around to her head to find out what was wrong, and discovered that I had guided her too close to a huge boulder, so that one wheel was on the road and the other half way up the boulder and we were in a tipping position. The horse's sense had told her that if she carried on we would be thrown out of the sulky.

I got back into the sulky and put the children down at my feet for safety, then I backed us a little way off the boulder; but I was not skilled enough to know how to get the horse past it, because Daisy was so awkwardly placed. The children cried, "Mummy, what's the matter, can't we go?"

"Yes," I said, "but we will have to have help."

"But there is no-one here to help us," they said.

"Yes, there is," I told them. "What do we always do when we are in trouble?"

"We ask Gentle Jesus," they said.

"So that is what we will do now," I told them, and together we asked Jesus to take the reins and guide Daisy away from the boulder. In a few minutes Daisy was happily trotting along, and how that happened I will never know, because there was only one way she could have passed the boulder, and that was by taking the wheel of the sulky up and over. That would have meant tipping the sulky and throwing us out, but we felt nothing, it was as if the boulder had been removed from Daisy's path. Yet when I looked back, the boulder was still there, and it was surely the power of prayer that helped us.

Eventually we came out on to the main road, and I drove Daisy on to the grass verge and tethered her to the fence opposite Emily's new home. Emily seemed a little embarrassed when she saw me – it was the first time I had visited her since she moved in. But her little girl Rae saved the day by screaming that her mouth was burning. Mrs. Smith had left all her big pot plants

253

along the verandah, and Rae had gone along sampling each one of them, and so burned her mouth. Emily said that yesterday Rae had burned her mouth eating corns off the peppercorn tree. It was lovely to stand out on the verandah and look out down the slope of the garden to the main road, and onto beautiful fields. This was farm country.

There were two men in the field opposite, building a pug wall. We went back into the house, and suddenly one of the men came rushing up to the door to tell me that I hadn't tethered my horse correctly. If the man had not come when he did, the horse would have strangled itself; I was so sure that I had tethered her properly, but being unskilled, I had not. Ivor was home when we got back, and he was very relieved that his beloved horse was all right, and that I hadn't smashed up the sulky.

Now that we had the horse and sulky, Ivor took us into town every Saturday, then went to the corn merchant, who was also the grocer, to order our groceries and pay for them. The grocer himself would take out the groceries and put them in the sulky; you could buy anything in his stores, from a pound of butter to a saddle for a horse. Meanwhile I would take the little ones to look round Stokes's store. I had no money to buy anything, but I wanted to see if he had any remnants of dress material, which were usually displayed on the counter if he had any. Then Pearl saw a dolly's bassinette pram for sale in front of the counter. She started to wheel it away out of the shop, wanting to show the 'dolly pram' to Daddy. She wanted me to buy it, but I tried to explain to her that I had no money and we would have to wait until Daddy could get some, so when she saw her father, she asked him if she could have a 'dolly pram'. I told him about the one in Stokes's shop, which was made of sea grass. Every Saturday after that, when we got into the sulky to go to town, it would be the same question: "Daddy, can you 'fford to buy me a dolly pram today?" and the answer would have to be, "Not today."

By now we had been in Australia for one year, and we hadn't seen a spot of rain. It had been very bad for the farmers, and most of the small farms around the bush had either lost their land or gone bankrupt, while thousands of sheep, after being sheared for their wool, were so thin through lack of feed and water that they were just bags of bones. They were driven miles to the top of a cliff and thrown over. We were told that Bert Ash

254

was next in line for bankruptcy. Now that I was able to go into town, I could meet the wives of the farmers who came into the stores to do their shopping. Many of them were very wealthy, but they lived miles away in the outback and this was their meeting place. While the men did their business and maybe had a drink, their wives would meet and walk together, dressed in beautiful dresses and big sun hats. Everyone I saw came up to me, shook hands and said, "How are you, Mrs. Webb, glad to see you have settled down, we hope you'll soon get used to our climate."

There was no class distinction in the outback; the motto was 'Jack is as good as his master.' The lowest paid man was equal to his boss, and what surprised me most was that every man that passed me touched his hat to me. I told Ivor that the Australians in the outback were rumoured to be hard drinkers and cursers, and according to the words of an old song, 'Northampton was an old mining camp, and the miners were made up of all sorts and classes, with many a scapegrace and many a scamp'; but to me these men were perfect gentlemen. "That's because they have accepted us," Ivor said. "They like you, and we are now regarded as Aussies."

The skies that had been an azure blue for the past twelve months were now beginning to gather, and we knew the cooler season would soon be with us. It was warm, but without the burning heat, and though we still wore thin clothing, it felt pleasantly cooler. On one particular visit to town, Pearl and Jack had a penny icecream cornet in the icecream parlour, and then we walked down to Mr. Barlow's, where Ivor was having his hair cut and listening to all the news, including an account of the day when our children were lost.

"We didn't include Snakey Patch in our search," said Mr. Barlow, "we didn't think any children would venture up there."

But Tom Pepper had told me, that fateful day, that if no-one else was going to look up there, he would go; and fortunately that was where he had found them. When he asked them what they were doing up there, they told him that they were going to Auntie's house because they wanted gloves like Beryl's. I couldn't express my feelings at how all these men had rallied to the cry of children lost. As we went down the road, we passed a group of men who called out "Hi, Ike" (the Australians couldn't

255

say 'Ivor' and always called him 'Ike'.) Ivor took me over and introduced me to them; they had killed a death adder, and were burning it in the gutter.

When the pub closed, at six o'clock, everyone went home; it was pitch dark and silent as the grave, and not a soul was seen after nightfall, so we left before it got dark. Ivor lit the candles on either side of the sulky, and away we went. Then, as we were nearing our house, we heard a baby crying. My two little ones had often prayed, "Please God, send us a baby", and now here was the unexpected sound of a baby's cries near our house. When we got into our paddock, Ivor handed me one of the candles, and while he unhitched the horse, I went into the house and lit the oil lamp, telling the children to stay on the doorstep while Daddy and I went to look for the baby. I thought that if a death adder could come into a busy street, it was possible for one of them to have come sneaking around our house, and I did not want to risk the children being bitten. (We knew that snakes went under our house to shed their skins; they would crawl out of their old shell into a new skin. leaving the old skin under our house. Ivor would have to rake out the old skins and burn them once a year.)

I wondered why, if someone had wanted to leave a baby, they hadn't opened the door, which was unlocked, and taken it into the house. However there was no sign of a baby – but there was a huge bull frog sitting in the glare of Ivor's lamp; he was the size of a large puppy dog, his eyes were bulging out, and he was crying 'Mama'. Ivor shooed him out towards the gully.

Next day we heard a pattering on the roof, and Ivor said, "It's started to rain." We looked out, and sure enough the wet season had started with a light rain. The children wanted to put their bathers on, so I dressed them in these, and we all went outside and stood in the rain. We were soaked through, but it was delicious. The rain came down heavier, and we turned our faces to the sky and let it wash over us, while the children danced about excitedly. It was the most wonderful feeling, and we couldn't have enough of it – the rain even seemed to unite us with South Wales, though we were thousands of miles away. (There are no grey skies in Australia, the land of perpetual sunshine. In England we have daylight without sunshine, but in Australia there is only sunlight, and without that light there is complete darkness. Hence winter in Australia is like summer in

Britain, and though storm clouds come into the sky, they do not obliterate the sun.)

Inside the house the noise of the rain beating down on the roof was so loud during the storm that we could not hear ourselves speak, but it was fascinating to go outside and see how the hungry earth swallowed up the rain. There was no beauty in the outback in the summer, not a blade of grass to be seen anywhere, nothing but hard, rock-like earth; and there was no variation of scenery, when you saw one part of the bush you had seen it all. Nothing could survive in that heat, no birds sang in the trees, and the trees threw out no leafy arms to shade you from the burning sun. The only leaves were on the uppermost part of the stringy trees, reaching up heavenwards as if asking for mercy. But now the first rains had fallen, and after the storm was over, the earth seemed like a hungry mouth licking up every drop of the rain; it left no trace of the storm. The air smelt sweet and fresh and lovely, and although the sun still shone, it was no longer merciless.

Next morning, after a night of heavy rain, the sun shone down kindly on a world transformed. Blades of grass were shooting up through the same earth in which it had seemed impossible for anything to grow, and we could go out and clean up, and start to dig our gardens. It was marvellous to be able to dig the spade into the earth and turn it over, something else which had been impossible before the rains came. We worked all day, through the light rain, the children enjoying themselves as if they were at the seaside. We learned to read the sky in winter, and tell whether the storm was going to be heavy or light. If it looked like being a heavy storm, then we ran for shelter long before it came, because the force of a tropical storm could batter a man's body black and blue, and had even been known to kill.

Every house had a corrugated iron tank running down the side of the house from the roof. My sister's was a seven hundred gallon tank, but some people had tanks holding as much as two thousand gallons of water, and the first rains on the roofs were like music to the people because it brought water into their empty tank. Emily's tank had been empty for weeks and she had had to buy her water from an underground tank quite a long way off. We didn't use the water from our tank because it was too small; Ivor had poured kerosene on top of the water to kill the silver-fish and stop the mosquitoes from breeding, and we used

257

that water for washing our hair, and drank the water from the well, which was good for us because there was magnesium in it, though it was too hard for washing hair.

Ivor planted the kitchen garden with vegetables – peas, beans, onions and other varieties, while I planted some bulbs that I had taken out with me from England. We found an old piece of netting wire which we placed in front of the verandah, and I planted sweet peas of all colours so that they would grow up the wire. We also planted cucumbers and tomatoes outdoors in the garden and we could actually watch the cucumbers grow; if we went out in the morning we could see just the tiny beginnings of a cucumber, but they grew so rapidly that by teatime we could go out and pick it for tea. In a very short time the outback had been transformed into what the Aussies call 'Chinaman's country' because the predominant colour was yellow. The trees, wattle and others, were full of yellow blossom, and everywhere we looked the ground was full of large yellow daisies; wild orchids grew in profusion, and arum lilies grew in large clusters on the roadside and anywhere where there was a grassy bank – if they grew in a garden they were considered to be weeds and were immediately chopped down. Sometimes a beautiful red cloud would pass over the house, turn and then change to silver grey, and by the squawking we knew it was a host of galahs (Australian cockatoos). We had one dead tree in our paddock, in sight of the house, and this was a favourite tree for budgerigars; sometimes it was a mass of colour with all the budgies nestled in it, leaving hardly a speck of tree to be seen. (They only settled on a dead tree.) But there seemed to be no singing birds in Australia.

THIRTY-ONE

Ivor was very much liked by the Australians, and had made many good friends, while now that I was going into town and was being accepted by the natives, life was a lot easier, and invitations to tea came from everywhere, though I lacked the time to go visiting. One day a man came by on horseback with a galah in a cage; it was a big five-foot cage, and he told me to keep it under my verandah where it would be company for me. But 'Cocky' soon became too much of a pet to be kept in a cage, so I clipped one wing and let him fly around the house. He would come for his food, and then fly back to his cage, but there was no fear of his flying away.

One of his favourite pastimes was riding on my shoulders and pulling the hairpins out of my hair so that it fell down. He got so jealous of Ivor that he would attack him if he came near me. One day a lady came to see me. She was middle-aged, and had walked three miles to bring me a kitten in a basket; she told me that her cat had mated with one of the wild cats, beautiful but vicious. She stayed for some time, and told me that I would soon tame the kitten; then, after making me promise to visit her, she left and walked the three miles back again to her home. The kitten dashed into the bedroom, under the bed, and there he remained, only coming out to eat his food and drink his milk, then back he would go under the bed again, hissing all the time.

Next day I took the children to visit Nellie Kiemc; Nellie's only daughter, Milly Beaumont, Emily's best friend, had died a few years before, aged twenty-nine, and had left two little girls, Delphie and Dody, and two little boys, Lennie and Kenny. The four motherless children were cared for by their grandmother, Nellie, who had also reared her husband's motherless daughter, Annie; she was a wonderful mother to the five of them. She lived in a bungalow that was very nice even though it had only earthen floors and was made from corrugated iron and weather board, built down on the ground. The whole of Northampton was feeling the depression, and there was very little money anywhere, but for our dinner Nellie had prepared meatless pasties; they tasted very nice after a three mile walk, and were very welcome. There was nothing else to eat apart from the pasties, but they were hot and tasty, and now I learned another lesson in cookery. I had already learned how to make meatless stew, and now I added meatless pasties. If a fly flew into our tea, Nellie would just throw the tea on the floor, as she did with the dregs; she said this was to harden the floor!

A family of Greeks had also come to live in the bush, and they had bought a large cleared paddock where they were going to grow peanuts. The parents were Mr. and Mrs. Sultana, and there were two sons, in their late twenties, Manolis and Vassilis, and a lodger, a man in his thirties, also a Greek, who was called only 'the lodger'. Mamma Sultana was a very stout lady. Their land was attached to the Hendleys' farm, but the land they had bought was some distance away from there. One day Mr. Sultana came down to ask Ivor to do him a favour. "Would Mr. Webb Ivor", as he called him, "please ride his horse up to Agina and fetch his cow back?" Agina was where they had lived before, and it would mean a journey of ten days there and back. Mr. Sultana had no money with which to pay Ivor, but he said he would give Ivor fifty incubator chicks instead. (The Sultanas were living rough, with no shelter around them.)

Ivor did not want to make the trip, but he didn't like to refuse the man, so he went, and once again we were left alone at night. We were without the dog now, because one day he and Ivor had gone out into the bush, looking for a wild turkey, and Ivor had come back some time later with no turkey and no dog. I asked Ivor where the dog was, and he said, "I lost him."

"Why didn't you wait for him or call him?" I asked.

"I did," said Ivor, "but I had to come away without him."

I worried all night about my dog being lost out in the bush, frightened in case he was savaged by dingoes. Then Ivor said, "I'll tell you the truth, Jack is dead, he was accidentally shot while we were in the bush." I was very upset about this, but Ivor told me, "Don't upset yourself. It's better this way, we couldn't afford to keep him when we have little enough food for ourselves."

"If you shot that wonderful dog because we couldn't spare enough food for him," I said, "I'll never forgive you." I thought of the time when the dog saved my life and the lives of our children when he pounced on the intruder, only to have this as his reward. I was very heavy hearted, though Ivor insisted that it had been an accident.

When Ivor had gone, and we were alone, I used to bring the budgie's cage in at night when it grew cool, and I would talk to it quite loudly, so that if anyone was lurking about outside, they would think I was talking to Ivor. One night, when Ivor had been gone for several days, I was sitting in my living room embroidering a tablecloth. It was a hot night, but not unbearable, and I couldn't pluck up enough courage to take the beds out on the verandah. The windows in the bedroom were just pieces of glass fixed into grooves, and I was able to push the whole window up into the roof and fix it so that it remained open; the two cots were near the window on the verandah side of the house.

The little ones were in bed, but not asleep, and now they both shouted excitedly, "Mammy, Daddy's home!" I said to them, "No, Daddy isn't home yet, go to sleep, there's good children." But they insisted, "Yes, Mammy, Daddy is home, he *is* home."

"No, Daddy won't be home for several days yet," I said, but they were adamant. "Yes, it is Daddy, he's got Daddy's hat on, and he's looking at us through the window."

Then I realised my mistake. If there *was* someone outside, and it seemed certain now that there was, he must have heard me tell the children that Daddy wouldn't be home for several days. The window was large, and whoever was outside could easily put his hands in and hurt the children. My husband's hat was a very wide-brimmed velour, so the man must have been six foot tall, wearing a similar hat. I quickly got hold of the gun, which already had a shot in it, pushed the curtain aside at the door, and stood in the doorway all through the night. I had two doors and two windows to guard, and he could have come in through any of them – but if he had attempted to do so, I would have shot him, and there would have been no prosecution because I was protecting my home and children. That was the unwritten law of the bush, intended to protect lonely women.

When I went to do the milking next day I asked Mr. Hendley if he had passed my way the night before, though I knew it couldn't have been him because he was a small man and didn't wear a wide stetson. Mr. Hendley knew that Ivor had gone to fetch the cow for the Sultanas, and he advised me to have nothing to do with them as they were spongers. Then he showed me a beautiful horse's saddle and said, "This is what Mr. Webb needs, it's hard going riding bareback."

"Yes," I agreed, "and if we ever have money again, he shall have a saddle, but I can't afford one at the moment."

"I'll make a bargain with you," said Mr. Hendley. "As you can see, this is a very expensive saddle. I don't use it myself now, because my horse has become too wild through lack of work. I'll exchange this saddle for that pair of large brass candlesticks on your mantelpiece."

"Mr. Hendley," I said, "I would love to present that lovely saddle to my husband, but what you are asking is impossible. That pair of candlesticks was given to Ivor's mother by her sister when she went to Canada, and she treasured them until she died – she was only thirty-seven, and Ivor was six years old when she died. His father gave them to me because he knew I would treasure them for her sake."

"I'll give you thirty shillings (£1.50) as well as the saddle," said Mr. Hendley. That was a lot of money, and it would have kept us in food for many weeks. "My wife has set her heart on those candlesticks," he added. "What more do you want for them?" He was very annoyed with me, but I told him it was impossible, they weren't mine to sell, and I couldn't consider parting with them at any price.

I'd had to bring the beds out on the verandah, because it was much too hot inside, and that night I didn't light the hurricane lamp because there was a moon out. I was just about to go off to sleep when I heard a rustling outside the garden fence. The air was so still that the sound could be heard clearly, and I knew it had to be something or someone out there; I thought it must be that same man. I put my slippers on because the ground was thick with double gees and they would pierce my feet. (Double gees are small seeds, like marbles, with three sharp points like spears, so that whichever way they lay on the floor, one spear always stuck up; and you could not help stepping on it. Australian children's feet are very tough and the seeds don't affect them, but if my children stood on one and it stuck in their feet, they would scream with pain. Emily's youngest girl used to get her feet full of them, then she would just sit on her behind and pull them out, declaring "Bugger double gees!")

With my gun at the ready, I went down the steps to the garden side of my shack, from where the sound seemed to be coming. I didn't lose sight of the cots on the verandah as I stood motionless, waiting to hear exactly where the sound was coming from, but I did lose count of time. I could not move, because I did not know in what direction the intruder would show himself – and then, by the light of the moon, I saw, near the clearing round my clothesline, what appeared to be a man kneeling, wearing a big hat. I thought that if I could see him, then he was bound to be able to see me, standing there as I was in a long white nightdress, with my gun pointed at him.

"I've got you covered. If you move I'll shoot," I tried to shout at him, but no sound would come. A twenty-two Winchester is a deadly weapon which will kill at twenty yards, and the man wasn't that distance away from me, but he did not move – and if he *had* moved, I don't think I would have been capable of shooting him, because I was far too terrified. Towards daybreak the moon moved and I had a clearer vision of my target; I had spent that entire night of terror covering nothing more dangerous than a bush! I took the cartridge out of the gun, threw the gun on the floor, and roared with laughter in sheer relief. (No wonder that every morning I woke up and shouted, "We're alive, we're alive, thank God!")

At the end of ten days, Ivor came home with the reward for all his hard work, fifty chicks. Every day the Sultanas sent their dinner down to be cooked on my stove; sometimes it was a leg of lamb garnished with potatoes and garlick, which made my house smell terrible.

One day the whole Sultana clan came down, wanting to know if 'Mr. Webb Ivor' would make a table talk for them. I asked Ivor what they meant, and he told me, "They've got some silly idea that I can get messages from the spirits for them."

"You can't do that here," I said. "I don't believe in Spiritualism." Ivor said that he would get rid of them, and he told them, "Can't make table talk, too light. Only make table talk at night."

"We'll wait," they said. Then Mrs. Sultana said, "We walk down again," and so we walked round the garden. It was still cool and everything was in bloom. First Mrs. Sultana gobbled up the petals of my roses, saying, "Make nice jam"; then we came to the beetroot, and she started to break off some of the leaves, saying again, "Make nice jam." In the end she tasted everything in my garden, saying all the time, "Make nice jam," until at last it was sundown and we were able to go back into the house. I made them a cup of tea, but I had no food to give them, so I tried to get rid of them by telling them, "Best go home now, I don't like table talk in my house. Want to go to bed."

Vassilis and Manolis spoke perfect English, the lodger and Mr. Sultana spoke no English, and Mamma had just a few words. They were determined not to go home until they had had their table talk, and sat around waiting, so I left them, and went to sleep, being very tired. They had been busy with this table talk for what seemed like hours when I woke up again and said to Ivor, "Haven't they finished yet?" There was a lot of wailing and crying going on, and one after another they were getting up and putting their arms round their adored Mamma who was also crying, and comforting her, while she kept asking Ivor, "Table talk true, Mr. Webb Ivor?" They were still getting messages, and all the conversation was in Greek except when they asked Ivor if the table talk was true; Ivor would say, "Yes, table talk true."

I said it was time to finish and to send them home, and Ivor said, "Tell me then, how to get rid of them!" So poor Mamma was helped out of the chair, and her family said to her, "Come on now, home, Mamma, lady tired;" and, all supporting Mamma, they left. As they were going out, the boys said that the messages had told them that Mamma was going to die, and it was plain that they really believed it was true. After they had gone, I asked Ivor if he could really get messages like that, and he said that of course he couldn't make a table talk; "they were all jabbering in Greek and asking questions, and I was just answering by knocking the table with my knees."

THIRTY-TWO

Ivor had been busy setting and planting the kitchen garden, and he surprised me one day by coming home with a dead calf lying across his horse. He said he had seen a man about to throw it down a mine shaft. "I asked him why he was throwing it down the shaft, and he told me it was a bull calf, and that was what they did when they didn't want to keep them." So then Ivor said to him, "Why didn't you eat it? It is good veal, very expensive meat. They can't get enough of it back home."

"O.K. cobber," the man said to Ivor, "you can have it, but don't tell the Aussies you are going to eat it, they think eating calf is cannibalism."

Ivor took the calf into the bough shade and cut it into joints; then I had to devise a way of keeping the meat fresh in the heat, and free from flies. I washed all the meat and dried it thoroughly, to make sure there was no blood to attract the flies, then Ivor put a hook through each joint, tied them with cord, and hung them in the bough shade. Next I took a lined pillowcase for each piece of meat, shook out each pillowcase to fill it with air, covered each joint from the bottom to the head, and tied each one securely, making sure that no part of the meat touched the sides of the pillowcase because otherwise the blowfly would blow it, and the maggots would eat their way through the bag. Next day I put a kerosene tin of water on to boil, and cooked quite a large amount of the meat into a broth; it had to be used up as quickly as possible, because it wouldn't keep.

That night Ivor told me that he would be leaving for Bluff Point at the weekend, since Mr. Ray, our landlord, who lived some fifty miles away, wanted him to put up wind breaks around his tomatoes. Mr. Ray made his living by growing and selling tomatoes, but this year his age had beaten him, and he could not afford to pay for the necessary labour. We owed Mr. Ray many months' rent, so Ivor had volunteered to do his tomato

265

planting and any ploughing, for his keep, and to clear off our debt. Ivor had already been down there several weeks ago, at the beginning of the wet season, ploughing and looking after the tomatoes, and now he was planning to go again, to put up the windbreaks against the hot March winds. I dreaded him going away again, for I had got so used to having him home.

We were living on boiled veal now. Ivor had made me a cooler box, a wooden box put on its side with the front open; he put four legs on it, made trays from kerosene tins to hold water, and covered the box with hessian which fell down over the opening instead of a door. Then he filled the trays with water, putting one under the cooler and over the top. Meanwhile I cut a number of wide strips from a flannel blanket, soaked them in water, and put one end of each in the water on the tray on top and the other ends in the water on the bottom tray. I placed these all around the box, the idea was that the water travelled up and down the strips, keeping them wet, while being in the shade kept both them and the inside of the box cool.

I hadn't seen my sister during the wet season. We had been cut off because the ground had become so boggy, and we couldn't take the sulky out because it would have got bogged down in the mud. On the day my sister visited us for the first time in three months, because the wet season had ended, I had made a four-pound bread tin of veal brawn. Emily liked my brawn so much that she asked if she could have some to take home. I cut the loaf of brawn in half, and gave one half to her, and she said, "I dare not tell the children what it is made from in case they tell Jim. Australians don't eat calf flesh." But later she told, "Jim said it was the nicest meat he had ever tasted, and he insisted on eating it for every meal until it was finished. He didn't know he had been eating veal!"

We had heard from Ted Manning some months previously, telling us that they were expecting a new baby, and they were hoping it would be a girl because they already had four boys. One night Ivor and I were asleep on the verandah, because the weather was too hot for sleeping indoors, and some time during the night we were awakened by a terrible noise coming from inside the house. We both jumped up in bed, and even the two little ones woke up, asking, "What's that?" It sounded as if a heavy vehicle had smashed into the house, smashing glass and splintering wood, and it seemed as if everything in the house was

266

breaking up. The noise was terrific, and it lasted for several minutes. We both jumped out of bed to see what had happened. The front door was open, but nothing had come out. Ivor told me to stay by the children's cots, away from the door, while he went round the back to see what was happening. A few minutes later he came through the house on to the verandah, and I never saw such a look on his face as then – shock, astonishment and fear all at once.

"What's the matter, Ivor? What's happened?" I asked.

"Nothing, Ray," he said. "Come into the house and see." And inside it looked exactly as we had left it before going to bed. We looked at each other in disbelief, not knowing what to think, and then suddenly I burst out laughing.

"I know what it is," I said. "Dolly's baby has just been born, and it must be a girl."

Dolly was Ivor's sister, and we both loved her, and rejoiced at the birth of her baby; she and Ted had been disappointed so many times. We went back to bed happy, but before getting in, we wrote of the night's happenings in our book of memories, recording the date and the hour of the event. We had to wait seven weeks for confirmation of what had happened; the letter from Dolly came then, confirming the birth of the baby at the exact time we had our experience, though the baby wasn't a girl, as we had thought it was bound to be, but a boy whom they called Lionel. We couldn't understand that night of fear; why, if it was a boy, did we have that premonition? We had to wait six years for the answer, but soon after little Lionel's sixth birthday, Dolly heard that very same sound, splintering wood and broken glass outside Lionel's school when she went to collect him. The driver of a double decker bus had lost control and failed to stop in time, and Lionel fell under the wheels and was crushed to death. (This happened in Billingham, Stockton-on-Tees, where they were living at the time.)

Ivor went to Bluff Point, and I was left alone, with the little ones. He would be gone for several weeks, and I wouldn't see him again until the job was done. I felt very depressed, and at night the beds were back inside the house, and the doors were locked, with a peg in one and a piece of stick in the other, but I was still nervous. Blackie the cow had dried up a long time before, so there was no milking to be done, and so no milk for the house, while Mrs. Davidson's son, the vicar, had come up and taken his mother back with him for a few weeks, and there was no washing or sewing for me to do while she was away. There was very little food in the house, and no money to buy any more.

I was sitting dejectedly on my makeshift sofa one day, just staring into space and wondering where it would all end. Ivor had left, thinking that we were all right – he didn't know that Mrs. Davidson would be going away – and for the first time I gave way to despair and homesickness. Then I heard a faint sound coming from behind the bedroom curtain. I looked in that direction, but didn't move; it was the kitten, grown into a full-sized cat now, but still untamed. He had evidently come in through the bedroom window, and he walked up to me, sprang up on to my lap, settled down and started to purr. I knew then that I was not alone, that God was speaking to me through the cat, and telling me that this was not the end, there were better things to come.

The next day, his job finished, Ivor came back from Bluff Point, and I told him about the cat. "I think our luck is going to change," I said. Mrs. Davidson came home from Perth and sent for me; she asked me how we had been managing because she knew how much I had missed her money, and gave me a present which she had brought back from Perth. This was six yards of smokey blue georgette, with a yard of pearl georgette for trimming, and buttons and cotton to match. There was also some white silk to make blouses for school for Jack, and some tussore silk for a frock for Pearl. Then Mrs. Davidson showed me a beautiful double bed eiderdown that she had bought for herself. When I told her how beautiful I thought it was, she said she didn't like the colours, and she showed me yards and yards of two-coloured satin, and said, "Now, I want you, my dear, to recover the eiderdown for me. Can you do it, my dear?" I had never before covered an eiderdown, but I said, "Yes, I can do it – but it is beautiful as it is." I knew she was only making work for me.

Soon after I reached home, I had two visitors, Mrs. Davidson's wealthy widowed daughter and her twenty-year-old son Jimmy; their daughter asked me if I would do her a kindness and accept a few things with which she was over-stocked. These were a shoulder of mutton, a large basin of beautiful dripping and a large pot of home-made jam, and she would accept no thanks for them, but merely repeated that I was doing her a kindness, and left. Apart from that, things went on just as they had been; I made tea just once a day, and kept the dregs for the following day. It was tinned milk for the children now, and Ivor and I went without sugar in our tea so that the little ones could have it. We would have fared much better in our garden, too, if we had had money to buy more seed, and our crop would have been better if the Sultanas hadn't been helping themselves! They were very nice people, but very greedy, giving nothing and taking everything – they even borrowed the last thirty shillings that Ivor had in his pocket without even a hint of giving it back, and they just came into our garden and took what they wanted without bothering to ask.

One morning Ivor went down the garden to see if there was anything left for us to eat. He was out there for some time, clearing away the tops of the vegetables and tidying up the garden, while the little ones were playing in their cubby house on the other side of the garden fence. Ivor must have been preoccupied with his thoughts while he was tidying up the garden, because he forgot the first law of the bush, that you must never put out hot ash or a piece of glass, or strike a match anywhere out of doors, except when the notices went up telling us to 'burn off now'. That happened for only one short period during the year, and this was not during that period. Still, it seemed the safest thing in the world to burn off a little garden waste on a patch of bare ground. Ivor was usually very cautious about such things; he was a very careful man, always warning me of the danger, but this time he was so preoccupied that he must have thought he was back home in England, and he set a match to the rubbish.

Next thing I heard him shouting, "Come quick, come quick, Ray," then, as I ran out of the house, he shouted, "bring sacks with you," and I could see what was happening. Ivor had put out the fire, but a blade of dry grass had caught in the flame, and a little streak of fire had travelled under the fence. I beat at it with the sacks, but the fire had such a strong hold that in only minutes, it seemed, the flames were almost to the tops of the trees and Ivor was shouting at me to go back, saying, "It's too late, Ray."

The fire had started from the garden at the extreme right hand end of the paddock, and now the undergrowth was all alight, and flames were climbing up the trees with frightening speed. It was so terrifying to watch that, in our fear, we had forgotten the children, who were separated from us by a wall of flame, but now I ran through the flames and brought them out, one under each arm. I didn't realize what I had done until I got them safely indoors. They had been inside a ring of fire, and yet their cubby house was not touched, and I hadn't even felt the flames as I dashed through them to the children. Divine Providence had helped us once again.

"It's no good, Ray," shouted Ivor, "we can't do anything." By now the fire was almost engulfing the whole paddock. Then suddenly there were men coming in from all directions, beating at the flames; they had been working out in the fields and had seen the smoke in the sky and known at once that it was a bush fire. They knew where the smoke was coming from, and rode instantly to our paddock. It was impossible to beat out the flames, so some of the men rode out ahead of the fire and started another one, beating these flames toward our fire; as the fires met, they went out.

The penalty for lighting fires is imprisonment, and Ivor knew that the police would soon be investigating, so he said, "Rit, for God's sake don't say I lit a fire in the garden." As he was saying this, a policeman was walking towards us. He could see we were shaken, and realised that this was our first experience of the dreaded bush fire. Our two little ones were standing by us, looking up into the policeman's face, and Jack stuck out his chest proudly and said to the man, "Pearly and me was lighting a fire, see, a little one, and then it was a big one, see." The policeman patted his head, and said, "I see, sonny, I see." – And that was that; he accepted the story, and we were free.

Once again we owed a debt of gratitude to the Australian people, for their promptness in coming to our aid. The fire did a lot of good, killing all the vermin in our paddock, but the marvellous thing was that the men had prevented the fire from spreading into the bush, and it was just our five acres that were burned. Now these looked like a field of telegraph poles; the trees were still standing, but they were blackened and their tops were burnt away, and the undergrowth too was all burned. The fire was out, but the horror of it remained in our minds for a long time. That night we discussed what we would do with the paddock now, and Ivor said that he would clear and cultivate it.

As he had no work just then, he was able to start right away, and he started by ring-barking the trees, which took him many months to complete. Then, when he had finished, he went back with his axe to the starting point and began to fell the trees.

By now it was nine months since Ivor had started to clear the trees, and in all that time not a penny had come into the house except for the five shillings from Mrs. Davidson. All through the nine months of summer Ivor had worked on the trees, felling and trimming them; (I had sent a letter to Mrs. Ray, telling her what had happened and we had had permission to fell the trees). Ivor told Mrs. Ray that he would sell the logs and give her half the money he got for them, which he did. Once most of the logs had been trimmed off, Ivor hired the local horse and cart and went out and sold all that he had chopped down; but once the wet season came, the cart kept getting bogged down in the earth, and was so difficult to move that we had to put sacks under the wheels in order to push it out of the bog. At last it had to be abandoned until the end of the wet season.

We had a little money now, and were able to go into town on the Saturday. Pearl, as usual, asked her father, "Daddy, are you able to afford a dolly pram today" and the answer was also the usual one: "Not today, you shall have one for Christmas." But I said, "If you *can* afford it, Ivor, let her have it now. It's her birthday next week, and she's waited a long time for the pram; otherwise some other child might have it for Christmas." Ivor said nothing. Meanwhile Pearl didn't go into a tantrum, she just looked up into her father's face and said, "Not today, Daddy can't 'fford it today, Zackie." When Ivor dropped us off in town, he usually left us and went on to the corn stores while we wandered around looking at the shops, but that day Pearl took hold of her father's hand and asked him, "Daddy, will you come Stokes's with me?" Then she led him up to where the doll's pram was standing, looked up into his face again, and said, "Isn't it a beauty, Daddy?" She melted him – he just couldn't resist that, and said to her, "All right, you can have it!" Ivor was a man whom you could lead, but not drive, and little Pearl had found his weak spot. From the moment the pram was hers, she would not let go of the handle, and going home in the sulky I had both her *and* the pram on my lap. Even while I was undressing her for bed, she kept one hand on the pram, and when she got into her cot, the pram had to go too, so that she lay there with the pram at

271

her feet until she fell asleep and I was able to take it out of the cot.

My sister and I had not seen much of each other because of the wet season, except for the visit when I gave her the brawn. Emily was a very secretive person, and did not discuss her business; she had never really explained why she left her old bungalow to go and live in Mrs. Smith's, and it came as a surprise to me to learn that she had moved again, and was now living in a little pug house, still on the main road, but quite a long distance from the town. The house belonged to Mrs. Davidson, whose father had built it about a hundred years ago, but the house had been neglected for many years and was in a bad state of repair. Emily must have been quite desperate to leave such a lovely bungalow and move into that place. Although she had moved from town, I was able to visit her, because when I heard of the move, Mrs. Hendley showed me a path which led past her land and the Sultanas' to a cart track leading to the Carruthers' estate, and on which we could walk, providing that the bull wasn't about. The track was difficult to find without Mrs. Hendley's help, but now I could visit Emily once a week, and she visited me, so it was less lonely in the daytime.

There was no social life in the bush, or in Northampton. Everything stopped at six; even the pubs closed then, and no-one was to be seen outside after that. Emily and I and the children planned to go to the beach on Christmas Day, and camp there for a few days, so on Christmas Eve Jim hired a horse and cart to take his family down to the beach, some sixteen miles away through the bush. He brought the horse down to our place and put it in the paddock with Daisy overnight, but didn't tell us that the animal was a biter. Early on Christmas morning he came down to fetch the horse; then, after collecting it, he came back to the shack and said, "I've got my horse, Ivor, but yours has gone. See you later." Then he went. Ivor searched, but there was no sign of Daisy. She had never attempted to get out before, but she must have been terrified of the strange horse and jumped the fence to get away from him.

The point of both families going together was that Jim and Emily would show us the way to the beach, but at ten o'clock they called to say they were off. They didn't offer to help look for our horse, and Ivor had to tramp into the bush on foot to look for her. He searched all day on Christmas Day and Boxing

Day, but there was no sign of her, and we had a miserable Christmas what with that and no Christmas dinner. Then somebody told Ivor that they had seen a riderless horse going through town towards Badra, and that was where he found her. She had a badly cut flank, so Ivor had to walk her back to our paddock. When he got her home, he told me, "Sorry, Ray, Daisy isn't fit enough to pull a full load in the sulky, so we'll have to leave our trip for a few days until she is fit. Either she ripped her flank by jumping over the fence, or Jim's horse bit her." After a few days of careful nursing, however, she was well enough to be harnessed to the sulky.

Ivor fastened a sack of chaff to the back of the sulky for Daisy, and then we all (including the cat) set off for the seaside. We were going for a holiday, but all we took with us was our tent, folded up under the seat, while our food was sugar, tea, tinned milk, salt, plain flour, onions and a billy can. We carried a large umbrella with us to give shade, and a bowl for our washing up – in fact we looked and felt like tinkers travelling along the road! We didn't know the way, but Ivor had a pretty good sense of direction, and we found our way eventually to the river mouth where Jim and Emily were camping. Ivor hobbled Daisy to a clump of tobacco plant in the shade.

Emily and her children were very badly sunburnt, and she told me that every time she came to the sea, the same thing happened, and her mouth became very cracked and sore. She asked us, "Why is it you Pommies never get sunburnt?" and I answered, "Because I take precautions. Do you?" "What do you mean?" she asked. Her children were crying with the pain of their sunburn, so I smeared vaseline all over them, and each morning all six children would come to me for this 'vaseline treatment'. Meanwhile Jim showed Ivor how to make bunks for the children so that they wouldn't have to sleep on the floor, and he made hammocks out of sacks and posts; we couldn't risk letting the children sleep on the sand because there were so many ear-wigs crawling about, and we were afraid they would get into their ears. There were also scorpions and centipedes.

We bathed in the river mouth, where all the streams flowed together to form a miniature lake. The water didn't flow out to the sea, but lost itself in the sand, no-one quite knew how (unless it flowed *under* the sand), and the water in the river mouth was calm and clear, like fresh water. A few yards' walk

273

away from the river mouth brought us to a steep bank, which led to the beach, and when we got to this bank, we had to run down to the beach because the sand was too hot to walk on. (The sand in Australia is not golden, as ours is in Britain, but silver.)

Emily's little boy was crying on the bank and refusing to go down; he had no shoes on, and the sand was burning his feet, so we had to wrap his legs and feet in wet sacks before he would go down. We wanted to paddle, but the sea just there was full of stingfish, starfish and jellyfish, all of which would give you a nasty sting if you stepped on them. Nearby the coral reef stretched out for some twenty-five yards, and the sea was very clear, with the coral looking like a cement floor under it. When there was a crowd of us in the water, we could just about keep away the stingfish, but at the end of the coral reef the sea was infested by sharks, so we could not bathe. (Many tragedies had happened on that beach.)

While we were walking at the edge of the water, the ground suddenly shook violently. Emily said we were feeling the tremor of an earthquake in New Zealand. The coral reefs round that shore are the most beautiful in the world, like fossilized flowers, of all shades and colours, sea dahlias and sea anemones, all crystallised in stone, washed in the most brilliant colours. Before we bathed, I covered the children completely, from ankles to wrists, to protect them from both the sun and the sea fish; we even kept our hats and shoes on. Ivor shot rabbits, which were plentiful and very fat, and we lived off them. I made stews and so forth, while Ivor made damper bread with just flour, bicarbonate of soda, cream of tartar and a little salt; he made these into a dough and rolled that into a ball, then to cook it, he dug a hole in the sand, lit a fire in the hole with pieces of stick, and when the wood had all burned away, swept the hot ash out of the hole, put the bread in the hot sand, covered it, and left it for a while till the damper bread was ready. Last thing at night, before the tide came in, Ivor and Jim would take the craypots, put pieces of rabbit in them as bait, and put them among the rocks; this could only be done on a moonlit night. Then at daybreak they would creep out of their tents and go down to see what luck they had had in the night. If they had been successful, they would come back with their craypots full of large red lobster-like crayfish.

We had each taken a chip burner down to the beach with us, in which to do our cooking. (A chip burner was a clean four gallon kerosene tin, with the top completely taken off; it was then cut half-way down each side of the tin, after which each panel was rolled down tightly, to make four handles. Next we made four holes on each side of the tin, and put iron or steel rods through them, so that they went in one side and came out the other, forming a shelf to put tins on; but before inserting these bars, the space that would be under them was filled with dry or chipped wood.) A kerosene tin full of water from the river was put on the bars of the chip burner to boil, then when the water was boiling, the crayfish were dropped in alive. While the crayfish were being cooked, I went as far away as possible, covering my ears to blot out the screams of the fish, which sounded just like a baby crying. Now we had a change of diet for breakfast; we ate crayfish with damper bread. The only parts of the crayfish that were eaten were the legs, which tasted delicious.

At first we were the only families at the bay by the river mouth, but a day later another family came rumbling down to the beach, and camped a little way from us. There were two women, a man and a teenage boy and girl. They did not talk to us during the day, but at night there was such a delicious smell of something cooking coming from their camp that I went up to them, and shook hands with them all and introduced myself. Then I explained that I had been attracted to their camp by the delightful smell of their cooking. They were Scottish, and had brought a bake-stone with them so that they could make girdle cakes on their chip burner. I invited them to come down to our camp and sit with us and have a sing-song, and though at first they had seemed a little standoffish, they were delighted to be asked.

They brought some hot girdle cakes with them, for us to taste, and it turned out that Emily knew them. The two women were sisters, from Scotland; one had married an Australian soldier and had insisted on bringing her sister with her, as they were orphans and had no-one to turn to. The husband had said that he had a beautiful farm waiting for them in Australia, but when they arrived in Northampton, all they found was a cantankerous old mother who lived in a shack with walls made from old sacks, and a way of life not far from hell. (This had been Emily's story, too; Jim had told us that she was going to a fine modern farm, but when they got to Northampton, they didn't even have a

275

shelter, because Jim's drunken old father had sold the farm and drunk the money. Like the Scots, Emily had vowed never to like Australia or the Australians as long as they lived there.) Still, for those few nights of holiday when we sat around the camp fire, we each forgot the hardships we had suffered in Australia, and sang Welsh hymns, Scottish songs and Australian ditties like one united family. Then, after a very pleasant Christmas time, we all went on our separate ways.

THIRTY-THREE

By now we were ready to begin cultivating our five acres. Ivor had finished cutting down all the trees in the paddock, and had been trying to sell the wood, but since the Aussies were surrounded by trees, and could get their wood for nothing, he was lucky to sell any; I think the Council must have bought it, and I doubt if they gave much for it. (Cutting, ringbarking and disposing of all those trees was a daunting task for one man, and only Ivor's determination saw it through). After the wet season the whole paddock was full of lovely green grass, and all we needed was a cow to help Daisy to eat it. However the land was not yet ready to be ploughed, because there were still thousands of tree stumps to be cleared out first, and that would be several months' work.

Bert Ash had gone bankrupt, like all the small farmers, but before the bailiffs moved in on him, he managed to smuggle out his one and only cow; now she was ready to calve. The family had moved down to his wife's little bungalow, just on the outskirts of town; it stood in just a quarter of an acre of land. One day I visited Mrs. Ash there, and saw the new-born calf tethered on the lawn. The cow was fenced in, in a small patch of green not much wider or longer than the cow herself, and she had been tied up like a mad bull, with a thick rope round each of her four legs. This had been her sixth calf, and she had never been milked by hand before because she was too nasty tempered, but now Bert was going to milk her, and he had spreadeagled her in this way before starting the job, so that she could not move at all. I went home feeling sick with pity.

The site of Northampton had once been the bed of the ocean, but long ago the sea had receded. Now Australia was a hundred years old, but this part of the bush had never been cultivated, and was regarded as untameable – until Ivor, a mere Pommie, a young man of twenty-six, attempted to do the job alone. The fire had destroyed the undergrowth, and Ivor had cut down the trees, but now the task was to remove all the tree roots, locked and intertwined under the soil, that made it impossible to plough. By now the ground had become so hard that one could not even get a spade into it, and I watched to see how Ivor would manage it. First he dug a hole at the base of each tree trunk, then filled each hole in turn with pieces of dried wood, poured kerosene over the wood, set each hole alight, and then covered it to prevent the flames coming upwards. Instead the flames burned underneath the earth, eating away the roots of the stumps, until Ivor could remove each one.

While Ivor was busy with his underground fires, I took the children for a walk, so that they were out of danger. We returned in time to make a meal for Ivor, and I found him down by the gully, strengthening the fence around the three acres of crown land which we had taken to be used for the horse. Ivor was quite excited as I came along, and he shouted out, "I've got a cow for you, Ray." I was delighted, and said, "That's lovely, we'll be able to have fresh milk again. Whose cow is it? Are you buying it?"

"Bert Ash has been up," said Ivor, "and he asked if we would let his cow run in our paddock. We can have all the milk, as long as you look after the calf as well."

As soon as Ivor said 'Bert Ash', I nearly died of fright, and told him to go and stop Bert Ash from bringing the cow. "That's not a cow," I told him. "It's a mad bull. Go quick, Ivor, I can't have it here, it will kill the children."

"Too late, Ray," said Ivor. "Here they are." There was Bert Ash, with a big stick in his hand, prodding the calf along, while behind him four men were dragging the cow along, roped securely with strong ropes.

"If it takes four men to drag a cow along when it's following its calf," I said, "What hope have we got of handling her? A cow should follow her calf without any need of coaxing."

Then I told the men, "Take her back, take her back, I've got two little children here, and I'd be afraid for their lives with that thing around here."

But they just laughed and put her into the three acres, saying, "Not likely, we had a cow of a job getting her here." The poor cow must have thought she was in heaven, to be free to run around the paddock with her calf, with plenty of good grazing, a gully to drink from, and trees for shade!

I told Ivor, "I'll never be able to milk her, she's too vicious, you will have to do it."

"I can't milk." he said.

"Well, now is the time to learn," I told him. Just then a man on horseback came cantering up, a Mr. McCaskill, who was a mounted policeman. He said, "Webb, I've got a couple of days' work for you; get your water bag and follow me."

I asked Ivor if he would be back that night, and Mr. McCaskill said, "No, not for three nights." So then I told Ivor that he couldn't go and leave me with that cow.

"Don't go, Ivor, don't go," I cried after him. "What if something happens to the children?" He just laughed and said, "You'll manage," then away he went. I took the children back into the house, not knowing what to do; I could only warn them not to go near the paddock. Later that afternoon I looked at the cow, so contented with her calf in the paddock, and I thought that perhaps it wouldn't be too hard a job to milk her, and perhaps I could manage. But when I took my milk pail down to the paddock, I very quickly got out again. I didn't have the courage to try a second time that day, but next morning I felt a little braver, partly because I was afraid that the cow might be feeling uncomfortable with all that milk; the calf was too small to drink much from her.

It was a three-cornered paddock, and I walked around looking for the best place to approach her. I knew that as soon as I got through that fence, she would come up to me, and I wanted to be sure I had some sort of protection. I knew too, that I wouldn't have any milk from her that day, but I just wanted to get near enough to talk to her, and let her know that I meant neither her nor her calf any harm. I found a few trees at one end of the fence which would afford me a little protection, though I still didn't know what I was going to do, or how I was going to approach her. Now, keeping the trees to the left of me, I came out into the open, called to the cow, and then, relying on faith and prayer, I waited. She ran up to me very angrily, but I was sheltered by the trees, and from their safety I spoke soothingly to her. My next actions were dictated by some power inside me – not by lack of fear, for I had plenty of that!

I grasped her two horns and threw myself at her head, putting all my weight into the effort to hold her head down; all the time I was talking to her, telling her what a good girl she was. She was shaking me backwards and forwards, trying to release her horns, but I held on until I found my strength leaving me, and then I let go the horns and dived to the safety of the trees. I hadn't hurt the cow, and while I was getting my wind back, she was trying to find out what had grabbed her. When I got my strength back, I did the same thing again, holding her head and talking to her all the time, so that she would know I was a nuisance, not an enemy, and then I repeated the treatment for a third time, after which I patted her and smoothed down her nose as I talked to her, but from the safety of the trees. Then I left her to run round the paddock. I had not attempted to take any milk from her, but I knew I had taken a step in the right direction.

I did the same thing again in the afternoon; three times I jumped out at her horns, and three times I let her go again, still without attempting to take milk from her. Then I repeated the same procedure the next morning, but by the afternoon I knew it was either make or break her. The first time she shook me off, but by the second time I realised she was easier, and her shaking was less violent. The third time I took her head and held it down, she didn't shake, and I knew she had given in; so I walked with her, holding her lightly by the neck, to the corner of the field where the fences came together. Then I called her calf and left her to feed it there – I wanted her to know that this was going to be her milking place. Lastly I patted her and left her.

Next morning I went with my milking pail and some bran and collard in my washing up bowl, and put the bowl in the corner of the field where the two fences met. I had fixed a bar from one fence to the other, for the cow to rest her head on while she ate. Then I went down the paddock to fetch her; she knew now where she had to go, and I just patted her flanks as she walked quietly up to the corner of the field, put her head through the fence, and started eating. While she was enjoying her meal of bran and collard, I made an attempt to milk her – but the next thing I knew, I was on top of the fence. I laughed, because I could see the funny side of it, and I sang at the top of my voice, "There ain't no sense sitting on the fence, all by yourself in the moonlight!" I laughed and laughed, and then through my laughter I heard Emily's voice crying out. "You fool, what are you doing up there?" So I told her I was trying to tame Bert Ash's cow, and she said, "Oh my God, I'm not staying to see that, I'm going in," and quickly disappeared indoors.

I had a length of rope, and tied just one of the cow's legs to prevent her from kicking me again, then I put my head in her groin and sang to her, as I had with Mr. Hendley's cow, and she gave me her milk freely. I had no further trouble with her. When Ivor came back, he asked me how I had got on, and I took him down to the paddock and called to the cow. She came up and took a titbit out of my hand. Ivor told me then that the men in town had been making bets with each other, saying that that was one cow that wouldn't be tamed by singing to it, because the only way to tame it was by putting a stick in its ribs.

Emily had called in to tell me that she had to go into hospital for a month, and she asked me if I would look after her four children for her. She brought them down, all carrying their hammock beds, and bringing with them their cat and dog. I went to meet them as they came along, to help carry their belongings. Emily was very down; she had never had an operation before, and she was a little frightened; then, to make matters worse, a little bird had flown into her sitting room and couldn't get out. Being superstitious, she had taken that as a sign that she was going to die, but I told her that probably an eagle hawk had frightened the little bird, and that it was just trying to find a way of getting out. I managed to convince her that birds often flew into my house and I was still alive.

The children settled in, though it was a bit of a crush with eight of us, plus a cat and a dog, in our little shack. Ivor had made some shelves for me in a corner of the room and I had displayed all the pretty ornaments that I had brought from home on them. In the middle of the night there was a terrific crash, and on going to investigate, I found that the dog had chased the cat which had been chasing a mouse; all three had been running around the room, and had crashed into my shelves, bringing them crashing down and so smashing my most treasured possessions.

With six children, two adults, two cats and a dog to look after, I was kept very busy, and I also cleaned the school all the time that Emily was in hospital. In the night, while Ivor was burning out the roots in the paddock, we loved to sit and watch the glow of the fires, and this reminded me of being in a town with all the lights glowing. We had plenty of milk now, from the cow, and Ivor bought a little corn grister and some wheat. Our last job at night was to fix the grister to the table, and we all took it in turns to turn the handle, which was very stiff, to make our porridge for breakfast. Altogether it was the happiest month that Ivor and I had spent in Australia. I felt like Old Mother Hubbard with all my children – and they were such lovely children, too, with no squabbles or arguments. I was sorry to see Emily's four going home when the time came, and they had been so happy with us that they didn't want to leave.

The burning of the underground roots went on for many weeks until they finally burned themselves out, and then it was time to plough the fields. Ivor borrowed a four furrow plough and three horses from one of the farmers, so that with Daisy we had four horses. We had no collar for Daisy, so Ivor borrowed an old straw collar from the Sultanas, and then the ploughing began. At long last what had once seemed an impossible task was actually being achieved!

Now that Ivor was ploughing the fields, we needed corn, but we had no money to buy any. On Sunday Ivor took us for a ride through the bush (it was the end of the hot season now, and becoming cooler), but when he told me we were going to steal corn, I didn't know whether he was joking or telling the truth. I said we had always managed without stealing and we were not going to start now; while the argument was going on, the sulky was driving along towards the Bowes estate. Eventually we came to a field of golden corn that seemed to stretch for miles, and Ivor said, "Get out and help me pick this corn. We are going to take enough to help seed our paddock."

"If you dare to touch one ear of that corn," I told him, "I will get out of the sulky, and I'll walk home, and never speak to you again."

"You stay here, then," said Ivor, "and I'll go up to the other end and start from there."

I was terrified, because I really believed he was going to steal that corn. After a while he came back, carrying a sack of corn, which had been left there by Mr. Drage of the Bowes estate for Ivor to collect – he had been teasing me all the time, and I had believed he was really going to steal! Of course, I should have known that growing corn could not be replanted in that way, but I was a greenhorn then. Still, thanks to Mr. Drage's generosity, we were able to plant the paddock with seed. We had no modern machinery to help with the planting, so that night, a beautiful, moonlit night, we decided to get as much of the seed corn planted as we possibly could, working till dawn if necessary. I showed Ivor how to scatter the seed as Jenkin Morgan used to do at Abergarw Farm in Brynmenin, and we walked up and down the field all night long, scattering the corn as we walked. We knew that the next shower of rain would wash the seeds right down out of the sight of the birds, and after that we must just wait for results.

Now that Summer was over and the wet season was on us, I was able to go to the chapel on a Sunday without fear of snakes. One Sunday night the minister's wife asked me if I would like to join the sewing guild, which met at her home; she said there would be a cup of tea and biscuits, but I also thought that this would be a wonderful opportunity to meet other people (though I could only go when Ivor was at home to look after the children). On the Tuesday evening I set out for the minister's house; however, due to the heavy rainfall, the gully was now a raging torrent, and I had to cross the gully to get to the road. (There was a little footbridge, but by now the water was so deep that it had washed over the bridge, which was just a plank crossing the gully with a handrail for support). I took off my shoes and stockings, and walked over the bridge, after that I had almost a mile to walk, on the old miners' road which was full of water-filled ruts, so I had to stay barefoot or the heels of my shoes would have sunk in the mud. When I got up on to the main road, I was able to wash the mud off my feet and put my shoes and stockings on again before getting to the minister's house.

Mrs. Meredith greeted me with, "Oh, I'm so glad you've come, Mrs. Webb. I've got someone here I'd like you to meet," and she introduced me to a young expectant mother, Mrs. Edwina Husband, who was staying with her until after her baby was born. I shook hands with Mrs. Husband and said, "You are Welsh, aren't you? What part of Wales are you from?" "Port Talbot," she said, so then I told her I was from Caerau (which is very near Port Talbot), and we immediately became friends (as we were to remain, life-long.) Edwina was the wife of Viv Husband, a farmer's son who, with his brother Tom, had emigrated to Australia; because they had emigrated, they had to go to the salt swamps, a few miles from Northampton, to work. (No Australian would work there, so they relied on emigrants as labour). The swamps were a breeding ground for fever, but the money was good, and as there was nothing to spend it on, no shops or pubs, they could save it up. Edwina had been Viv's fiancée and had gone out to Australia to join him in the swamps after their wedding in Perth, but now that she was expecting a baby, she had to leave for a while, because of the fear of malaria. The two brothers did not want to be separated, so now they were looking for a spot where they could make a home for Edwina and the baby.

About two miles from our shack was a farm which had not been lived in for years; the farmer who owned it had had to leave because of debts to the council, and though the land was cleared, it included no water, so it would not be easy to make a living out of it. Viv and Tom paid the farmer's debt and took the land over, in order to make a home for themselves; then, after Edwina's baby was born, the boys left the swamp and made their home in the old pug house in Northampton, cleaning out the water tank so that the rains would fill it with fresh water. Being farmer's sons they were used to working with animals, but they could not have any on the farm because of the lack of water. However they vowed that one day they would make it into a real farm. They bought a milking cow, and they were given a bull calf free (to save it from being thrown down a mine shaft, the usual fate of the young bull calves), and then they let it be known around town that they would be willing to pay for live bull calves. After that they bought a horse and cart, and made pens; when they were given a bull calf they reared it until it was ready to kill for beef. They would go round taking orders from anyone who wanted fresh beef, and then, once they were sure of having enough customers to buy all the meat, because there was nowhere to keep anything unsold, they would kill the bull and deliver the meat to the customers. Fresh beef was a novelty to their customers, who usually only got salted meat. The brothers worked very hard, as a team, determined to make a success of butchery and farming.

One day Edwina walked over to my place, very excited, and exhausted too, after her walk. She showed me a piece of voile she had bought, to make a christening dress for her baby, and asked me if I would cut out the frock for her; she could not afford to by a dress and had no idea how to make one. However I realized that a yard of material was not enough to make any kind of christening dress, and so I took my scissors and cut the voile up into long strips, holding them up like lengths of bandage. The colour drained from poor Edwina's face when she

284

saw what I had done to her lovely material. "Oh!" she said, "what *am* I going to do with that?" I laughed, and said, "Cheer up, Edwina, you're not dead yet! Leave this with me and go home. I'll make you a frock."

"Can you come over to tea on Sunday?" she asked fearfully, not really expecting that I would make a frock out of the strips.

"All right," I said. "We'll be over on Sunday."

Mrs. Davidson had given me a beautiful white voile blouse with insertions in it, and as she was a large woman, the blouse was quite big, so I knew I could use it to make the frock. (The blouse had been very expensive, and was well made, but it would have been far too big for me to wear.) I picked away every stitch of insertion in the blouse – each strip was two inches wide, – the width of the strips I had cut from Edwina's voile – and then for every strip of voile I put in an insertion; when it was finished, even I was amazed at the beauty of the frock.

After dinner on Sunday, Ivor harnessed Daisy into the sulky, and we all went over to the Husbands' for tea. I showed Edwina the frock, and she couldn't believe her eyes; she held it up and danced around with it, saying that she had never seen anything so beautiful. The men took Ivor round the farm, while Edwina showed me how to separate the cream from the milk. Marjorie, the baby, was in her cot on the verandah, and Edwina made a delicious meal for us. Their house looked like a stone house, but it was built of pug, made from mud, and it had a corrugated iron roof. While we were eating our meal, I heard a strange pattering sound. I looked up towards the ceiling and saw that there was a ledge going round the room, just below the roof, and on it were whole families of rats calmly walking around the room, as if they were out for a stroll. I must have gasped in astonishment because Edwina looked at me and said, "Don't worry, Ray, they are quite harmless. They're very inquisitive creatures, they always come out and walk round the room when we came in to eat."

Later Edwina and Viv had two more children, a son, named Viv after his father, and a daughter, Dorothy. Some years later Tom married a very nice Australian widow, and the couple lived very happily until Tom's death.

THIRTY-FOUR

A while back, in the summer, Ivor had built a little bough shade, attached to the house between the door and the window, in which he kept his tools. He put in a high shelf, to keep the more dangerous tools, including an iron shoe last, out of the reach of the children. (Originally Ivor had made this bough shade as a place where he could sit in the shade while I cut his hair – which I had been doing for some time, as the barber in town was inclined to shave all your hair off once he started on you.) One day Ivor was working somewhere around the paddock and I was in the little bough shade; I bent down to do something, and the iron last fell off the shelf on to my back, knocking my shoulder out, and leaving me lying on the floor. The little ones tried to lift me, but every time I attempted to get up, I fainted with the agony in my shoulder.

I couldn't risk sending the children to look for their father, I could only hope that he would soon come in for his food. I knew he wasn't far away, but I didn't know exactly what he was doing, whether he was attending to the cow or working in the fields. However I did know that the longer I waited, the harder it would be to get my shoulder back; something must be done, but what? I tried pulling myself along on my good side, hoping to get into the bedroom, though first I explained to the children what I was trying to do, so that they wouldn't be frightened. Eventually I managed to get to the rail of the bed, and then I asked Jack to get me a stool, which he did. All this took a very long time because I kept losing consciousness with the severity of the pain. Jack put the stool by the rails at the foot of the bed, eventually I was able to get myself onto the stool by hanging on to the rail. Next I managed to raise my body so that the rail came underneath my arm, and put the arm over the bed, so that the rail acted as a sort of crutch. Finally, when I was in a suitable position, I kicked the stool from under my leg and the weight of my body pulled the shoulder back. As I kicked the stool, I let out a terrific scream so loud that Ivor could hear it where he was working, and he came running to the house – but my shoulder was already back in place. I felt weak and sick, and all the colour had drained from my face, but Ivor made me a cup of tea, and I felt a little better. For a few days I didn't feel too well, so Ivor had to do the milking, but he had watched me doing it, and he managed all right, even though he had never milked a cow in his life before.

Soon the corn was beginning to show little spikes above the ground and we knew we would have a good crop. Our problem was to keep the chickens and our pet emu away from it. We had been given the emu by Dick Raymond who had found it on his farm one day. There was a price on the head of all emus because they were so destructive to the farms, but ours had been a little gosling-like creature when we first had him; now he had grown tall and strong enough to carry a man. Still, we needn't have worried about Jimmy; he wasn't a bit concerned about the cornfield, he was more at home in the kitchen, watching me cooking, He would follow me round everywhere, and was quite an entertainment for us in the evening.

Soon Ivor had to go to Bluff Point to help Mr. Ray with his tomatoes, so we were on our own again; I didn't know how long he would be away this time. Meanwhile he had forgotten to give the collar he borrowed for the ploughing back to Mr. Sultana. Ivor had not mentioned this to me, and one day, when I was doing my washing out in the back yard, Mr. Sultana called, to ask for the horse's collar. It was only a working collar, made of straw, and as I didn't know we had borrowed it from him, I couldn't understand what he was talking about. He motioned and put his hands around his neck as if he was trying to strangle himself, but I could make no sense of what he was doing, and he could speak no English. And it must have looked to Mr. Sultana as if I was doing a dance, because Jimmy the emu was standing at my side, nipping at the flies. (I wasn't wearing stockings and the flies were landing on my bare legs, whereupon Jimmy would nip at my legs and I would have to jump out of his way.) I was puzzled; this old Greek owed us thirty shillings, and yet here he was, asking me for a collar worth only a few shillings. I held out my hand to him, saying, "You give me thirty shillings you owe me, I give you collar." At that he said, "No money, collar," and I said, "No collar, money." We kept this argument up for some time, and I got annoyed with the old man because we needed that money badly. Then he said, "I fetch a policeman." I put my hands on my hips, pointed to my house, and said to him, "Quick way, you get policeman." At that he got fed up with the discussion, and went away, sighing deeply.

Now it was time to start Jack in school. He was six years old, and I had been busy making him blouses and shorts, and had bought him a little satchel. He could have had his education by correspondence course as we lived so far out in the bush, but I wanted him to go to a real school, not to be educated as a bush boy. The great day came, and we started out early, Jack had his little satchel in which he carried his food, a flannel and soap, exercise book and pencils, a towel and a drinking mug. When he got to the school, I waited to see him go in. The daily drill was this: the boys were lined up on one side, and the girls on the other, then they would march a little way down the track to the flag pole, and form a ring around it. There were two flags flying from the pole, the Australian flag and the Union Jack; the children would salute the Union Jack, and sing 'God Save the King', but a little differently from the way we sing it back home:

> God save our gracious King,
> God save our King:
> Far from our Empire's heart
> Make us a worthy part,
> God save the King.
> Keep us forever Thine,
> Our land Thy southern shrine,
> And by Thy grace divine,
> God save our King.

Then they would salute the Australian flag and sing:

> Australia fair, I love thee, dear land of my birth,
> To me you are the sweetest, the dearest place on earth.
> I love thy golden sunshine, and thy skies of azure blue.
> Australia, I salute you.

Then they would walk to the verandah, still boys on one side and girls to the other, and go to the wash basins and wash their hands, after which they would leave their towels, flannels and soap by their own basins.

Near each side was a water bag, which looked like a soldiers kit-bag, hanging from the roof of the verandah, but within reach

288

of the children. It had a little wooden top, and any child needing a drink would take it then in an orderly fashion, with no pushing. Next they would go towards their classroom where a teacher was waiting to inspect their hands, necks and heads. The children were allowed to go barefoot if they wanted to, but though shoes were not compulsory, any child whose clothes were found to be less than fresh and clean was given a note to take home to their parents. Cleanliness played a vital part in their education.

Jack had a little friend who started the same day as he did, named Tuppenny Drage; they were put to sit together, and they were identically dressed, though Tuppenny was the richest boy in Northampton and Jack was the poorest. But this made no difference anyway: the saying in Australia is 'Jack is as good as his master, one man is as good as another.' There is no class distinction there, and the boys became the best of pals throughout their school days. I went to collect Jack from school and met Mr. Drage, who was there collecting Tuppenny; as we waited, we spotted them coming out arm in arm, and Mr. Drage said, jokingly, "Look at the twins! Which of them is yours?" Tuppenny wasn't willing to get into his dad's car, he wanted to walk with Jack; but of course he had to get into the car because he lived miles away from the school, then Mr. Drage suggested that in future I should bring Jack to the crossroads each day, so that he and Tuppenny could pick him up in the car, and bring him back again after school and drop him off at the crossroads where I would be waiting for him. When we got home that afternoon all we could hear from Jack was what he had learnt in school:

> 'Cookaburra, cookaburra,
> Sitting on a gum tree.'

and we had to sit and listen to that over and over again for the rest of the day.

We were told that now the wet season had started, Jack would have to be dressed in the regulation winter outfit – oilskin coat, sou'wester and galoshes, with slippers to change into for classes. When Ivor came home from Bluff Point on Saturday, I gave him the list of clothes that we had to get for Jack, and asked him if he had any money. Some time previously, while we had been discussing hardships and the lack of work for the men, Emily had told me that Mr. McCaskill, the head of the mounted police (a tall, handsome, but big-headed man who thought he was the cat's whiskers!) had the authority to give a little help, providing the women went themselves to ask for it. She told me that Mrs. Raymond had had money off him for boots for her little boy, so I thought I would try my luck, because I needed winter shoes for Jack. I asked Ivor not to go back to Bluff Point that morning, but to stay in and look after Pearl while I took Jack to school, and then went into town on business. (I didn't tell him what the business was.) I handed Jack over to Mr. Drage at the crossroads, and then hurried into town.

Mr. McCaskill's office was the first place I came to as I reached town, but when I got to the office my courage failed me, and I couldn't go in. I walked along the street aimlessly, hoping my courage would come back, until I came to the one and only butcher's shop. The window was empty and dirty, and the only signs that it had ever been a butcher's shop were the blood spattered walls and a meat cleaver. A dirty old man, between seventy and eighty years old, came to the door to talk to me. He was an Englishman who had run away many years ago to live in the bush, later he had married a young woman of twenty, and they now had eight children, with less than a year between each one. He apparently wanted to sell me meat, though I could not see any in the window, as I told him. He told me to come inside, and showed me a barrel of a horrible-looking liquid which he said was brine. Then he said he only sold salted beef, but he added, "Anything you want, you tell old Cloey and I'll get it for you." I explained that I hadn't come in to buy meat because I had no money, so he asked how I managed and I told him we ate rabbits. He offered to give me meat, and said I could pay for it when I had money, but though I thanked him, I said I would prefer to wait until I had money to buy it, and then I would be sure to come and get it from him. "Everybody owes old Cloey money," he told me. "You are the only bloody Pommie who doesn't."

"Aren't you lucky, then, Mr. Cloe," I replied, "that there *is* one who doesn't owe you money."

With that I left him, and went back to Mr. McCaskill's office. I had to go round to the back door, and after I had knocked timidly, the door was opened and a voice said, "Come in, Mrs. Webb." It was Mr. McCaskill, who was sitting at his desk, with no-one else in the office. I had never asked for charity, and I

290

didn't know how to begin to ask for his help, but he said, "Don't stand there, Mrs. Webb, come up to the table and tell me what you want." I went and stood by his desk and explained that I needed shoes for Jack for school.

"You've got twenty-five pounds in the bank," he said. "Why don't you use that?"

"Mr. McCaskill, that money doesn't belong to us, it isn't ours to use," I said, and I told him that we had some Defence Bonds back in Britain, but they were of no use to us in Australia. My husband had therefore written to his brother, asking him to sell the bonds and send the money out to us, as we were in dire need of it, but since my brother-in-law had been unable to do this, he had sent us twenty-five pounds of his own money, which we intended to return to him immediately.

"Why don't you spend it?" said Mr. McCaskill. "He's sent it to you, spend it."

"My brother-in-law is an unemployed miner," I told him. "He has a wife and four little boys to support, and he has heavy commitments. If we spend this money, we might never be able to repay it, and their hardship is worse than ours."

Mr. McCaskill put out his hand, and drew me towards him. "Your husband is working at Bluff Point, isn't he, and you are all alone in that old shack, aren't you?" he said.

"My husband works down there for his keep and our rent," I said. "He has no wages to bring home, and all my children and I have to live on is the five shillings a week I earn at Mrs. Davidson's."

He told me then that my little boy could go to school without shoes on, the same as lots of other little boys did, to which I replied, "Your children are very well fed, aren't they, Mr. McCaskill? Do they go to school without shoes on?" By now his arm had gone round my waist, and he pulled me towards him and attempted to kiss me. At that I slapped his face with all the force I could muster, and he staggered back in surprise, saying as he did so, "You spitfire!"

"Mr. McCaskill, I came here looking for help, not insults," I said, and started walking to the door; then I turned back and told him, "If you ever do anything like that again, I'll go straight to your wife."

Just as I reached the door, he called me back, and though I wanted to walk out of the office, I felt I must try for those shoes,

291

so I walked just a little way from the door, keeping a safe distance between us.

"You wouldn't really go to my wife, would you," he said.

I didn't answer him, but said only, "Do I have the shoes or don't I?"

"Come here," he said. "I can't shout. I promise I won't touch you again."

I went closer to his desk, but still keeping a safe distance, and then he tried flattery. Once again he asked about the shoes, but he said, "Oh, don't be in such a hurry, stop and chat with me for a while. Aren't you lonely up in that old place when your husband is up in Bluff Point? A beautiful woman like you shouldn't be shut away in the bush on her own. Suppose I were to come around there one night, would you invite me in and give me a cup of tea?"

"Certainly, Mr. McCaskill," I said. "If ever you are passing my way, you would be most welcome to a cup of tea. But be sure you call when my husband is there."

"Oh, that's no good," he said. "It's when you are alone that you need company."

At that, I told him that I had a twenty-two Winchester, and that I was a good shot. He stared at me in surprise, and said, "You wouldn't shoot me, would you?" I looked him straight in the eye and said, "You or any rat that crawls around my place at night when I am alone." Then I walked out of the office in disgust.

Ivor found the money and Jack got his shoes. Meanwhile, by the time I got home I had fully composed myself, and Ivor did not hear of my visit or of my reason for going to Mr. McCaskill's office. Jack came home from school in his new outfit and proudly told us what he had been taught that day. Pearl and I had to be his 'pupils' while he 'taught' us the poem he had learnt:

> 'Ducks go out on rainy days,
> They never wear galoshes,
> No-one calls to them and says,
> 'Put on your macintoshes.'
> Oh how I wish that I could go
> Splish splashing around the yard,
> And be a dripping duck.
>   End of poem!

292

Now the wet season had ended, and police notices went up all over town (they were even fixed to trees), warning people that the snakes were waking up. The children now had to learn snake protection; each child had to take a matchbox to school, carrying one live match and a woman's hairpin, and they were told to walk like the Chinese people. This meant that instead of raising each foot as they walked, they were taught to shuffle their feet when out of doors. If they were bitten by a snake, they were to strike the match on the box and hold the end of the hairpin in the flame until it was red hot, then quickly jab the two hot ends of the hairpin into the two punctures made by the snake's fangs. After that they were to go as quickly as they could to get help from someone who could get them to a doctor. Even if the doctor attended them immediately, it was not a hundred per cent certain that the children would not die, but that small act at the very beginning afforded them at least a chance of recovery. All the snakes out in the bush were deadly poisonous, and the children were acutely aware of this.

Now that Jack had started school, Pearl was lonely without him, and I had to give a lot of time to amusing her and keeping her happy. One Saturday morning, Jack and Pearl were playing in their cubby house when suddenly the cat came dashing in, making a terrible noise. I knew he wanted me to follow him, and he led me to the side of the cubby house, taking me up to what appeared to be a car tyre – though I knew from the cat's excitement that this was no tyre. On closer inspection I could see it was a large adder, curled up fast asleep. I knew that if I waited for it to wake up, it would be very dangerous, but I didn't know what else to do with it. There was an unwritten bush law that no man should pass a snake and let it live, but no woman should try to fight one because of their skirts. However, there was no man with me, so I had to do something myself, and quickly too. I picked up a heavy piece of wood and struck it on the head time and again, until it was dead.

The corn was growing so high now that the children would get lost in it. Ivor was almost six feet tall, and when he walked through the cornfield, we could just about see the top of his hat moving as he walked.

A scheme had started now to give unemployed men a job of work to do; each man worked for one whole day, and then so many hours and minutes of the following day, the same length of time for each man. The job they were given was repairing the roads. One day, after this scheme had gone on for some time, Ivor came home and told me that he had been made foreman of one gang, which would mean a little extra work each week. I asked him why he had been given the foreman's job, when he was a Pommie, and he explained that each man had been allotted a certain part of the road to work on; when the council came to inspect their work, they wanted to know who had worked on one section, and when they were told 'Ike Webb', they had asked him about his work on the road. He had told them that a road was no good unless it was sealed, and that was what he had been doing. They had no knowledge of sealing roads, and they had been so impressed by Ivor's work, that they had appointed him foreman and had asked him to teach the men how to seal a road.

One day Mrs. Ray came up from Bluff Point, being curious to see the corn field. She had come up on the train and was staying with my sister. She was so pleased with the corn field and the other work we had done that she said she thought the rent should be put up to ten shillings a week. After all our hard work in making our home so beautiful and growing our corn so high, our reward was to have our landlady raise our rent from five shillings to ten!

By now Ivor was working two days a week, and he had been busy working in our kitchen garden too during the winter season. Since the corn was now ripe and ready to cut, we had to discuss how we were going to get it in, because there was always a danger of fire breaking out in the bush, and if that happened, there wouldn't be a hope of saving our corn. When I mentioned this to Ivor, he said, "Oh don't say that now we have worked so hard and done so much. Mr. Drage is the only one that has a harvester – it cost him thousands of pounds, so he hires it out and it is already booked up for the season. In any case we couldn't afford to hire it for such a small paddock. It makes me feel sick to think of that lovely corn going to waste, but what can we do? We've got nothing to cut it."

On the Monday I tried to persuade Ivor not to go to Bluff Point that day, but to stay at home and try to find a way of clearing the corn, because I was so frightened of fire, but he got on his horse, said, "I'm sick of worrying about it," and rode off. However I couldn't stop worrying about the problem. It was very hot, the chickens were pulling at the heads of the corn, and the hens were coming out from under it with the clutches of chicks that they had hatched there. I lay awake all night worrying, my loneliness forgotten. A train went up on Monday and back on Friday, and many fires had been caused by a spark from the engine.

Then, during the night, I had an inspiration; I had to save at least a little of the corn. The children were on holiday – the school had been closed because of the intense heat – so I got them up at four o'clock the next morning and told them we were going to play at being a farmer's boy. I gathered up all the old rags and cut them into bandages, then I got the children washed and covered them completely with vaseline, before dressing them in very light clothing to cover their nakedness, and putting large hats on their heads; I did the same for myself.

We took the tin bath and some tin buckets down to the edge of the paddock, and I filled a bucket from the well, then filtered it from one bucket to another to get the frogs out of it. When this was done, I bandaged the children's fingers, each finger separately, and put a glove on each of their hands and tied them at the wrist, after which I did the same for myself, the children tying my gloves for me. (The need for gloves was due to the fact that the stalks of the corn were so brittle that they were razor sharp on the edges.) Pearl pulled the stalks down, and Jack cut off the heads and let them fall into the bath. All day long we worked at cutting off the heads, going a yard at a time, and when the bath was full, I would empty it into a sack. We stopped only for a short time to eat our sandwiches, and continued until it got too dark to work in the fields, though I had to stop occasionally to rebandage the children's hands, because the stalks were cutting the rags to shreds.

We did this all through the week, spending each whole day in the field, and making believe, for the children's sake, that it was a game. By the end of the week we had cleared a row, a yard wide, from the top of the paddock to the bottom, and on the Saturday we started on our second row, again a yard wide. I let the children rest as much as possible, but I kept going for as long as I could. When Ivor got home on the Saturday afternoon, he was amazed and delighted at what we were doing, and said he had been worrying about the corn all week, though he knew he could do nothing about it. He thought that what we had done had been a wonderful idea, and he promised us a shilling for every bag we filled.

Early on the Monday morning Ivor left again, and we carried on gathering the wheat. It was still stiflingly hot, and though our labour was a game to the children, I had to push myself hard to make every minute count. My anxiety was great and the sun was so hot that it was shimmering on the corn; it was like a burning weight on my back and made me feel dizzy. The heat made it thirsty work, but the children had great fun bailing out mugs of water for us to drink, and having them with me meant that I did not have to worry about them.

Even when we had worked for two weeks, we seemed to have made very little progress; it was such a very large field, and working out in the open in such terrific heat (124 degrees in the shade) made it an even harder task. I felt very exhausted, but determined to carry on. One day I was startled when I suddenly heard a man's voice coming from the lower end of the paddock where we were working. I looked up and saw a tall man, which surprised me because no stranger ever came that way. He repeated what he had already called out to me, "What are you doing out in this heat, missus, get inside at once." I stopped work and looked at him. I couldn't tell who he was because of the glare of the sun; he was coming towards me from the gully, but I told him that I was trying to save the corn in case of a fire, and this was the only way I could do it.

"Go in out of this heat," he said again. "I will come tomorrow and take the corn off for you."

I didn't want to disobey him, but I couldn't really imagine him coming back to take the corn off for me, I thought he was just saying it. Ivor had told me that there was only one harvester, on the Drages' estate, and I couldn't believe that the man would come to work in my field. It was too hot to go indoors, so we went and sat in the bough shade, but I was worried at the thought of a half day's work wasted. What if the man didn't come back?

At half past four the next morning, after a largely sleepless night, I woke to the sound of what seemed to be a tremendous roaring. I went out to the paddock to see what it could be, and there was the same tall man, seated in a tremendous iron machine. In fact it was the wealthy Mr. Drage himself, stripping our paddock with his harvester, and in a very short time he was dropping large sacks of corn, winnowed and sealed, ready for the miller. He wouldn't even wait to be thanked, and when I tried to ask him how much I owed, he just waved his hand, saying "So long, lady." My heart was filled with gratitude, to think that a man with his wealth would bother to bring such an expensive harvester all those miles to work in my field. And not only that, where it would have cost other farmers a great deal to hire such a machine, he had provided it for me out of the kindness of his heart, without even the need of thanks. (It seemed that Mr. Drage had been keeping an eye on our paddock; having given us the corn, he knew when it would be ripe for harvesting, and he had walked a mile from the main road where he left his car, through Mrs. Magee's land, out of concern for us.)

Ivor couldn't believe his eyes when he came home and saw the field stripped and the corn all taken in, especially when I told him that Mr. Drage himself had done the work for us. Next Ivor hired a cart to take the corn to the mill. I had no idea where that was, and I hadn't thought of asking Mr. Drage, but Ivor found the place, and since we had no money to pay the miller, he took corn instead. It was marvellous to see a two hundredweight sack of flour standing in my living room. I covered it with a cloth, but it was our pride and joy.

THIRTY-FIVE

We didn't have Daisy now. Mr. Hendley had lent Ivor a horse to help him plough the field because Daisy wasn't strong enough for the work, and then he had asked Ivor if he would like to keep that horse, while Mr. Hendley himself kept Daisy. (Mr. Hendley only needed a horse when he went to the burial ground, so Daisy was ideal for him, though she was too old now to carry Ivor about.) Mr. Hendley wanted to get rid of his own horse because he was afraid of her; as he told Ivor, she was a bolter, and had run away with him, though she worked well with the other three horses at the plough. Ivor decided to take a chance with the horse, although she had never pulled a cart, and the first time he tried to put her in the sulky, he asked me to come out and help hold her. She went right up on her hind legs, and if Ivor hadn't been quick enough, she would have come down on the sulky and smashed it. I was terrified.

One day Ivor decided to take us for a ride in the sulky; we got in, and set out for the Husbands' farm. The horse was all right until we got out on the main road, and then she bolted. There was a long stretch of road ahead of us and no traffic, and Ivor shouted to me, "Hold on tight, I'm going to break her of this fear." The faster the horse galloped, the more Ivor used the whip on her, to make her go faster, knowing she would soon be exhausted. The Drages had been widening the road, and had cut down a belt of trees on the grassy verge, but the stumps were still sticking up out of the ground, and when the horse got up on the verge, we could feel the wheels going up over the stumps. Still Ivor did not rein her in, but gave her her head, and when we got back onto the main road, he kept her at a gallop, not letting her slacken speed, but using the whip to urge her on, until eventually she gave in, and Ivor knew that fear of the whip had conquered any other fear, and we would have no more trouble. After that we had no fear of going in the sulky, and though we hadn't wanted to part with Daisy, she had a good home, and we

298

had a younger, stronger horse.

We were coming to the end of the hot season, and Ivor had had no work for some time – even the council scheme had come to a stop. We had flour to make bread and biscuits, but it was still a very lean time and I felt very depressed. In the hope of cheering me up, Ivor suggested that we go for a run down to the coast, to the river mouth. It was just a short break, we couldn't stop because of our cow. There was no-one about at the beach (which was usual), so we just rested the horse, then turned around and started on our way back. The weather was breaking by then, and Ivor said if we didn't get back soon, we would get caught in the storm. The craypots had been empty and there seemed to be no sign of rabbits, though we had hoped to be able to take both crayfish and rabbits home with us. However, we had just got up on to the road, Ivor having led the horse up through the sand, when we spotted a large rabbit ahead. For one moment Ivor forgot that it wasn't Daisy pulling the sulky, and shot the rabbit, but on hearing the shot, the horse bolted, with the sulky, the children and me.

Ivor dropped his gun and ran for the horse's head. I could do nothing, because the reins had slipped to the floor, and the horse had run half a mile before Ivor could control it and bring it to a stop. He was as white as a sheet, and said to me, "I'm sorry, Ray, for a moment I forgot. I don't know what I was thinking about, shooting so close to the horse, I'm so sorry." We had to go back for the gun, and Ivor said again, "My stupidity could have killed you all."

Once the horse had calmed down again, we went on our way. If I had felt depressed before, I felt worse now – and then the storm broke, a tropical electric storm. The lightning was pretty to watch, but very frightening too, because there was such a lot of metal around the sulky and the horse's harness; the lightning was striking the harness and playing round the horse. Ivor had to get out and walk at the horse's head, leading her through the storm, and soon he got the tent out from underneath the sulky and covered both that and the horse with it. He walked at the side of the horse, holding the tent securely round him. When we got into Northampton, the men asked Ivor how we had managed to come through the storm, and when he told them, they said we had been very lucky, and would most certainly all have been killed if the lightning had struck the sulky.

Now that the wet season had come, Mr. Rae from Bluff Point sent for Ivor to come and prepare the ground for the tomatoes. Ivor did not want to let the old man down, so he took the sulky and rode off, leaving us alone again. If I had told Ivor I was afraid of being left alone, he would have told me that there was nothing to be afraid of, there were no aborigines around now. It seemed that the aborigines had been moved out some miles, a few years before, to a settlement some way away. It was said that they had been sent there because of the rituals they performed on moonlit nights, known as corroborees. At these, they would paint their naked bodies and faces, making themselves look grotesque, then they would form a circle out in the clearing and do a war dance, working themselves into a frenzy and screaming and shouting. It was said that before their corroboree ended, they would take one of their own men, kill him, roast him and eat him, because they were cannibals. I believe they were put into a compound for the safety of the white people, probably because of the murder of the little boy who had once lived in my shack.

The day I arrived at my sister's house in Northampton, she had taken me for a walk to see some aborigines who still lived at the back of the town. These hadn't been taken to the settlement, so I knew that there were still about twenty families living near town; they had been told they could live there as long as they caused no trouble to the whites. Their homes were just tea-tree hovels, covered with potatoe sacks, and the aborigines themselves were short people who looked very ugly to us, with their thick faces and flat noses; they sat around wearing almost no clothes – the men had loin cloths, and the women were naked to the waist. They seemed unconcerned at us looking at them, although Emily had warned me not to stare at them. She said the Government had told them they were not allowed to come into town or go into a pub, or even come into the street for anything (although it was known that they came into the streets after dark, looking for any clothes that they could find.) The aborigines were given an allowance of tea, sugar and tobacco once a month, and a blanket every six months, but if they were ever caught mixing with white people or doing anything they were not supposed to be doing, they were sent to the compound.

One night, while Ivor was away, the children and I were sitting in the living room; it had been my practice, since coming

300

out to Australia, to give the children one hour of lessons every night after tea. I would take the chenille cloth off the table and put a piece of linoleum on it; then I would give the children a piece of chalk each, and they would sit with their backs to the wall while I taught them the simple basics of nursery school. When I wrote a letter home, they would each write a little note to put in with it. On this particular night the children had settled down for their lesson (which they thoroughly enjoyed). It was between five and six o'clock, and the night was very still, with nothing to be heard but the sound of the frogs in the gully. Then suddenly there was a terrific noise of screaming and whooping; it was like being part of a cowboy film and being attacked by Indians, and the screaming was horrific.

I hadn't heard anyone approaching, but this noise was coming from inside the back yard, right underneath the window where the children were sitting. They were terrified and ran to me, clinging to my skirts, frightened out of their wits, while they cried out, "What is it, Mammy, what is it?" But the noise outside was so deafening that I could hardly hear what they were saying. I put my arms round them and said, "It's all right, loves, it's only some silly clowns trying to frighten us. We are Welsh people, aren't we, and no-one can frighten Welsh people, can they?" With their little voices shaking, they said, "No, Mammy, we is Welsh, they can't frighten us 'cause we is Welsh."

I knew that whoever was outside could see what was happening inside, because there were no curtains at the windows and the lamp was alight in the room. The gun was prepared, but I did not want to show any fear, so I walked slowly over to the weapon and reached it down, then I pointed it in the direction of the noise. I knew now that it was the aborigines, who were still howling and screaming outside, but I could do nothing while the noise was going on and I just waited, expecting them to attack the house at any moment. I told the little ones to sit on the settee, then stood in front of them, not knowing whether any attack would come by the window or the door. There was the noise of their feet shuffling; my hair stood on end, and the top of my head felt as if it was frozen. If I had not had the children, I could have attempted to get away through the front of the house, relying on my swift running to get me to safety, but I couldn't run with two children.

It seemed to me that I had been waiting for hours, in a never-

301

ending nightmare. And then there was a hush, a dead silence, and I thought, 'This is it, either they are going to kill one of their own people, or they are going to come in after us.' (It was a well-known fact at that time that they loved to eat white children – we elders were too salty, but they found our children delicious – or so the story went!) I called out to them, "You can make as much noise as you like out there, we're not worried. But if one of you dares to put a hand on this shack, I'll put a bullet through you."

At that my little ones cried out, "Mammy, you won't kill them, will you?"

"No, loves," I said, "Mammy won't kill them, but I'll mark them so that Mr. McCaskill can identify them." I could not have said anything more useful than McCaskill's name, because I didn't hear a sound after that. His was the one name they feared because he was the man who could put them in the settlement. They must have gone as quietly as they had come, but I didn't know then whether they were still waiting their chance outside. I told the children to get into their cots and go to sleep; Mammy would watch over them all night, and nothing would happen. Then I spent another night standing in one doorway, with three windows and another door to watch. There was no fear of falling asleep!

Next morning my brother-in-law Jim came down. He had never come to our house alone before, and I was both surprised and pleased to see him. "What's the matter, Rit?" he asked. "Are you ill? You're as white as a sheet." I told him about the previous night, and then it was his turn to go white under his tan. He said, "God, Rit, you've had a corroboree here." Then he looked around the ground from which the noise had come, and said he had been uneasy about me all night and had wanted to come down. "I wish to God now that I had come," he said. "We could have had the black trackers out, but it is too late now, the chickens have disturbed the ground too much."

It was Monday, washing day at Mrs. Davidson's, and now that Jack was in school, I only had Pearl to take with me. The pile of washing waiting for me was enormous. The wash-house was just a corrugated iron shelter, and although it was sheltered from the rays of the sun, the iron drew the heat and made it very uncomfortable washing on the old washing board. Mrs. Davidson usually used the 'dolly' in the dolly tub when she did the washing – or so she told me – but after carrying Pearl piggyback

302

for a mile and half, I didn't have a lot of stength left for dollying, and I preferred to use the rubbing board. Pearl was missing Jack very much, and needed a lot of attention, so I settled her in the shade on the verandah, with her doll and books and pencils. The day was intensely hot, and I would occasionally have to throw cold water over my feet because the ground was burning them where I stood. Then Mrs. Davidson came to help me peg out the washing. I hadn't noticed that Pearl had left the verandah and was sitting on the earth floor, near where I was standing at the wash tub. Suddenly she let out a scream, and Mrs. Davidson and I ran over, to see black ants crawling all over her. I picked her up quickly, and Mrs. Davidson and I worked frantically, trying to beat the ants off her body. Mr. Davidson ran to see what was happening, and to help us, and he told me that, given the chance, the ants would have picked Pearl's bones clean in half an hour.

When it was all over, and Pearl was safe, Mrs. Davidson told me that when she was a young girl, living with her parents in the pug house that Mrs. Douglas now lived in, they had called them 'execution ants'. If the bush people wished to dispose of anyone, they would take them to a clear piece of ground where the ants had their nests, then they would strip that person and peg him (or her) to the ground with arms and legs stretched, and leave him/her to the ants. In half an hour there would be nothing left of them but bones.

One day Mr. Ash came up, very sheepishly. I hadn't seen him since the day he had left the cow in my paddock, and the calf was now six months old or more. He hadn't wanted to show himself before, because he was afraid I would ask him to take the cow back – he didn't think I would ever have been able to tame her. Of course, he didn't want the cow back while his bankruptcy was going on, or else it would have been taken away from him to help him pay his creditors, and meanwhile he was having the cow and calf paddocked and fed free. He asked me how the cow was doing, and I said, "Come and see for yourself," and took him over to the paddock. I had called her Beauty, because she was such a beautiful cow: she had not had a name before, Mr. Ash had just cursed at her to get her attention. When she heard her name called, she and the calf came trotting up to the fence and nuzzled the hand I held out to them. Mr. Ash was astonished, and said he wouldn't have thought it possible, but I told him, "Brute force will get you nowhere with animals. You see what a little kindness will do."

Unfortunately, when he saw how tame she was, he said, "Oh, I can take them back with me now." I was so upset when I heard that, I felt I had betrayed the animal in showing him how tame she had become; it was like parting with someone I loved, but there was nothing I could do about it, though I dreaded being parted from her and letting her go back to that ill treatment. I begged him to let her stay with me a little longer, but it was no use, he took them both and left. Ivor was very annoyed when I told him what had happened, and said it was a dirty trick for Mr. Ash to have played on me.

THIRTY-SIX

One day we went up to visit Emily, and she said, "If tomorrow isn't too hot, we will go for a picnic." I laughed, and said, "Back home we say if it isn't too wet, we'll go for a picnic!" The following day I packed a picnic basket and took the children to meet Emily, and then we all set off to what Emily said was a nice picnic spot, through the bush and up near the Carruthers' land. It was a little cooler in the bush; although the trees did not give much shade, the undergrowth made it a little cooler than it was out in the open. However it was still stiflingly hot, and in my opinion not suitable for picnicking. The path was narrow, and we had to walk in single file, while there was no place where we could sit down and rest, but Emily said there was a little clearing up ahead, and we would soon reach it.

The children all wore shoes, to protect their feet from the 'double gees', but Emily's youngest little girl, six-year-old Ray, sat down on the path and took off one shoe, saying there was something in it. We were walking quietly on ahead, when suddenly we heard Ray scream and we ran back to see what was wrong. There was a soldier ant on her, and Emily beat it off, caught Ray by the hand, and told us all to run as quickly as we could away from that spot.

"What are we running for, Emily?" I asked.

"I can't stop to tell you now," she said. "Keep running until we come to the clearing, then I'll tell you."

Eventually we got out of the bush, and Emily said, "That ant was a scout for the other soldier ants. They stand on long legs, about two inches from the ground, and they are very tall; they walk on two legs, swinging the other two like arms, and they move like a battalion, usually four abreast."

I had been living in the bush now long enough not to discredit anything that I heard, and I believed what Emily had said; she explained that we had been running because by now there would be thousands of those ants looking for us, and we had to get away quickly before they picked up our scent. (There is an account of these ants and their behaviour in the Encyclopedia Britannica.) The incident had frightened Emily and the four children so much that we didn't have our picnic, and had to walk miles out of our way to get back to the main road, because it would not have been safe to go back through the bush again and risk meeting the ants.

By now Ivor was able to buy us a cow of our own with some money we got from our wheat, and our family of animals was complete. We had a cow and young strong horse, as well as a few hundred chickens – though unfortunately there was no sale for chickens or eggs (and in the summer the eggs were seldom fit to eat anyway, because in the intense heat they were cooked almost as soon as they were laid). However, the chickens cost nothing to feed, since there was plenty of food and seed in the bush for them. We also had a cat, two galahs, an emu and a pet lizard which we encouraged to live in the house with us because it ate up all the flies. One day an exhausted half-grown kangaroo wandered into our yard, and I gave it food and drink. It stayed with us for quite a while, until we found one day that it belonged to our neighbours, who had lost it some time before, and reluctantly we had to part with it.

At one time we had occasion to go to the doctor because I had pains in my head. However he could not give me anything for the pain, because, so he said, the blood wasn't pumping quickly enough round my brain, and this caused the blood to be sluggish; the only thing he could do, he said, was to bleed me. I did know that I was suffering from severe eyestrain caused by hours of sewing, because I had been making a bedspread for Mrs. Davidson, and had kept on at it until it was finished. (She had been so pleased with it, that she had carried it around with her, showing everyone.) The bank manager's wife, who said the bedspread was beautiful, asked me if I would cover her eiderdown for her, and I said I would, but I didn't really want to do it. I needed the money, but I knew it would be a tremendous strain on my eyes. As it happend, I was relieved of that job, when her husband committed suicide that weekend. When I discussed the tragedy with the doctor, he said it was a common complaint in that country; he called it 'melancholitis', caused by sheer boredom, which made people so melancholy that they committed suicide.

Early one morning I heard a cooee coming from outside the fence. I went out to see who it was, and found Jimmy M'Gee, Mrs. Davidson's twenty-year-old grandson. "Mrs. Webb," he said, "Grandma sent me over to tell you that the three girls are ill with typhus fever. They are very ill and Mamma is all in, and Grandma said if I came to tell you, you would be sure to help Mamma."

"Yes, Jimmy," I said. "I'll come straight away." Ivor was home now, and I told him about Jimmy's message. Then I said I was going over now and he would have to stay with the children. Ivor was alarmed, though, and said, "You can't go over there now, Ray. Typhus is a very dangerous tropical disease, and you might get it – or the children might."

I said, "Mrs. Davidson has asked for my help, and God knows she has helped us enough; if it's God's will that I shall help Mrs. M'Gee, then He will protect me and our children."

Before going over, I filled a bucket with water from the well and put Jeyes Fluid in it. "Watch what I'm doing, Ivor," I said, "because you'll have to do this every day for me. I'll put this outside the fence, in the bush, then I'll travel through the bush, and come back the same way, so that I can't come into contact with anybody. I shall be back before sundown."

I put some clean clothes together, and told Ivor that before sundown he was to hang them on the tree by the bucket, so that I could change into them before coming home. Then I told the children to stay with Daddy; I would be back before dark, and they were not to wander away.

When I reached Mrs. M'Gee's house, she told me the three children had come home from boarding school in Perth for their holidays, and had brought the fever home with them. "I have sent to Perth for two nurses trained in fever nursing," she said (she was a wealthy woman), "but though they came, they were not allowed to get off the train, and there is no-one in Northampton who knows anything about the fever except the doctor. Then Mamma remembered that you had told her you had been nursing fever before coming out to Australia."

"Well, yes," I said, "I have been trained for typhoid nursing, but we never had typhus in Britain. But if the doctor will provide the right drugs, I will provide the nursing care, and with God's help we'll make your children well again."

The doctor had not taken precautions to prevent the fever

from spreading out of the sickroom, so I told Mrs. M'Gee that I wanted as many sheets as she had doors in the house, and some Jeyes Fluid. Then I soaked every sheet in water to which I had added Jeyes Fluid, and asked Jimmy to tack one over each door. The girls had very high temperatures and needed a lot of sponging; at the end of the day I took all the soiled linen and towels out of the sick room and put them in the wash-house. There I soaked everything in the washtubs, filled the tub with disinfectant, and left it all to soak overnight; I left instructions that no-one was to go into the wash-house until I arrived next day. As soon as I got there that day I had sent Mrs. M'Gee to bed, having decided that she should sleep by day and nurse by night, while I slept by night and nursed by day. Now Mrs. M'Gee came down to relieve me, so that I could go home through the bush before darkness descended.

When I arrived at our paddock fence, I stripped off all my clothes (I knew there would be no-one around to see me), took the pins out of my hair, and put my head into the disinfectant water, and then washed my whole body in the water, to kill off any typhus germs that I might be carrying. Everything that I had taken off I put into the disinfectant, and added the towel that I had used, after which I dressed myself in my clean clothes and knew that I could safely go back to my husband and children without fear of infecting them. That was the procedure every morning and night, and every day I followed the same route home through the bush.

Initially, when the children were taken ill, the doctor's wife had assisted Mrs. M'Gee, but after her first day there the doctor had stopped her going again, and that was when I was called upon to assist. One morning, as I was nearing Mrs. M'Gee's, I saw her running through the paddock to meet me; she was crying bitterly, and as she came near the fence, she called out, "Don't come in, don't come in!" I wondered what had happened, because the children had been improving nicely when I left the previous night.

"What has happened, Mrs. M'Gee?" I asked. "Why are you so distressed. Has something happened to the children?"

"The doctor has told me I am not to let you in again," she said.

"Why did he say that, Mrs. M'Gee?" I asked her.

"He said, 'Mrs. Webb isn't strong enough to nurse those children through typhus. If Mrs. Webb caught the fever, she would never recover from it, and if anything happens to her, I shall hold you responsible. She isn't well enough to be sick nursing,'" she explained.

"Mrs. M'Gee, if you don't want me, tell me yourself that you don't."

She was still crying bitterly, and said, "Of course I want you – what am I going to do without you? But I can't let you come in, the doctor has warned me."

Then I said to her, "Stand aside, Mrs. M'Gee, I am coming in. You need me, the children need me, and I demand that you let me come in, Now, get out of my way, and you can tell that to the doctor. If it's God's will that I nurse your children, He will give me strength, and I will only answer to Him." I went in, and nursed those children through their fever until they were completely well again, and we also prevented eighteen-year-old Mary and twenty-year-old Jimmy from contracting the fever. The sickness was confined to the M'Gee bungalow only, and there were no further outbreaks of typhus.

During the whole of the six weeks that I nursed Mrs. M'Gee's children, Mrs. Davidson had to do her own washing, but Mrs. M'Gee insisted on paying me the five shillings a week that I would have been having from her mother, because I wouldn't take payment for nursing. I had been glad to help, to repay some of the kindnesses shown to me by her mother.

These weeks of anxiety and the strain of the nursing, coming so soon after the shock of the corroboree in the back yard, had had a lowering effect on my health, and there had been no money coming into the house except for the five shillings from Mrs. M'Gee. However now I was home, Ivor was able to go and look for casual work, picking peaches, oranges and tomatoes, all in their seasons. These jobs could only be found a long way away, so Ivor had to sleep near his job and was unable to come home at night. I was able now to do my two days washing for Mrs. Davidson, but that was all the money we had to live on, because the farmers who employed Ivor were able to give him only a little actual cash, and sometimes all he would have would be a few perks, such as a kerosene tin of whatever he happened to be picking at the time, together with his keep. Still while he was having food out, it meant that our food lasted a little longer, with one mouth less to feed.

All the things that had happened in the past when I had been left alone at night, had left me more nervous than ever. I just couldn't bring myself to put the beds out on the verandah now. Just before darkness fell, I would pull up a bucket of water from the water hole and bring it into the living room, then build up a log pile on the hearth; (I would have to take them all out again in the morning, but I had to do the same thing every night in case the water and wood were needed for anything.) I would shut the two doors, putting a stick behind one and a peg in the other, and tell myself 'Now we are safely tucked away behind these doors' – but deep in my heart I knew that just a puff of wind would blow them wide open.

One night I was sitting in my usual place on the settee, giving the children their nightly lesson; they wanted their cocoa and were ready to go to bed, saying they were tired. With them in bed the loneliness was frightening. At one time I would have eased my nervousness by singing, but now I was too frightened to make a noise, so I tried to conquer my fear by concentrating on a tablecloth I was embroidering. Then, in the stillness of the night, I heard a sound in the distance, moving in the direction of our house. I went to the front door, but didn't open it; I just looked through a little peephole in the door, which had at one time been the door knob. I tried to think what the sound could be – it was like someone with a wooden leg stumping along, but the night was so dark that I couldn't see a thing. By now I knew it was coming up our track; the ground was hard and I could hear first a shuffle, then a tap, just like a blind person walking along with a stick. I looked up at my gun, but I felt I had no strength even to get up and take it down, I was so petrified, and my tongue seemed to cleave to my mouth, as if to stifle the sound of my breathing. Nearer and nearer came the sound of the shuffling and the stick, and louder and louder it got, and this seemed to frighten me more than anything else that happened before. All I could do was pray, "Oh God, help me, I am so frightened."

By now the sound was on my verandah. I looked through the peephole to try to see what was outside, but I could see nothing in the blackness of the night; the noise was right outside, and I knew that there was just the door between me and whatever it was. Suddenly I heard something groping for a door handle. I called out, "Who's there?" but there was still no answer – and then I heard a cough, and I thought, "Oh thank God, I know who that is!" It was Mr. Davidson. He hadn't heard me calling because he was deaf, and because he had not been to my house before, it hadn't occurred to me that he could have found his way there. I opened the door, and had to restrain myself from throwing my arms around him, I was so relieved.

I stood aside, and Mr. Davidson came in and made himself comfortable in my fireside chair, which was a decorated, cushioned deck chair. Then I made him a cup of tea; it was pointless to try to make conversation with him because he was stone deaf. He was a small, stocky Swede in his early eighties, and he started to tell me stories of his sea voyaging days. My fear had left me, and I was able to relax with my embroidery and listen to the wonderful tales he told of his early life at sea. Several hours passed most enjoyably, and I was sorry when at last he got up and said, "Goodnight," and disappeared into the darkness. (I had not seen his torch when he was approaching the house because I was looking the wrong way. I had been looking towards the town, but he had come by the old miners' track that Mrs. Davidson had once shown me as a short cut to get to her place.)

Mr. Davidson had promised to come again. He seemed to have enjoyed himself talking and found me a good listener, and he came several times after that, when I was alone. The shuffling and tapping noise he made was to frighten away snakes if any happened to be on the track, and, in fact, his visit had helped me to get back my self-confidence, so that I was less nervous than I had been. He called several nights a week for a number of weeks, and was the only person who ever called after dark. I was very much at ease with him, and it was wonderful listening to the tales he had to tell of his native country.

I was at Mrs. Davidson's, one cool day, when she had lit a fire in the room where I was sewing, and while I was there, two lady friends called on Mrs. Davidson. the three ladies sat by the fire, chatting over a cup of tea, and I sewed away as usual. Mrs. Davidson had once told me that her husband would never come into the house, night or day, except when these ladies visited her, but then he would walk across the room and back again, glare at the ladies, and say, "Bloody cows!" They had been coming every week for years, and each time they came he would do exactly the same thing. This time, though, he did not appear, and after a while I packed up my sewing and went home; later I

311

was told that as soon as I had gone he came in to give them their weekly treatment.

When I went over to do their washing the following Monday, I could tell that Mrs. Davidson was very excited about something, and she could scarcely wait to get me into the house and tell me her secret. She whispered to me, "Mrs. Webb, I've got to tell you something. What do you think, the old man has got a fancy woman somewhere!" I didn't take a lot of notice of what she was saying, because first I had to get Pearl settled down, and then there was a tremendous amount of washing for me to do, after which I had to get back in time for Jack coming home from school. I really didn't have time to stop and listen to her, but Mrs. Davidson wasn't going to be cheated out of her tale, so she said again, "What do you think of it, Mrs. Webb? The old man has got a fancy woman somewhere!"

"Oh, Mrs. Davidson, not at his age!" I said.

"Yes, indeed," she told me. "He's been disappearing several times a week now, for a long time. I've been around all his friends, and he's not been going to their houses, so it must be a woman somewhere. I've had my suspicions!"

I laughed, and said, "Do you really want to know where he goes, Mrs. Davidson?"

"Oh yes," she said. "Have you heard anything?"

"No, I haven't heard anything," I said, "but I've had a gentleman caller visiting me for quite a long time now. He is a wonderful old gentleman, and I hope he will continue to call on me for as long as possible."

"Do you mean the old man?" she asked.

"Yes," I said. "And he entertains me with some of the most fascinating stories I have ever heard."

"Do you listen to his stories?" she enquired.

"Well, it wouldn't do any good me telling him my stories, would it?" I told her. "He couldn't hear me."

"No wonder he calls you 'lovely little woman, lovely little woman'" she said, "if you listen to all his tales! But I'm so glad you told me about it, now I know where he's been going. Every woman who comes to visit me is a 'bloody cow' according to him, and you are the only woman who comes to this house who is *not* a 'bloody cow' – *you* are a 'lovely little woman.'"

THIRTY-SEVEN

On Sunday we went to visit the Raymonds, who were no longer living in Badra, but now lived in a little pug house in North-ampton. The farmer whom Dick had worked for had gone bankrupt, like so many of the other farmers, and Dick was now out of a job; Mary had had another little boy whom she called Barry. We didn't stay long, and when we reached home it was still daylight. The beds were indoors at this time, and we always left the doors and windows wide open when we went out, because of the heat. However, with the house being left empty for a few hours, it was necessary to take a few precautions in case snakes had got into the house for shade from the sun. I went to turn the bedclothes back, because the favourite hiding place of the snakes was curled up at the foot of the bed. The covers had to be turned back very carefully, and as I approached the bed, I noticed that there was a thick brown cover over it.

"Come and see, Ivor," I said. "Someone has been in here and changed our gold and violet quilt for this brown one."

"That's not a brown cover," said Ivor. "It's ants. I'll get rid of them now," and he went out to get the tin of kerosene. There were millions and millions of ants on the bed, clustered so thickly that we couldn't see them moving. Ivor went out, following their track to an old tree stump in the garden, and there he poured the kerosene down into the hole and set it alight. As soon as he did that, I could see the ants moving, and in no time at all the bed was cleared. Next Ivor soaked rags in kerosene and put them across the doors and windows to prevent the ants from coming in again. We used a tremendous amount of kerosene as preventative against ants and other pests, and it was a must to anyone raising chickens because 'stickfast flees' were a menace in Australia. These fleas would not attack humans, but they buried their heads in the young chicks and fed off the brains, and we would try to prevent this by hanging strips of flannel soaked in kerosene all around the place where the

313

mother hen lay, hoping that some of the kerosene would get under her wings, and so prevent the fleas getting at the young chicks. This was not very successful, and we lost a great many chicks through the stickfast fleas.

Our tomcat and the chickens got along very well together. The chickens were not cooped up, because they had to be free to feed in the bush, and to roost in the trees at night. It was quite a common sight to see a chicken lying flat on the ground, with its wings spread, and the cat lying with his head on the chicken's body, while another chicken was lying with *its* head on the cat's body, all three friends together. The intense heat was very upsetting for the chicken's, and made them most uncomfortable, so that they would stand with wings spread out and flapping, while they gasped for air. Many a time, too, I have heard a chicken scream in terror, and when I went to investigate, I would see a snake menacing and mesmerising it – a snake could hold a chicken still for any length of time just by staring at it; the bird would not be able to move. If our tame domestic cat saw this, he would turn into a wild bush cat, and a tremendous fight would occur – which the cat regularly won; he had many fights with the snakes found near the chickens.

My brother-in-law Jim Douglas was over six foot tall, and my sister Emily was so short that she could walk under his arm, but she ruled the roost in their household. She was very much against his drinking, and if at any time he happened to have had one too many, he would be too frightened to go home, and would come to our place to sober up first. The pubs closed at six, and one vey hot, breathless night, just after six, Jim, who had had a drink, made his way up to our house as usual before going home. The little ones were already asleep in their cots on the verandah, and I had sprinkled camphorated oil on their pillows and over their cots as usual, in the hope of keeping the mosquitoes away. Ivor hung the hurricane lantern outside the back door and sat there, trying to get some air; we were like the chickens, with our mouths open, gasping for air. It was quite frightening, we felt as though our lungs were going to burst for want of air.

I thought we would enjoy our supper more outside, so I rigged up a table out of some boxes, and I was just carrying the supper out when Jim arrived. I teased him about being a naughty boy (meaning his having a drink!) and then I brought out a chair for

314

him to sit on. Jim was very placid, and became even more so after he had had a drink, as well as being quite entertaining, and he sat there chatting to us while I prepared the supper. We had intended to enjoy a pleasant supper out of doors, but when we went to sit at the table, we found what appeared to be a cloth covering the whole table; the cloth was made up of the wings of flying ants, which were flying round the hurricane lantern and then dropping down on the table. We had no supper that night; but we sat down supperless, to have a chat with Jim. Suddenly he said in a whisper, "Don't anyone move or make a sound. There is an adder nearby." Then we saw it, slowly crawling around the back yard, near us – too near for us to make a move; but as it came near Ivor's feet, he acted swiftly. His spade was lying near him, and he reached out for it, jabbing at the head of the snake – though he cut off about a foot of its tail instead. (The snake was eight feet long.) Jim said, "It will go away now, and it will have to wait until tomorrow's sundown to die."

Jim decided to sleep in the bough shade that night, where it was nice and cool. Next morning I went to call him in, to give him a cup of tea, and found him lying on his back, fast asleep, with his arms under his head to keep it up off the floor; sleeping by his head was a huge iguana. I couldn't call Jim, because he would have moved his hand, and if he had done this and wakened the reptile, it could have caused the creature to bite his hand off; they have a fierce bite. I went quietly back into the house, and said to Ivor, "What can we do? We can't wake him, and if he should wake suddenly, of his own accord, it could be disastrous."

"There's only one thing we *can* do," said Ivor, "and that's to try to get the iguana away without waking Jim."

I remembered that one day I had seen an iguana drinking out of the cat's saucer, and Emily had told me once that she had got rid of the snake by using a bowl of milk. So I put some milk in a bowl and took it up to the other end of the bough shade, which was shaped like a bus shelter, open at both ends; I left the milk there for a moment or two, for the iguana to get the scent of it, then I took the bowl as close as I safely could to the reptile, and drew it away again. After doing this several times, while Ivor called quietly to Jim, warning him not to move, we managed to get the iguana away from Jim's head.

One night we were in bed out on the verandah when there was

a terrible noise from the chickens. I thought a snake had got up into one of the trees where they were roosting, but next morning there were a dozen young pullets lying dead with their heads bitten off. The same thing happened the following night, and this time Ivor saw something like a wild cat and shot at it. Next day we were unable to find our own cat, but he turned up in the evening with a bullet hole through his body. Each night we had the same trouble, and each night Ivor shot at the creature, but it got away and our own cat turned up with a fresh bullet hole in his body; still he did not die. Soon thirty-six young laying hens had died in the same way. We could not eat them, they had to be burnt and buried in the ground.

I told Ivor that he would have to kill the cat once and for all; it didn't seem to be in pain, but as I said to Ivor, "If you don't kill it, the holes will turn to gangrene and he will be in agony. He'll go wild with pain." Several times Ivor got the gun, but each time the cat saw it, and jumped clear over the eight foot fence; he always came back later and went to sleep on the verandah.

One day Mr. McCaskill rode up to our gate and shouted, "Bring your water bag and follow me, I've got a couple of days' work for you." Quickly Ivor got his horse, but I said to him, "Shoot this cat first, Ivor, you can't leave me with him like this, he might go mad and attack the children."

"I can't shoot it again, Ray," Ivor said. "I've shot through it eight times and I still cannot kill it, it's not a cat, it's the devil incarnate!"

The cat feared Ivor, and I was afraid it would one day jump at him and perhaps scratch his eyes out, but the animal trusted me. We all loved it, but by now it was a dangerous menace and I knew that eventually it would go mad with pain and possibly maim or kill one of the children. Just now the cat was sleeping peacefully on the verandah, and the children were playing in their cubby hole. I went in to get the gun, but I did not come out on the verandah with it as Ivor had done; instead I took the gun through the back door and came around the back of the house to the front where the cat was sleeping. My eyes were blinded with tears because the cat had been the children's playmate and my friend for several years, but I had to destroy it, for their sakes. I couldn't see through my tears to get the cat in my sights, so I crept up, put the barrel to its head and fired, and all was over. It was the first time in my life that I had ever shot anything.

One Saturday it was so hot, and the little ones were so languid with the heat that I put the tin bath in the bough shade where it was cool, and filled it with water from the well to make a paddling pool for them. Suddenly a horse galloped past the front door, and its rider shouted out, "Get your water bag, cobber, fire at the Bowes place!" He was gone in a cloud of dust. Ivor got his horse, and I filled his water bag (no man ever went off without his water bag hanging from his saddle), then he too had gone off in a cloud of dust.

"Let's go up to see the fire," I said to the children. I covered them with something cool, and set off towards Mrs. Hendley's which was the track that Ivor would have taken to get to the Bowes estate. That was several miles away, but I thought that if we got up as far as the Hendleys' house, which was on a high rise overlooking the Bowes place, we would see the glow of the fire in the sky. As he galloped off, the rider had shouted, "You are safe as long as the wind doesn't change," and as there wasn't even a breeze blowing, I thought it was safe to take a little walk.

Little Jack ran on, a few yards ahead of us. Soon we could feel the heat of the fire coming towards us, and Jack stopped, looked up at me, held up his hand and said, "It's all right, Mam, you've got your little Jackie with you." We went as far as the Hendley's place but it was too hot to go further, what with the heat of the day itself, and the hot breeze from the fire. Jack stopped and looked back at me again, and I realised that he was old enough to understand the danger of a bush fire, especially having lived through such a fire in our own paddock. I knew *this* bush fire was frightening him, and when he said again, "Don't be afraid, Mammy, you've got your Jackie boy with you, I won't let the fire hurt you or Pearly," I realised that my little boy saw himself as a man, who mustn't show fear, protecting his family. I knew it was wrong to press on in that terrible heat, so I said to Jackie, "I thing we had better go back, we have to protect Jimmy Emu, and the cow, and all the chickens, they'll be lonely without us, won't they?" The relief spread across his face; he had wanted to go back, but didn't want to show he was a coward.

We turned around and went back, and when we were safely in our paddock, Jackie stood in front of me and said, "You weren't frightened of the fire, were you, Mammy? Because you had your little Jackie boy with you, and I wouldn't let any harm come to you or Pearly. You're a lucky mummy, aren't you,

317

because you've got me for your Jackie boy. Some mummies haven't got a little boy, have they, it must be very sad for them, don't you think so, Mammy?"

"Yes, my love," I said, "I am a very lucky mummy to have you for my son and Pearly for my little girl."

Then we dismissed the fire from our conversation, but I was very worried, because I was afraid that the wind would change and the fire would come in our direction before the men got back. I filled as many buckets as I could from the well, and hoped that these would be enough to help us, and perhaps save our lives. Ivor did not come home that night, but the fire did not come our way, and all was well.

Before I left England I was supposed to have gone into hospital for treatment to repair the damage I had suffered after the birth of my little girl, and while I was staying with my mother a letter came, telling me to report to the hospital. When I reported there, I told them that I was sailing for Australia in a fortnight, at which the specialist told me that the operation I needed was urgent, but if I had it, I would not be allowed to travel for at least a year. At that I said that I could not stay, I had to go to Australia because my husband was alone out there, and I would leave the operation and have it when I got out there.

All I knew at that point, of course, was that I was voyaging to the land of perpetual sunshine; the advertisements called it 'the land of milk and honey', and urged 'Come to the land of opportunity.' No mention was made of the fact that Australia too was going through a depression that meant there was no work, only starvation, so that we would find it hard to buy a loaf of bread, let alone cover the cost of medical treatment.

When at last I could afford the twenty-five shillings needed just for knocking on the doctor's door, he told me that unless I returned to my native land, he would give me just two months to live. "And although the sun has been good to your little boy," he added, "you will have to take your girl home. This intense heat has weakened her heart, and she could develop epileptic fits." After that I had no choice but to tell my husband that we would have to go back to Wales.

Now we had to think of a means of getting the money to go back, and to provide warm clothing for the voyage. There was no way Ivor could come back with us then, and it was going to be almost impossible to gather enough money to pay for one full

318

fare and two half fares; we sold everything for which we could find a buyer; and Ivor arranged to go and live with Viv and Edwina Husband, where he would work for his keep, until he could perhaps join us in Wales. (Though he would be happier if we could rejoin him in Australia once I was well again.

Eventually my passport arrived, just two weeks before my two months was up. Emily and her children walked with me to the railway station on the morning of our departure, and I could hardly hold back the tears as we waited for the train. But we had no choice, and once again, as so many times before, I went forward into a new chapter in my life.